Making Money in Foreclosures

How to Invest Profitably in Distressed Real Estate

Second Edition

ANDREW JAMES MCLEAN

McGraw-Hill

New York Chicago San Francisco Lisbon London
Madrid Mexico City Milan New Delhi San Juan
Seoul Singapore Sydney Toronto

1 2 3 4 5 6 7 8 9 0   FGR/FGR   0 9 8 7 6

ISBN-13: 978-0-07-147918-9
ISBN-10: 0-07-147918-X

This publication is designed to provide accurate and authoritative information in regard to the subject matter covered. It is sold with the understanding that the publisher is not engaged in rendering legal, accounting, or other professional service. If legal advice or other expert assistance is required, the services of a competent professional person should be sought.
 —*From a Declaration of Principles Jointly Adopted by a Committee of the American Bar Association and a Committee of Publishers and Associations*

McGraw-Hill books are available at special discounts to use as premiums and sales promotions, or for use in corporate training programs. For more information, please write to the Director of Special Sales, Professional Publishing, McGraw-Hill, Two Penn Plaza, New York, NY 10121-2298. Or contact your local bookstore.

This book is printed on acid-free paper.

Contents

Preface

Welcome to *Foreclosures and How To Profitably Invest in Distressed Real Estate*. It's all about how to invest successfully in foreclosed residential real estate, specializing in single-family homes and small multiunit apartment buildings, and how to do it profitably in your spare time without quitting your job. In this useful guide book you'll learn all about the fundamentals of foreclosed realty and how it can progress through the traditional three phases of foreclosure—the default phase, the foreclosure auction, and, if it fails to sell at auction, the lender's real-estate-owned phase—and how you can profitably invest in any of the phases the distressed property may evolve.

Beginners will appreciate the introduction to the specialized terminology used in the foreclosure process, and well-experienced investors will value the different types of profitable holding strategies not available in other foreclosure books. Whichever you are, if you like the idea of buying bargain-priced real estate, then this book was designed especially for you. With basic hands-on guidance throughout, this book will serve as an excellent guide for both layperson and professional. You'll find a wide range of topics along with proven guidelines that will help you along the path to profitable foreclosure investing. In creating this work, I tried to cover all the angles and make it the all-in-one guide that covers everything you need to know to avoid uncertainty, and invest in today's foreclosure market safely, confidently, and profitably.

My experience is yours for the taking

Written in an easy to read conversational style, the book blends my knowledge of investing with a broad working experience in real estate.

Preface

Throughout the book I, on occasion, reminisce about a few of my memorable investment experiences, including the time in 1976 I managed multi-millions in foreclosed realty for a 39-branch savings and loan, along with 32 years of real estate investing on my family's behalf. Also, I was fortunate to acquire extensive experience working with some of America's mighty real estate moguls, including George Ross, the executive business and legal advisor to Donald Trump and co-star of *The Apprentice*. (I had the great honor of being the co-author of Ross' *Trump Strategies For Real Estate; Billionaire Lessons for the Small Investor*). Additionally, over the years I had the opportunity to work as a real estate appraiser, a property manager for a major developer, a loan officer, and a resident manager of a luxury 363-unit apartment complex.

Yet this foreclosure handbook is more than just reminiscing about my varied experiences. It also incorporates my core principles with proven expertise to provide lessons for first-time foreclosure investors or midlevel buyers that they might not otherwise have. So, for example, when you're preparing to bid at a foreclosure auction, this book answers the pertinent questions: How do I determine what to bid? How do I know if the real estate I'm looking at is a good deal? Where and what kind of financing should I get? And then once I own the property, what are my holding strategies? How do I find good-paying, long-term tenants?

This useful guide answers many other questions too. For instance:

- How do I gain position of the second loan?
- Once I own the property, what improvements should I make, and which ones should I avoid?
- What types of foreclosed properties make the most profitable investments?
- How do I avoid deadbeats and find good-paying tenants who will care for my property?

Furthermore, this book offers sound advice on:

- How do I go about evaluating foreclosed real estate and what should I look out for?
- How do I go about dealing with lenders that own foreclosed realty?

Preface

- What are the strategies for earning a great return on a modest investment?
- How to gain financial independence by pyramiding your investments?

This book is *not* a get-rich-quick scheme or some far-fetched no-money down plan that you might see on late-night television for earning mythical millions overnight. Although buying foreclosures, given the proper guidelines will, in fact, eventually make you rich, but that milestone achievement won't come without the investment of time and effort. And you will be pleased to know that compared to other types of investing, real estate investing (foreclosures in particular), yields an extraordinary ratio of profit generated given the amount of effort exerted to produce it. The reason foreclosures are so profitable is that, unlike a traditional realty purchase, they are usually purchased at a fraction of market value.

To that end we have included several profitable long-term holding strategies for your consideration. Also, we added a special section on key guidelines to making a superior realty investment. This way you know exactly what to look for in a profitable real estate investment, along with what to avoid. (See in Chapter 5 "Key Ingredients To Making a Superior Real Estate Investment" and Chapter 6 "How To Spot a Real Estate Lemon".)

This book is easy to follow, featuring methodical ways of first acquiring one property, then fixing it up, and renting it and perhaps later converting it to more profitable office space, or perhaps giving your tenant an option to buy, in contemplation of acquiring additional properties. It also features how to manage your investments efficiently, without many of the hassles unskilled or inexperienced landlords have to deal with.

Above all, this book features the essential know-how of acquiring distressed realty during all three phases of foreclosure, although we highlight and recommend the reader to focus his or her endeavors investing in the third and final phase. That's because it's usually less risky and not as complicated, nor as competitive as investing in the first two phases of foreclosure.

We begin by introducing you to the foreclosure process, then defining all the terminology involved, along with the three phases of foreclosure, and why foreclosures occur. Then we merge into the essentials of how to acquire foreclosed property prior to the sale and how to deal with troubled owners and lenders. From there we discuss acquisition procedures and how to determine a bid price at a foreclosure auction. And, of course, if the foreclosure sale was unsuccessful (lack of acceptable bids) we detail procedures for buying a lender's Real Estate Owned (REO), which is a lender's inventory of foreclosures that failed to sell at the foreclosure auction.

Foremost, this book not only explains how to profitably invest in foreclosures, it has a special invaluable feature that should prove very useful to the reader: We included several profitable holding strategies for your consideration after you acquired the property. These holding strategies include renting, renting with a buy-option, land banking, and profitable conversions (converting homes to office space and apartments to condominiums).

Other chapters in the book focus on such topics as the appraisal and the financing of distressed real estate, along with where to find other sources of foreclosed realty.

The featured sections in the book"Key Ingredients To Making a Superior Realty Investment" and "Hassle-Free Techniques to Efficient Property Management" are styled from the Investing in Real Estate course I teach at the Jefferson Davis campus of the Mississippi Gulf Coast Community College. This is the true bread and butter section of the book, which the reader should find valuable in any realty investment situation.

In the section on Key Ingredients To Making a Superior Realty Investment, you'll learn:

- The six key ingredients to making a superior realty investment.
- Time-tested advice to investing in improved real estate.
- How to use three key principles to maximize your investment.
- How to spot a real estate lemon.

In the property management section, you'll learn:

- How to find quality tenants that pay on time and will care for your property.
- How to take the hassle out of being a landlord.
- How to maintain harmony by profiling your tenants.
- How to use success-proven strategies to optimize rental income.

Preface

You'll also discover in this book how to:

- Find the best low-cost financing
- Shop for the best mortgage loan
- Avoid adjustable-rate loans and prepayment penalties
- Make practical improvements that pay, and avoid ones that don't

Why this book is special

It's special because it offers the reader an easy to follow blue print from an experienced author who's done it: who not only managed large amounts of foreclosed realty, but also bought and managed it for his own account. It's also special for the following reasons:

- Each chapter opens with an introduction which outlines its content and describes highlights within that will help the reader.
- We offer four different profitable holding strategies for your consideration.
- It will point out potential pitfalls at foreclosure investing, so you can avoid them.
- It includes the author's "Landlord Tales," which are heartfelt personal experiences he had over the years of working in the industry.

This book will also give you sound guidelines to:

- Using the comparative sales approach to evaluating real estate
- Knowing what types of property to buy, and which to avoid
- Gaining financial independence from profitable foreclosure investing
- Learning foreclosure terminology and how to invest in foreclosures in any of the three phases that can occur

While this book is aimed primarily at beginning and midlevel real estate investors—owners of one or two rental properties—it will also be of interest to:

- Anyone interested in purchasing bargain-priced real estate
- Anyone unsure of the foreclosure process and the terminology used
- Anyone unsure of what type of real estate financing to choose
- Anyone who wants to learn hassle-free methods for attracting good tenants and maximizing profits

Preface

- Anyone who wants to learn how to appraise real estate
- Anyone interested in learning how to retire on his or her real estate investments

With basic know-how logically portrayed throughout, this book will serve as an excellent guide for both layperson and professional. But more importantly, *Foreclosures* will help you to achieve your real estate investment goals, safely, confidently, and profitably.

Best of luck with your realty investments.

Sincerely,

A.J. McLean

Introduction

There are many reasons improved real estate—foreclosures in particular—are such a great investment. Its finite supply, of course, makes habitable well-located property desirable, and therefore eternally increasing in value. But other factors on the demand side of the economic equation make it a great investment. These include a steady future growth in America's population, growth in the number of U.S. households, and growth in second-home ownership. Low interest rates also increase the demand for improved real estate, not to mention insufficient housing starts and bureaucratic red tape that stifle its supply.

But there are other benefits to investing in real estate. For example: You have personal control, it's easy to learn the how-to's of profitable foreclosure investing, you don't need much to get started, you earn tax benefits, and you get forced savings from the equity buildup benefit. And then there's inflation, and its positive effects on the appreciation of improved real estate.

In the following chapters we will describe the foreclosure process, define the special terminology involved, and give you guidelines to investing in foreclosures during the three phases that a distressed property can evolve.

Why Foreclosed Real Estate
Is a Great Investment

In classic economic theory, supply increases to satisfy demand. Shortage of a product increases the demand for it, which inevitably makes its price rise. One of the significant reasons real estate is a great investment is because of its finite supply—and in the foreseeable future there's no way of making any more of it. Thus, we're faced with the fact that although the United States is blessed with an abundance of land, unfortunately, most of it is situated where people don't want to live. Most of the desired habitable land is already built on, and land that is still unimproved costs plenty to own and in the future will cost much, much more.

On the demand side of this economic theory, future demand for real estate in the United States will increase faster than the future supply. There are three reasons why:

1. *United States Population Growth.* Conservative growth expectations indicate that the U.S. population over the next 20 years, primarily from immigration, is expected to increase from its current figure of 291 million to 337 million, an increase of 46 million people. Thus, in just two decades the United States will add more people than are currently living in Florida, Michigan, and Texas.

2. *Growth in the Number of Households.* Presently, Americans average 2.2 persons per household. However, that number has been declining recently. It is expected to decrease to about 2.0, given the latest trends of families having fewer children, more singles living alone, and more baby boomers born in the 1940s phasing into retirement. Then 25 million additional housing units will be required just to adequately house the 50 million people who will be added to the population.

3. *Growth in Second-Home Ownership.* Currently, more than 8 million American households own a second home. Considering the present market conditions that encourage more real estate investment—a growth in population of 50 million more people who need housing, low interest rates for home loans, and dispirited stock investors bailing out of unpredictable markets to invest in real estate—economists

predict this number to increase significantly over the next 20 years. They're forecasting that by 2025 more than 20 million households will own at least two homes.

Twenty years of vigorous growth in the U.S. population, as you can see, will result in record numbers of people needing adequate housing. Yet there's another reason why real estate is a great investment, and that has to do with interest rates.

Low Interest Rates Increase the Demand for Real Estate

During the hyperinflationary 1970s and 1980s, when double-digit inflation was the rule rather than the exception, interest rates for home loans ranged between 9 and 17 percent. But beginning in the mid 1990s something happened to America's economy that had a major impact on the housing market. Inflation began to moderate, usually below 3 percent, and often below a negligible 2 percent. This led to a substantial reduction in the rate of interest homeowners had to pay lenders for a new mortgage loan. So instead of borrowers having to pay 10 percent interest or more on their home loans, they began paying on loans at substantially reduced interest rates, at times below 5 percent.

These interest rate reductions set off a flurry of homeowner refinancing of high-interest home loans. Also, and more significant, the rate reductions gave more people the financial ability to buy a home. Some of these people were low-income renters who were now able to qualify for a home loan at the lower interest rates. The lowered rates also permitted homeowners to buy additional investment property and/or to trade up to larger, more expensive homes. Previously, at interest rates of 10 percent or more, these investments had not been possible for many people. When the rates went down to 6 and then 5 percent, monthly payments went down too, making these investments feasible. Buyers who could previously afford only a $90,000 home at 10 percent could now afford a $130,000 home at 6 percent. (The monthly principal and interest payment on a $90,000 loan at 10 percent for 30 years is $790, which is the same amount a borrower would pay on a $130,000 loan for 30 years at 6 percent.)

Therefore, with lower interest rates for home loans, more demand was created for homes as more people entered the home-buying market. This easing in credit conditions stimulated homeowners to not only trade up, but also to begin investing in rental homes and vacation homes. Today, affluent baby boomers, rather than selling their homes as they near retirement, are buying second houses. According to the National Association of Realtors (NAR), investment homes were nearly a quarter of all purchases in 2004, and vacation homes were an additional 13 percent.

Insufficient Housing Supply and Red Tape

With low interest rates raising the demand, there's also pressure pushing down the supply of housing. Home builders say that because of immigration the current elevated level of 2 million housing starts annually is insufficient to meet higher-than-predicted growth in new households. The housing supply is very tight in some areas of the United States because now it can take years to get new developments approved by the environmental protective agencies and the zoning authorities. The end result has been a huge increase in real estate values that has lasted since the late 1980s and shows no signs of dissipating.

The Effect of Inflation on Real Estate

Historically, and for the most part during the last 20 years, improved real estate has been extremely sensitive to the effects of inflation—so much so that when the rate of inflation averages 5 percent annually, an average improved property increases 8 to 10 percent (14 percent or more in coastal areas such as Boston, San Francisco, or Los Angeles) during that same period.

Several factors account for this appreciation. One has to do with what is called *replacement cost*. Every time a plumber, carpenter, or electrician receives a new union contract for higher wages, the cost of new residential construction goes up. And every time the cost of building supplies increases—lumber and concrete, for instance—the cost of new construction likewise spirals upward. The result is that the house you own becomes worth about what it would cost to build it at today's prices. This is one reason why improved real estate has more than doubled in value during the last 10 years.

Another key factor, as mentioned earlier, is the limited supply of habitable land. As the land available for residential building becomes more scarce, the cost of that land increases proportionately, and the increase is added into the appreciating value of your realty investment.

To more fully understand how both the factors of inflation and appreciation affect you as a realty investor, consider the following pertinent facts.

Research shows that the median price for homes in the United States more than doubled in the 10 years from 1977 to 1987. In 1977, the median price of a home—that is, half sold for more, and half sold for less—was $44,000. In 1987, the median price of the same home was $95,000. That's an increase of 116 percent over a decade, or an average increase of 11.6 percent annually. During that same period, the rate of inflation averaged about 5.6 percent, which is less than half the annual increase of a median-priced home.

More recently, according to the NAR, from 2002 through 2004 the median price of single-family homes saw an average annual increase of 8.8 percent, while the rate of inflation during the same period was moderate and under 3 percent. The rate of inflation in 2002 was 1.59; in 2003 it was 2.27 percent; and in 2004, 2.68 percent. In 2002 the median single-family-home price was $158,100; in 2003 in was $170,000; and in 2004 it was $184,100. Notably, the average annual increase in home prices in the western states was 14.1 percent, with Las Vegas, Nevada, showing a whopping annual increase of 47.3 percent. (Two key factors most responsible for this huge increase in Las Vegas real estate values were the tremendous growth in population and the fact that most of the available habitable land in the Las Vegas valley, which is surrounded by mountains, has already been built on. Therefore, land available for residential construction is extremely scarce.)

Investing in Foreclosures Offers Boundless Opportunities

Why should you invest in foreclosed real estate? Because you can buy distressed real estate at bargain prices, and often with below-market financing and with reduced closing costs. Usually, when purchasing real estate through normal channels you're required to pay near market value prices. But foreclosed real estate often sells far below its market value, and often at the amount loaned against it.

Not only that, but you have the opportunity of investing in any of the three phases that a foreclosed property may evolve: in the default phase, at the foreclosure auction, or from a lender's inventory if the property fails to sell at the auction.

Investment During the Three Foreclosure Phases

In a typical scenario, a distressed property evolves through three phases during the foreclosure process. When the delinquent borrower becomes significantly past due with mortgage loan payments—usually 90 days—the encumbered property emerges into the default phase of the foreclosure proceedings. In the second phase, if the delinquent borrower fails to make the loan current, the lender arranges a foreclosure auction in order to recapture his losses. If there are no competing bids at the foreclosure auction, the property evolves into the third phase: It is taken by the lender and put on their books at a cost of the outstanding loan balance, including incidental late fees and costs to repossess, and is now identified as the lender's real estate owned (REO) inventory.

The Default Phase

In Chapter 2 we discuss the first opportunity to purchase foreclosures, before the auction, in the default phase. During this phase investors can not only make a good deal for themselves, but also assist delinquent property owners by purchasing the property directly from them prior to the foreclosure sale. The property owners benefit from the preauction purchase because they preserve their credit rating—avoiding the negative stigma of a foreclosure—and steer clear of incurring additional costs involved with the delinquent loan. Buyers benefit from the preauction purchase because they can acquire the property before all the incidental foreclosure costs are added on to the auction price.

At the Foreclosure Auction

The second opportunity you'll have to invest in foreclosures is at the foreclosure auctions. Here we describe what you can expect at a public foreclosure auction, including how to prepare a successful bid. In Chapter 3 we go into more detail about what you can expect at a public foreclosure auction and the process of making a successful bid, including how to do your homework to prepare for the auction.

Being fully aware of all the procedures will aid potential foreclosure investors in deciding if bidding at a foreclosure sale is appropriate for them. If not, they have the opportunity to invest in foreclosed property after the auction.

In the Lender's REO Phase

Should the foreclosed property fail to sell at the foreclosure auction, the property then is listed as real estate owned inventory of the foreclosing lender. It is now a superior investment compared to investing in the other two phases of foreclosure. Why is it a superior investment? Because when you purchase in the lender's REO phase you don't have to worry about any outstanding liens against the property. When the lender took it back, it was cleared of any outstanding liens against it, and any outstanding property taxes were paid. Furthermore, because there is no auction, you won't have to compete with other bidders. And finally—the biggest advantage—since the seller is also a lender, you can usually finance your purchase at below market interest rates and at reduced closing costs.

In Chapter 4 we discuss in more detail the advantages and the how-to's of buying foreclosures after the auction, when the property becomes the inventory of the foreclosing lender.

Other Benefits of Investing in Foreclosed Real Estate

Besides the advantages of buying at bargain prices with great financing, beating inflation, steady appreciation, and having the option of investing in any of the three phases that a foreclosed property may evolve, there are many other benefits of investing in foreclosed real estate. They include:

- You have personal control.
- It's easy to learn the how-to's of profitable foreclosure investing.
- Anyone can buy.
- You don't need much to get started.

- You earn tax benefits.
- You get forced savings from the equity buildup benefit.

We will briefly explain each of these advantages.

You Have Personal Control

Unlike investment in common stocks or bonds, which can increase or decrease in value with the whims of a changing marketplace, real estate offers the investor a much greater opportunity for appreciation in historically stable markets. Owning a home or other income-producing realty not only gives you a wonderful feeling of pride in yourself, it also gives you confidence because it's a tangible asset. You can see it, feel it, and improve on it. More important, you can rest assured that your real estate investment will likely increase in value because real estate, in general, has appreciated consistently for hundreds of years. Yes, in the short term, values can become depressed, but over the long haul almost every well-located improved property will appreciate in value.

Simply stated, there's virtually no better investment available—none that give you total control, none that exist in a market that traditionally appreciates, and none that give you as great a hedge against inflation. The emphasis is on *total control*. Unlike investing in stocks or bonds, with real estate you don't have to rely on third-party agents to handle or manipulate your hard-earned investment money. That's because *you* make the critical decision as to what to invest in. Granted, you may heed the advice of knowledgeable realtors or friends, but it's you who will ultimately either live in the property and care for it or decide who rents it. And it's you who will thereby have command of its usage.

It's Easy to Learn the How-To's of Foreclosure Investing

Successful foreclosure specialists didn't get that way by recklessly throwing their money around, making ill-advised decisions such as paying too much for the wrong type of property in a poorly located declining neighborhood. To the contrary, they made educated, informed decisions based on well-defined guidelines. In Chapter 5 we give you a blueprint of exactly what you need to look for—the six key ingredients to making a superior realty investment.

Anyone Can Buy

To be successful as a foreclosure specialist you're not going to need a real estate license or a college degree. You don't even need experience. You don't even have to be a citizen of the United States to purchase property in foreclosure. There are no restrictions whatsoever as to who can buy. Information on foreclosed real estate is a matter of public record without reserve to anyone. What you do need is perseverance, commitment, and a willingness to learn and apply the lessons given in the following chapters. That, along with a good knowledge of your local area and property values, along with knowledge of terminology involved in the foreclosure process (see Chapter 1), will take you a long way toward achieving your realty investment goals.

You Don't Need Much to Get Started

A few thousand dollars is all most people need to get started with buying a foreclosed property, especially if you intend to make it your home. And under certain circumstances, some people don't even need that. This book features several high leverage financing techniques (see Chapter 7 "Financing Foreclosed Real Estate"). If you're a qualified veteran, for example, you can borrow up to $203,000 with no money down. Or almost anyone with reasonable credit can borrow up to $208,000 with just 3 percent down under an insured FHA (Federal Housing Administration) loan.

Unlike buying common stock, you can purchase a $100,000 home with as little as $3,000 for a down payment (or nothing down if you're a qualified veteran). To buy $100,000 in common stock, you have to come up with at least $50,000 in cash (50 percent). And if the stock you purchase declines in value, you'll unfortunately get a margin call requiring that you add cash to the account. If you do not meet the stockbroker's margin requirements, the stock could be liquidated to satisfy the deficit, and you'll be stuck with the loss. The good news is, there are no margin calls in real estate investing. Even in the unlikely event that your real estate investment declines in value, your lender cannot require you to invest more cash into the property just to maintain a specified loan-to-value ratio.

Furthermore, not only can you invest in improved real estate with far less cash than you would need to invest in an equivalent amount of stock, but financing real estate is not nearly as risky, and it's much less complicated than using leveraged margin accounts to buy stocks. Using margin accounts to invest in a volatile, unpredictable stock market is a risky game played mostly by daring speculators.

You Earn Tax Benefits

More good news for real estate owners. Current income tax law favors homeowners and real estate investors. As a renter, you get absolutely no tax relief. But as a homeowner, the loan origination points, mortgage interest, and property taxes you pay are deductible against your federal, state, and local income taxes. And notably, compared to the fully taxable dividends you receive from stock ownership, when you sell your home, the capital gain of up to $500,000 is exempt from income taxes. In addition, *active* income property owners are allowed to shelter some of their rental income from federal, state, and local income taxes.

You should also know that if you sell a winning stock intending to move the proceeds into another stock or managed fund, you'll be required to pay a good portion of your gain to the IRS. With an individual retirement account (IRA), 401(k), or other tax-sheltered retirement plan, you may defer some of the taxes on the gains; yet many regulations and restrictions apply to these plans. However, you avoid these kinds of income taxes in real estate, which means you get to keep your entire accumulated wealth as long as you own properties. Additionally, there's another great benefit: Through home equity loans, refinancing, or installment sales, you can extract cash out of your realty holdings with little or no payment of income taxes.

You Get Forced Savings from Equity Buildup

Table 0.1 shows what happens to a $10,000 down payment on a $110,000 home over 30 years based on conservative appreciation rates of 5 and 7 percent annually. Note that based only a 5 percent annual rate of appreciation, as the loan pays down over 30 years, the homeowner can expect his or her value to grow to $491,370 in 30 years. And at 7 percent, a similar down payment would grow to $892,760 by year 30.

You can see from Table 0.1 that over an extended period an initial down payment of $10,000 can increase significantly—from both the factors of

Table 0-1.
Building Wealth with Appreciation and Equity Buildup

Appreciation Rate		Year 0	Year 10	Year 20	Year 30
5%	Value	$110,000	$181,380	$298,300	$491,300
	Loan	$100,000	$86,780	$58,900	$0
	Equity	$10,000	$94,600	$239,400	$491,300
7%	Value	$110,000	$220,900	$441,100	$892,700
	Loan	$100,000	$86,790	$58,900	$0
	Equity	$10,000	$134,110	$385,200	$892,700

appreciation and loan pay-down—into hundreds of thousands of dollars. Better yet, if you buy in a hot real estate market (properties in the western United States have appreciated at 14.1 percent annually between 2001 and 2005), and make practical improvements to your property, you can pyramid your wealth by trading up to larger properties that much faster. (See Chapter 11, "Gaining Financial Independence Through Foreclosure Investing.")

What Does the Future Hold?

"Yes," you might be saying, "you've convinced me that real estate is a great investment. But what about the future of foreclosure investing? Will there always be different sources of foreclosed property to choose from? And then once I own the property, what about troublesome tenants who don't pay their rent? Who needs that kind of headache?"

Good questions. That's the reason Chapter 10 shows you how to efficiently optimize profits using proven hassle-free methods to manage your property. When you follow the guidelines discussed later in the book, you learn how to attract good tenants, supervise your resident managers, and make your property more desirable.

Regarding the question about future sources of foreclosures, liberal lending policies, along with borrowers taking out adjustable-rate loans and overextending themselves, will always result in an adequate future supply of foreclosures. As long as primary lenders and government-backed loan programs allow buyers to finance their homes with nontraditional financing, such as interest-only and adjustable-rate loans, there's more risk of the borrower becoming delinquent on his loan, which in many cases will inevitably lead to foreclosure.

The future looks bright for foreclosure investors. Not only is inflation on your side—real estate values typically appreciate more than twice the rate of inflation—so is time. As time passes, rents can be increased, while most of your operating expenses, such as your fixed-rate mortgage loan, remain the same. This means that the property you initially purchased, which had little or no cash flow then, can in time develop positive cash flow from annual rental increases.

Owners who wisely held onto their properties over the long haul are eventually able to live off the rental income earned on them. In other words, income property purchased today with a minimal down payment is unlikely to net a positive cash flow. But as time passes, the property appreciates and the rents are periodically increased, and over the long term these will produce more and more income for the owner. Therefore, the longer you own the property, the greater the net income from it becomes. Furthermore, during the time of ownership, you continue to enjoy the tax shelter benefits from the property. In other words, *buy all the income property you can when you're young, then enjoy the income benefits when you're older.*

There's more good news for future foreclosure investors. Besides the benefits of years of increasing income, appreciation, and tax sheltered income, you also have a great refinancing benefit. You can periodically refinance your realty holdings as the loan balances diminish and your equity position becomes substantial. Every five or 10 years you can refinance certain properties, pulling out cash to reinvest in more properties, or doing whatever you want with it.

Still another method of income production can be created when the owner of real estate decides to sell. After you have owned property for an extended period, you will more than likely realize a sizable capital gain from the sale. You have the option of taking all cash from the gain, or of accepting an interest bearing note for your equity in the property. And it's worth noting that as of this writing the IRS allows an individual taxpayer who owns a home and lives in it for two out of the last five years prior to the sale to completely avoid taxes on up to $250,000 in capital gains, and to exclude up to $500,000 in gains if the taxpayer is married filing jointly.

As you can see, investment in foreclosures can provide tax sheltered income for its owner in a variety of ways. But it can be more than just a part-time income. By making continued selective investments, over the years real estate can eventually make you extremely rich, which of course is the financial achievement of almost every working person.

But it is up to you to decide how prosperous you want to be in the future. Should you wisely opt to take control of your financial well-being and become a prosperous real estate investor, then all you have to do is diligently put into operation the guidelines described in this book.

An old proverb comes to mind: "A journey of a thousand miles must begin with a first step." Your first step on your journey to financial independence is the purchase of this book, and your second step is to implement its guidelines and lessons. This could be the purchase of a bargain-priced foreclosure property for you and your family to reside in, or, if you already own a home, it could be the purchase of a rental house. Whatever the situation, when you become knowledgeable and experienced about foreclosed real estate, you can use this knowledge and, with careful planning, take control of your own financial future. The end result is freedom to do as you please; freedom from working for someone else, if you desire; by joining in the general prosperity enjoyed by those who are prosperous homeowners and landlords.

1

Learning the Terminology and Understanding the Foreclosure Process

In this chapter we'll introduce the foreclosure process and the terminology involved and discuss why investing in distressed realty offers virtually boundless profitable opportunities. In the ensuing chapters you'll learn how to invest successfully in any one of the three phases foreclosure realty may evolve.

Knowledge of the specialized terms and of the three phases that occur during the foreclosure process will help potential distressed property investors: (1) determine which phase is most profitable and appropriate for their particular investment plans and needs, (2) become more knowledgeable in this very specialized and lucrative field of investment, and (3) begin a new investment career with a solid foundation to build upon.

In the ensuing chapters we reinforce that foundation with proven guidelines for acquiring foreclosures in each of the three phases. You'll also learn the how-to's of appraisal, the key ingredients in making a superior investment, financing, and how to make practical improvements to your acquisitions. We also featured chapters on strategies after the sale, such as several profitable holding strategies and how to profitably manage your real estate holdings hassle-free.

How Foreclosures Occur

What exactly is "foreclosure"? A definition appropriate for our purposes would be: It is a lawful method of enforcing payment by taking and selling the secured property when the loan is substantially delinquent. Foreclosure is the termination of rights of an owner of real property (real estate) that is secured by a mortgage or deed of trust, applicable when payment of the debt was not made when it was due.

A Typical Foreclosure Scenario

Suppose, for example, a homeowner has a mortgage loan with terms specifying that the loan will be in default after he is 90 days late with the monthly loan payments. In our scenario, the principal balance owing on the mortgage loan is $140,000, and the monthly payment for principal and interest is $1,000.

After neglecting to pay monthly payments for three months (90 days), the borrower will owe the lender $3,000 in accumulated monthly payments plus all incidental late charges. Once the borrower missed the third consecutive payment, the loan obligation is 90 days delinquent, and in accordance with the 90-day default provision, the due date of the mortgage loan accelerates and the lender has the right to demand the entire principal balance (including late charges) that is due, and payable in full. That is, instead of the borrower owing just three overdue payments and late charges, he owes the entire principal balance of $140,000 plus incurred late charges. And should the delinquent borrower in our scenario be unable to pay off the entire balance he owes, or implement an alternative repayment plan with the lender, the lender has the legal right to recapture his losses by selling the encumbered property at public auction.

The foreclosure auction will usually be held at a specified advertised location open to the public, such as the county courthouse, town hall, or corporate lobby of the foreclosing lender. Notification of the foreclosure auction is accomplished through local custom, usually through postings on public buildings and published advertisements in local newspapers. A trustee or appointed referee is on hand to accept verbal bids, usually beginning at the delinquent balance that is owed, on behalf of the foreclosing lender from those who attend the auction. The *Contract of Sale* is awarded to the highest bidder. If there are no competing bids, the foreclosed property is then taken by the lender and put on their books at a cost of the outstanding loan balance, including incidental late fees and costs to repossess, and is now identified as the lender's real estate owned (REO).

The duration of the foreclosure process, from its inception to its completion, is predicated on whether the instrument that secured the debt and created a lien against the encumbered real property was a trust deed or a mortgage.

Reasons for Foreclosure

So, why do so many property owners allow their homes or other real property to be foreclosed? Believe it or not, the federal government and some innovative primary lenders are inadvertently the culprit at instigating the majority of single-family foreclosures. Due to federal home loan assistance programs, such as the FHA and VA, which offer a very low, or virtually no, down payment, a recent homeowner doesn't have much to lose if he cannot meet the mortgage obligation and is eventually foreclosed upon. Under these government-backed programs the borrower merely has to come up with nominal closing costs, and can often move in a property for less than a $700 investment. All that's required is a fair credit rating and steady employment. Primary lenders are also inadvertently at fault because of funding risky financing, such as adjustable-rate mortgages, graduated mortgages, and interest-only loans.

It is not our intention to criticize or demean these helpful housing assistance programs. They are definitely a boon to many families who normally could not afford adequate housing. We are merely trying to point out that a lack of adequate homeowner equity often causes the majority of foreclosures.

In most cases it takes years for the low-down-payment buyer to build up equity in his home. If poor financial times occur within a few years of purchasing the home, the owner may feel that he hasn't much to lose since it was purchased with such a small down payment. His attitude might be that he has merely paid rent during that period, or has plenty of time to catch up on payments. If the mortgage loan is government backed, such as an FHA or VA loan, he often has up to six months without making mortgage payments because it will take two to three months just to get the default recorded. During this period the delinquent borrower will receive late notices, payment demands, and a variety of collection devices. Only if he totally ignores these will a default be recorded. By then, the tiny amount of equity in the home will be consumed by the delinquency charges. As time passes the actual foreclosure proceedings are held and the owner has probably moved away, leaving the house for that particular government agency to repossess.

There are many other reasons why residential foreclosures occur. Frequent among them is when the primary breadwinner of a household loses his or her job or is no longer able to work. A divorce in the family will often cause a property to become distressed and inevitably cause a foreclosure. In this case, the home will be the responsibility of only one spouse, instead of two. In which case, the new sole owner might not be accustomed to making the mortgage payments, or he or she may have difficulty making such payments without the aid of spousal income.

A death in the family can also cause eventual foreclosure. Such a sad event often causes remorse, and meanwhile none of the survivors bothers to take over the responsibility of making the mortgage payments, as a "devil may care attitude" sets over the stricken household.

Income property often faces foreclosure when owners defer maintenance beyond a point of no return. When a property, such as a multiunit apartment building, is not budgeted properly for preventive maintenance— for instance, funds for future replacement of such items as carpeting or roofing are not set aside—it may physically deteriorate to a point of foreclosure. If a building is not kept up properly, the owner loses income because quality tenants will refuse to reside in deteriorating units. Therefore the owner cannot get adequate rent to meet expenses. Then, in order to keep his head above water, he continues making the mortgage payments but does not put any money into keeping up the building. Meanwhile, as the condition of the building continues to worsen, more and more tenants move out. Finally, so many tenants have moved out and the building has deteriorated to the point that the owner cannot continue to make mortgage payments, and a foreclosure sale results.

Regardless of the reasons, primary lenders who hold a lien on the secured property still require regular monthly payments of principal and interest, or a notice of default will be recorded and the foreclosure process instigated.

There are myriad reasons for foreclosure. But why do so many property owners allow their homes to be sold out from under them when it can be saved in so many ways? Essentially, the reason stems from the fact that the distressed property owner thinks he can save his home at the last moment, and that he waits too long to protect his interest. Most often he continues to ignore the potential trouble until it's too late. While time passes, the delinquency charges continue to add up, the default period elapses, then the foreclosure period begins; and seemingly all of a sudden, the foreclosure sale occurs.

Nevertheless, in many cases distressed property in the foreclosure process can be salvaged by the alert property owner. Among the many alternatives available, he or she can outright sell the property, refinance it, take out a new loan, communicate directly with the lender for a postponement, sell other assets, etc. But these procedures take time to act upon, and unless a timely decision is made by the property owner, it will be sold at a foreclosure auction.

Foreclosure Terminology

Why should you learn foreclosure terminology? Because it is important that you become knowledgeable with the procedures and the terminology involved with the process of foreclosure in order to present yourself as a knowledgeable person to the owners of the distressed property with whom you will be dealing. This, in turn, will make it easier for you to function efficiently and effectively at acquiring worthwhile investments.

Before we get into some specific terminology, let me note: *Foreclosure laws and customs vary throughout the United States.* Due to the country's huge expanse, complicated further by the fact that about half the states use a mortgage as a security instrument while the other half utilizes a Deed of Trust, it is impossible in a book of this nature to set down standards of practice for all of them. Although the terms are very similar, and for the most part laws regarding foreclosure and real estate are somewhat uniform nationally, it is sound judgment to consult a trusted real estate attorney or professional knowledgeable in foreclosures to answer specific questions in your particular area.

For the purpose of clarity, throughout the book we refer essentially to a *Deed of Trust*, or *Trust Deed*, instead of continually describing both it and a mortgage, when each instrument is mentioned. For all practical purposes, both instruments are similar; the only major difference is their method of enforcement during foreclosure proceedings.

One further disclaimer: In the preparation of this book I have endeavored to offer good, sound advice in overall strategy and procedure at investing in foreclosed real estate. But by no means am I offering legal advice. While the procedures offered will most likely work in every county of every state, there are some variations in local laws and customs with which readers will have to familiarize themselves.

Mortgages and Deeds of Trust

Mortgages and Deeds of Trust are written instruments that create liens against real property (real estate). Should the borrower default on the loan (fail to make payments when due), mortgages and trust deeds will allow the lender to sell the secured property in order to satisfy the loan obligation.

The two parties involved in a mortgage are referred to as the *Mortgagor*, who is the property owner or borrower, and the *Mortgagee*, or lender. There are two parts to a mortgage: the *Mortgage Note*, which is evidence of the debt, and the *Mortgage Contract*, which is security for the debt. The note promises to repay the loan, while the contract promises to convey title of the property to the Mortgagee in case of default.

Should the Mortgagor fail to make loan payments when due, the secured property can then be sold through foreclosure in a court action. In order to implement such an action, the Mortgagee must first obtain from the court a *Foreclosure Judgment*, which orders the sheriff to sell the property to the highest bidder (usually over and above what is due the lender). Should a successful bid be made, the bidder receives from the sheriff a document known as the *Certificate of Sale*. The bidder must then hold the certificate for one year before he will be issued the deed to the property. If, within that year, the Mortgagor pays the bidder sufficient monies (bid price plus accrued interest), the Mortgagor then retains ownership of the property and the foreclosure sale is nullified. The period during which a Mortgagor is entitled to redeem his or her property is referred to as the *Mortgagor's Equity of Redemption.*

Trust Deeds are similar to mortgages except that (1) an additional third party is involved, and (2) the foreclosure period is much shorter in duration.

With a trust deed, the property owner or borrower is called the *Trustor,* and the lender is the *Beneficiary.* The intermediate third party, whose job it is to hold title to the property for the security of the lender, and if necessary handle the foreclosure sale, is called the *Trustee.* This is the key difference between these two instruments and why mortgages are more difficult and time consuming to foreclose on. The Mortgagor has title to the property, and it has to be seized from him in a court action, but a Trustor doesn't receive title to the property (the Trustee holds title) until debt on the secured property is paid off.

Should the Trustor default on his loan obligation, the subject property will be sold by the Trustee at public auction through a *Power of Sale* clause contained in all trust deeds, without court procedure.

Foreclosure is initiated by a *Notice of Default*, which is recorded by the Trustee, with a copy sent to the Trustor. After three months, a *Notice of Sale* is posted on the subject property, and an advertisement for the sale is carried in local newspapers once a week for three weeks. If during this period the Trustor fails to pay the Beneficiary sufficient funds—overdue loan payments plus interest, penalties, and late fees—to halt the foreclosure, the sale will then be conducted by the Trustee. Proceeds from the foreclosure sale are disbursed to the Beneficiary, and then to any other junior lien holders.

As mentioned earlier, throughout the United States, about half the states still use the traditional mortgage as a security instrument for real estate loans, though a few states use both the mortgage and a deed of trust as a security instrument. Primary lenders prefer the deed of trust overall, because in that case a foreclosure can be effected in one-third the time of a traditional mortgage, and notably without the need of court action.

You should also familiarize yourself with the following terms:

Assignment of Deed of Trust is a written financial document that transfers rights of the Beneficiary of a deed of trust to another party.

Lis Pendens (Notice of Action) is a legal notice that a lawsuit is pending on the subject property. It gives notice that anyone acquiring an interest in the property after the date of notice may be bound by the outcome of the pending litigation. Obviously, you should be very careful with such a notice attached to a property you're interested in. Unlike most other liens and attachments, a foreclosure sale usually does not wipe out this pending litigation.

Power of Sale, which was mentioned above, is a clause written into all Deeds of Trust. It gives the Trustee the right to advertise and sell the secured property at public auction if the Trustor defaults on the loan. This clause enables the Trustee to sell the property without a court order. When the sale is completed at the public auction, the Trustee will convey title to the purchaser, use the funds from the proceeds to satisfy the Beneficiary, pay off any junior lien holders, then return surplus monies, if any, to the Trustor. Once all this is accomplished, the Trustor is entirely divested of his or her property without any right of redemption.

Recission is the act of nullifying the foreclosure process. It places the property back to its previous condition, before the default was recorded. Recording a recission removes the default from the title records.

Substitution of Trustee is a written document, often located on the back of a Deed of Trust, that transfers trusteeship. Transfer or substitution of Trustees are made for reasons of convenience, more personal service, etc. Legally, the Beneficiary can also be the Trustee. His purpose in doing so might be to gain control of a trustee sale.

Trust Deed Foreclosure vs. Mortgage Foreclosure

The key differences between a Trust Deed foreclosure and a mortgage foreclosure are:

Understanding the Foreclosure Process

1. A Trust Deed has an additional third party intermediary involved called the Trustee, who holds title on behalf of the Beneficiary, and if necessary handles the foreclosure sale.
2. The Trust Deed foreclosure sale can be held at public auction *without* court action.
3. With a Trust Deed the duration of the foreclosure process is substantially shorter, such as four months compared to a duration up to 18 months with a mortgage.
4. Under a Trust Deed, the Trustee holds title to the property until the entire principal balance owing is paid the lender, whereas under a mortgage, the borrower holds title to the property during the term of the loan. And since the Trustor *does not* receive title to the property until the debt is paid, compared to a mortgage, with a Trust Deed it's much simpler to foreclose on the borrower because it's not necessary for a court action to acquire the title.
5. The successful bidder at a mortgage foreclosure receives from the sheriff a document known as the Certificate of Sale. The bidder must then hold the certificate for one year before he will be issued the deed to the property. If, within that year, the Mortgagor pays the bidder sufficient monies (bid price plus accrued interest), the Mortgagor then retains ownership of the property and the foreclosure sale is nullified.

Trust Deed Foreclosure

As mentioned earlier, the third party intermediary involved in a trust deed, the Trustee, holds title to the subject property on behalf of the Beneficiary as security for payment of the incurred debt. And if the Trustor fails to make the loan payments, the Power of Sale clause, which is written into all trust deeds, gives the Trustee the right to advertise and sell the secured property, without a court order, at public auction called a *Trustee Sale*. Usually when the Trustor is 90 days past due, the Beneficiary orders the Trustee to instigate the foreclosure proceedings by recording a Notice of Default. A copy of the default notice is also sent to the Trustor, and after a statutory period elapses and the Trustor neglects to remedy the default, notice of a Trustee Sale is posted on the subject property and advertised in local newspapers.

When the sale is completed at the public auction, the Trustee will convey title to the purchaser, use the funds from the proceeds to satisfy the

Beneficiary, pay any junior lien holders, then return surplus monies, if any, to the Trustor. If, by chance, the Trustee Sale fails to have a successful bidder, the foreclosed property then reverts to the beneficiary and put on the books as REO at a cost of the outstanding loan balance, including all late fees and costs incurred in the foreclosure.

Mortgage Foreclosure

In those states that utilize a mortgage as a security instrument to secure real property against default on a mortgage loan, the Mortgagor (borrower) signs two separate instruments: the *mortgage*, which is security for the debt and creates the lien against the encumbered property; and the *note*, which is evidence of the Mortgagor's promise to pay the incurred debt. Should the Mortgagor not make loan payments when due, the Mortgagee (lender) has the legal right to take action and recover the entire amount owed.

The usual procedure institutional lenders take when Mortgagors fall behind in their mortgage loan payments begins when the Mortgagee sends a letter notifying the Mortgagor that the payment is overdue, and requests the payment to be remitted immediately. If payment is not made, the Mortgagee will usually telephone the Mortgagor in an attempt to make contact. The Mortgagee essentially wants an explanation of the delinquency. He or she will want to know when the payment can be expected, or if the situation is temporary, or perhaps if the borrower is having financial difficulties. Whatever the case, if the Mortgagor has not made a payment for 90 days, or if the delinquent Mortgagor is unresponsive or uncooperative, the Mortgagee will instruct their attorney to initiate a foreclosure action in order to recover the amount owed.

The foreclosure is initiated by the attorney, who orders a *foreclosure search* on behalf of the Mortgagee. It is a written report issued by a title company providing the attorney with information about the Mortgagor, such as creditors who have an interest in the property and may have recorded liens against it. This foreclosure search ascertains that the party named as the defendant in the foreclosure proceeding is, in fact, the legitimate owner of the subject property. Other junior lien holders could, for instance, be second or third Mortgagees, contractors who recorded a mechanic's lien, utility companies, and state or federal income tax agencies.

Understanding the Foreclosure Process

The foreclosure attorney next files three legal documents with the clerk of the court in the county where the property is situated. These include a *Complaint*, which is the plaintiff's (Mortgagee's) allegations of entitlement to relief and the relief sought; a *Summons*, which orders the defendant to appear in court; and the Lis Pendens, which gives notice that anyone acquiring an interest in the property after the date of notice may be bound by the outcome of the pending litigation. In other words, any liens or judgments filed against the subject property *after* the date of the Lis Pendens may be excluded from the foreclosure action, and those creditors must instigate legal proceedings against the delinquent owner's assets separately.

Once the necessary documents have been filed with the court, each party named in the court action are served with the legal notices. Those served include the delinquent Mortgagor, all creditors who have an interest in the subject property, leasehold tenants, the Trustee, etc. As mentioned earlier, foreclosure laws and customs vary throughout the United States, and each state has laws that regulate the time periods these documents must be filed and who should be served. Some states, for instance, require that the delinquent Mortgagor be served within 30 days of the filing of the Lis Pendens. In another instance, the delinquent Mortgagor may have a leasehold tenant residing in the property that the Mortgagee is foreclosing on. In this situation, some states require that the successful bidder at the foreclosure sale honor the terms of the leasehold agreement until it expires, and that tenants are named as parties to the foreclosure action and served with notices.

Should the Mortgagor be uncooperative and fail to respond to the Complaint within the specified time limit, the Mortgagee's attorney reports to the court all the facts of the case and requests the court to appoint a referee. The appointed referee reviews all the pertinent facts and circumstances relevant to the foreclosure proceedings and then issues his or her report to the court. Then the court issues a Judgment of Foreclosure and Sale in favor of the foreclosing Mortgagee.

The date and location of the foreclosure auction is set and advertised according to local statutes and practices. The referee begins the auction by identifying the property being sold and then reads the terms of the sale to the auction attendees. The bidding on each particular property starts at the "upset price," which is usually the loan balance plus all incidental late charges and fees incurred during the foreclosure process.

The successful bidder is usually awarded a Contract of Sale, and will be expected to pay a required down payment (usually 10 percent of the bid amount) immediately in the form of a cashier's check, money order, or certified funds, as required by the referee. The successful high bidder will be expected to "close" with the 90-percent balance due, typically within 30 days after the Contract of Sale is signed. See Ch 3 for detailed guidelines to buying foreclosures at the auction.

And as mentioned earlier, the successful bidder does not receive a deed to the property. Instead, he or she receives from the sheriff a Certificate of Sale. The bidder must then hold the certificate for one year before being issued the deed to the property. If, within that year, the Mortgagor pays the bidder sufficient monies (bid price plus accrued interest), the Mortgagor then retains ownership of the property and the foreclosure sale is nullified.

Soldiers and Sailors Civil Relief Act of 1940 The SSCRA, which was revised in 2003, provides a number of significant protections to service members. Among them, when a person is on active duty, in certain cases a lender must revise a foreclosure action to comply with the SSCRA. In compliance of this act, when a property is owned by a service member and the mortgage loan was originated before the commencement of that military duty, then no seizure, no sale, nor foreclosure for nonpayment of any sum due will be valid if it's made during the time of the military service, or within several months thereafter. However, this is not applicable if it's the belief of the court that the ability of the delinquent borrower to comply with the terms of the loan obligation is not materially affected by the borrower's involvement in military service, or if the foreclosure sale was ordered by the court prior to commencing active duty.

Other protections for service members include: staying court hearings if military service materially affects the service members' ability to defend their interests; reducing interest to 6 percent on preservice loans and obligations; requiring court action before a service member's family can be evicted from rental property for nonpayment of rent if the monthly rent is $2,400 or less; and termination of a preservice residential lease.

Understanding the Foreclosure Process

The Servicemembers Civil Relief Act (SCRA) of 2003 was written to clarify the language of the SSCRA to incorporate many years of judicial interpretation of the SSCRA, and to update the SSCRA to reflect new developments in American life since 1940. The new law, SCRA, as revised December 2003:

1. Extends the application of a service member's right to stay court hearings to administrative hearings. It now requires a court or administrative hearing to grant at least a 90-day stay if requested by the service member. Additional stays can be granted at the discretion of the judge or hearing official.
2. Modifies the eviction protection section by precluding evictions from premises occupied by service members for which the monthly rent does not exceed $2,400 for the year 2003. The act provides a formula to calculate the rent ceiling for subsequent years.
3. Extends the right to terminate real property leases to active duty soldiers moving pursuant to permanent change of station (PCS) orders or deployment orders of at least 90 days. This eliminates the need to request a military termination clause in leases.

Historically, the SSCRA applied to members of the National Guard only if they were serving in a Title 10 status. Effective December 6, 2002, the SSCRA protections were extended to members of the National Guard called to active duty for 30 days or more pursuant to a contingency mission specified by the President or the Secretary of Defense. This continues in the SCRA.

NOTEWORTHY

Always consult with a knowledgeable real estate attorney or mortgage expert who specializes in foreclosure acquisitions about the specialized laws and procedures that apply in your state.

You Have the Opportunity to Buy in Any of the Three Phases of Foreclosure

As a foreclosure specialist, you will have the opportunity to buy at any of the three phases a foreclosed property may evolve. In the first phase, the default period, you'll have the opportunity to work with distressed property owners prior to the actual foreclosure sale in an attempt to buy the distressed property from them. Or perhaps you like the idea of bidding and competing with others for foreclosed property at the public auction, which is the second phase in the foreclosure proceedings. Then, if the foreclosed property fails to sell at the auction, you'll have the opportunity to buy it from the foreclosing lender during its third phase, when it reverts back to the lender and put on the books as real estate owned.

Default Period

This is the period prior to the foreclosure auction when the borrowers are usually more than 90 days delinquent on their loan and a notice of default has been recorded. During this initial phase of foreclosure, the foreclosure specialist can enter into negotiations with the troubled owner and acquire the property through various means, which we will detail in the next chapter.

Foreclosure Auction

During this second phase of the foreclosure process the borrower has defaulted on his or her loan, and the lender takes action to recover the entire amount owed by selling the encumbered property at public auction. What you can expect at a public foreclosure auction along with how to successfully bid are detailed in Ch 3.

After-the-Sale or REO Phase

Should the foreclosed property fail to sell at the foreclosure auction, it reverts to the lender and is put on the books at a value of the outstanding loan balance, plus all late fees and costs incurred during the foreclosure process. In Chapter 4 we provide guidelines on how to purchase foreclosed properties from inventories of primary lenders and government agencies.

2

Guidelines to Acquiring Foreclosures Prior to the Sale

In this chapter you'll learn how to purchase foreclosures during the default period, which is the first phase of the foreclosure proceedings before the foreclosure auction. We recommend you follow the 10 key guidelines for acquiring properties prior to sale. Among them is featured a Business Plan and how to implement it. Also included are strategies for dealing with troubled owners and institutional lenders, and how to gain position of the second loan. In addition, we included two helpful forms necessary for gathering important data: the Property Information Form and the Cost Estimate Sheet.

In Chapter 3 we provide detailed guidelines to buying foreclosures at the public auction. And in Chapter 4 you'll learn how to purchase foreclosures after the public auction.

Before digging in and discussing the details of available approaches you may wish to take, it is essential to your success that the terminology used in this specialized field of foreclosure be studied (see Chapter 1), and that you follow these investment guidelines to acquiring properties.

Overview of the 10 Key Guidelines

When you know the proper guidelines and procedures for acquiring fore-closed realty, you will have a better chance of being a successful distressed realty investor. The following is a summary of the 10 key guidelines, after which each is discussed in more detail.

1. *Learn the terminology of the foreclosure process.* In the previous chapter we presented the specialized terms and definitions that are relevant to this very specialized business of foreclosure investing. As mentioned before, you must become knowledgeable with the procedures and the terminology involved with the process of foreclosure in order to present yourself as a knowledgeable person to the owners of the distressed property with whom you will be dealing. This, in turn, will make it easier for you to function efficiently and effectively at acquiring worthwhile investments.

2. *Acquaint yourself with the sources of distressed property.* You have a variety of sources of foreclosed realty to choose from. Prior to a foreclosure sale, you can acquire lists of default notices and foreclosure sale notices published by legal newspapers and fee subscription services. Also, there's the Country Recorder's Office, which records Notices of Default and is available to the public for inspection. Then there's real estate owned (REO), which is the repossessed realty that failed to sell at the foreclosure sale of primary lenders, and federal, state, county, and local agencies.

3. *Decide on a specific territory to operate in.* It is virtually impossible to become an expert on real estate in distress when the area of concentration is too large. You're better off concentrating your efforts and focus on a specific small area—for example, within two or three counties in your own state—where you can learn property values, keep tabs on events that can affect property values, and acquaint yourself with local professional people (such as realtors and contractors) who can be helpful in that area.

4. *Specialize in detached single-family residences.* They are the wisest choice, especially for the newcomer to foreclosure investing. Avoid investing in condominiums, cooperative apartments, vacant land, industrial real estate, and commercial real estate.

5. *Prepare a list of potential investments.* Now that you are acquainted with your territory and have tapped various sources of distressed realty, you can begin, through the process of elimination, to narrow down those properties that show a good profit potential.

6. *Prepare an investment analysis and a business plan.* Once you've narrowed down a number of properties that should be given further consideration, make a careful written analysis of what kind of offer you will make to the seller and what you intend to do with the property after acquiring it.

7. *Meet and negotiate with the owner.* If you'll be meeting with a distressed owner prior to a foreclosure sale, you want to instill a mood of mutual assistance. You will fully explain the procedures, gather all the pertinent data, and stress the fact that only the specialist investor can truly remedy the distressed owner's precarious situation.

8. *Estimate the costs.* Now that you have gathered all the relevant facts about the property, you can make an estimate of all the costs involved and prepare for the next step.

9. *Gather all the data and close the deal.* During this step, you have to do some research and become acquainted with all the forms necessary to close the deal and how to complete them inexpensively.

10. *What to do now that you own the property.* In this final step, you want to be sure the deed is recorded, the utilities are turned on, and eviction procedures are initiated if unwanted tenants are occupying the property. Then utilize the strategy you intended in your business plan in the disposition of your newly acquired investment, which could be to do any of the following: simply rent it to a quality good-paying tenant, give your tenant a buy option, land banking, or make a conversion to a higher rental usage.

Key Guidelines to Buying Foreclosures Prior to the Sale

Now that you've been introduced to the 10 keys, we will go into each of them, one by one in more detail.

1. Learn the Terminology of the Foreclosure Process

You should have carefully read the terminology we presented in the previous chapter. To reiterate, if you are unfamiliar with the language used in this very specialized field of foreclosure, the people you will have to deal with will likely try to avoid doing business with you. In contrast, a knowledgeable foreclosure expert who presents an image of confidence will quickly gain the respect he or she will need to compete in this very specialized business.

2. Acquaint Yourself with the Sources of Distressed Property

Sources of information regarding real estate in foreclosure are available through a variety of outlets. Services that provide such information vary throughout the country due to each state's legal requirements. Some states require the Notice of Default to be published in a legal newspaper. Many legal newspapers publish these notices simply as a community service.

Besides legal newspapers, some companies make available public record services on a fee subscription basis. Both newspaper and fee subscription services get their information directly from the County Recorder's Office. For the customer's convenience, the information they sell is rearranged into a more easily read form. Of course, you can get information about recorded defaults directly from the County Recorder. This data is recorded daily, and is available without cost for public use.

Once the default on a Deed of Trust has been recorded and the 90-day redemption period has elapsed, the Trustee is legally required to publish the Notice of Trustee Sale. This legal notice *cannot* be found at the County Recorder's Office because the Trustee is only required to publish, not record, this notice. You can attain this information from subscription services, legal newspapers, and often in local newspapers authorized to publish these legal notices. Further legalities require the Trustee to post the Notice of the Trustee Sale on one or more public buildings within the same county and on the subject property itself. Thus, you'll often notice these postings on bulletin boards at your county courthouse.

Keep in mind that services publishing Notices of Default are not liable for the accuracy of the information they publish. It is not uncommon to find incorrect addresses or other erroneous data. The only data that can be deemed reliable are the actual recordings found in the County Recorder's Office.

Most of this vital information about defaults also can be attained by ordering preliminary title reports from a title company. But this type of service can be prohibitively expensive. In order for you to become a professional specialist in the field of distressed realty, you should take the trouble to examine the records available at the County Recorder's Office. By doing so you can gain the experience necessary to be an expert in this specialized arena of investment.

You also need to know that these published services do not state whether the instrument in default is a first, second, or third Deed of Trust. To correctly determine which of the liens is in default, you'll have to make a personal visit to the County Recorder's Office and look it up yourself.

Occasionally, these legal notices of default omit the exact street address of the subject property. If this is the case, you can get the correct address by consulting the map books available while at the County Recorder's Office. The address can be attained by matching the given legal description with those in the available map books.

There was a time when the Trustee would provide necessary information about the default to the public as a professional courtesy. This service, unfortunately, is not given so freely anymore due to the increasing popularity among speculators in this interesting field of foreclosed realty investing. Nowadays, besides holding public auction of the subject property, the Trustee is not obligated to provide information except for date, time, and location of the sale. (See sample of a published Notice of Default in Figure 2-1.)

By the way, once you attain needed information about a distressed property and decide to pay a visit, you'll note a certain aura about it. Property in foreclosure, virtually 99 times out of a 100, always has the same appearance. You can spot the neglected property a mile away. In a typically nice neighborhood it's the only house on the block with a dried-out, unmowed lawn with debris scattered about. You may notice a broken window or two—especially if the structure was not boarded up—possibly a roof in need of repair, and it most likely requires paint. These "tattered ladies" stand out in a nice neighborhood like a man wearing a pair of polka dot tennis shoes dressed in a black tuxedo.

Figure 2-1 Sample of a Published Notice of Default

PUBLISHED NOTICE OF DEFAULT

NOTICE OF DEFAULT AND ELECTION TO
SELL UNDER A DEED OF TRUST

Loan No. MI-XXXXXXXXX

Foreclosure No. S-XXXXXX

Original 'Notice of Default' recorded 7-9-78,
File No. 78-46 XXXXX, in Office of Recorder
of Los Angeles County, California.

NOTICE IS HEREBY GIVEN:

That XXXXXXXXXFEDERAL SAVINGS AND
LOAN ASSOCIATION , a corporation, is Trustee
under a Deed of Trust executed by XXXXXXXXX
and dated January 3, 1975, and recorded January
I4,1975, page no. 472, Document No. XXXXXX
Book XXXXXX, of Official Records in the Office of the Recorder of the County of Los Angeles,
State of California, and given to secure payment
of a promissory note for $10,670.20, dated January
3,1975, payable with interest thereon and therein
provided, in favor of XXXXXXX FEDERAL
SAVINGS AND LOAN ASSOCIATION, a
corporation.

That a breach of the obligations for which said
Deed of Trust was given as security has occurred
in that the following payments due upon said note
were not paid when due, and still remain due,
owing, and unpaid:

> The monthly installment of principal
> due March 1, 1978, and subsequent
> installments thereafter, thereby decl-
> aring the entire principal balance of
> $8,974.66 due and payable, and late
> charges as set forth in said Deed of
> Trust, and together with any and all
> sums advanced by the Beneficiary
> under the terms and provisions of
> said Deed of Trust, and delinquent
> taxes, assessments, and insurance pre-
> miums. if any.

That by reason thereof, the undersigned,
present beneficiary under said Deed of Trust, has
executed and delivered to said Trustee a written
declaration of default and demand for sale, and
has surrendered to said Trustee said Deed of
Trust and all documents evidencing obligations
secured thereby, and has declared and does
declare all sums secured thereby immediately
due and payable, and has elected and does hereby
elect to cause the property described in said
Deed of Trust to be sold to satisfy the obligations secured thereby.

NOTICE

You may have the right to cure the default
described herein and reinstate the mortgage or
deed of trust. Section 2924c of the Civil Code
permits certain defaults to be cured upon the
payment of the amounts required by that section without requiring payment of that portion
of principal and interest which would not be due
had no default occurred. Where reinstatement is
possible, if the default is not cured within three
months following the recording of this notice,
the right of reinstatement will terminate and the
property may be sold.

To determine if reinstatement is possible and
the amount, if any, necessary to cure the default,
contact the beneficiary or mortgagee or the succ-
essors in Interest, whose name and address as of
the date of this notice is: XXXXXXXFederal
Savings and Loan Association of Los Angeles
(Mailing Address: XXXXXXXXXXXXXXXXX
XXXXXXXX

Dated   March 21,1978

Lot 7, Block 13, Tract XXXXX, as per map
recorded in Book XXXX, Pages XXX through
76, except the Northerly 35 feet thereof,
County of Los Angeles, State of California.
XXXXXXXFEDERAL SAVINGS AND LOAN
ASSOCIATION OF XXXXXXXXXXXXXXXX

By XXXXXXXXXX
Assistant Secretary

3. Decide on a Specific Territory to Operate In

For the purpose of efficiency, it is important that you restrict your operations to a specific area near your residence. The designated area could be
within your city limits or no larger than the adjoining counties where you

reside. The primary reason for working within a certain designated area is both to develop contacts in that area and to get to know local property values so you can ascertain market value in order to expedite an efficient purchase. The designated area you choose should have the potential for growth, which will eventually lead to an increase in property values.

Once the territory has been selected, you can begin accumulating data relevant to important events occurring in the area. Purchase a large, detailed wall map of your area of interest and then note the sales prices of homes, where schools are located, and specific streets where resales offer higher dollars per square foot of house living area. Additionally, you can note areas that show signs of reduced value, possibly due to higher crime rates, poor land planning, or local traffic jams.

When you become a specialist in this designated territory, you don't have to confine your activities just to single-family homes. Get to know the values of small one- to four-unit apartments and what they rent for.

A large wall map of the area you're interested in can be attained from the County Assessor or at the County Clerk's Office. Make notations on your map in colored pencil denoting trends and certain events as they occur, either positive or negative, that may have an economic impact on your designated territory.

Similar to specializing in detached single-family residences, when you keep your operations within a limited designated area, you get a good feel for the territory. Not only that, but you also become more familiar with the roads and terrain, so that you can more efficiently get around.

4. Specialize in Detached Single-Family Residences

Specialization is important because it leads to efficiency, and usually means that one is better at their profession, whatever it happens to be. For instance, most doctors concentrate in one particular field of medicine, and many attorneys specialize in one specific area of law in order to be an expert in that specialized field of endeavor. It's more practical, and probably easier, to be an expert in one particular field of expertise than to become a jack-of-all-trades, master of none.

And why should you specialize in detached single-family residences? Because, of all the different types of housing—such as attached homes like condominiums and cooperative apartments—DSFRs have historically held their value better in weak markets and have appreciated more in strong, booming markets. Moreover, American homeowners have always had a deep-seated love affair with detached homes. It's likely that they will always be the most desired style of home and always in demand for most potential home buyers.

For the small investor, or the newcomer to foreclosure investing, specializing in DSFRs is the wisest choice. There's a plentiful supply, along with strong demand created by other small investors and first-time home buyers, which means there's an adequate supply and plenty of demand for homes to make it worth your while. On the other hand, the category of "attached homes"—condos and co-op—represents less than 10 percent of the overall residential marketplace. So, we do not recommend that you invest in them, with the exception of condominiums in great locations, but then only if they can be purchased at a bargain price.

5. Prepare a List of Potential Investments

This procedure begins by narrowing down the total available supply of distressed property that you have compiled from various sources. Start, for example, by selecting worthwhile prospects from all the real estate owned listings that you acquired from REO managers. Then compile available property through the sources we mentioned earlier: legal publications, subscription services, and the County Recorder's Office.

Compile all pertinent data of each potential investment on the Property Information Form (see Figure 2-2). This form lists all vital information on each potential distressed property acquisition, which will provide you with adequate data to make an accurate financial analysis, and, hopefully if everything goes right, effectively close the deal.

Additional potential investments can be developed while the distressed realty investor is getting acquainted with his or her territory, simply by just cruising neighborhoods. Often, property that will eventually be in a distressed condition can be spotted with an alert eye. Run-down homes with debris scattered about are usually rented out by absentee landlords (owners who live out of state). Due to varying circumstances, they are often abandoned by the tenants, and the absentee landlord should be contracted immediately to procure a sale. Some of these owners who have vacated

Acquiring Foreclosures Prior to the Sale

Figure 2-2 Property Information Form

Lot no._____ Block no. _____ Map page no. _____
Owner's name: _____
Property address: _____
Phones: Cell _____ Home _____ Work _____
Date default action taken: _____ Final date to correct: _____

First Loan
Lender's name: _____ Loan No.: _____
Type: _____ Is it assumable? _____ Rate of interest: _____
Original principal owing: $_____
Balance as of: _____ is $_____
Monthly payments (P&I): $_____

Payments in Arrears
First loan $_____ No. of months at $_____ = $_____
Second loan $_____ No. of months at $_____ = $_____
Third loan $_____ No. of months at $_____= $_____
Total late charges = $_____
Total default and foreclosure fees = $_____
Total amount in arrears as of _____ is $_____

Description of Other Liens
_____ as of _____, total owing including penalties _____
_____ as of _____, total owing including penalties _____
Square footage of livable area _____ Lot size _____
No. of bedrooms _____ No. of baths _____ Dining:_____ Garage: _____
Estimated cost to repair interior (describe rooms and work required):
_____
_____
_____
Estimated cost to repair exterior:_____
Total estimated repair cost of interior and exterior: _____

Property Location Factors (indicate whether good, average, or below average)
Lot: _____ Shopping: _____ Public transportation: _____
Schools: _____ Parks and other: _____ Freeway access: _____

Preliminary Cost Estimates
Total cost of all delinquencies   = _____
Title and escrow expenses   = _____
Loan transfer or origination fee   = _____
One month's P&I, taxes, and insurance   = _____
Cash required for additional liens   = _____
Total cash required to make current   = _____
Total interior and exterior repair costs = _____

rentals often board up the windows and doors to protect their property from vandals. If you spot a boarded-up property that is not already on your list of potential investments, find out who the owner is and try and make a deal.

6. Prepare an Investment Analysis and a Business Plan

Now that a list of potential acquisitions has been made, it's time to prepare a financial analysis of those properties that deserve further consideration. On the Property Information Form you can list more detailed information about the property, such as the date the default was recorded, final date to remedy the default, and all necessary financial data. This will take us to the next step, which is writing a business plan.

The Business Plan. It's crucial to write a business plan before you buy. That's because when you develop a strategic plan it forces you to think through the most important factors of owning a particular property—such as how to finance it, what improvements to make, and what to do with it once you own the property. It also compels you to think about your future goals and objectives with the property you intend to purchase.

By starting with a business plan before you make any investments, you will have already made some fundamental decisions as to what you're looking for in a particular property. Are you looking for a safe return, or for a situation in which you're going to buy and do something to the property—perhaps dramatically increasing its value based on your creative vision—and then renting or selling it to earn a profit? Is it going to be a short- or long-term investment?

Your business plan will also serve as a basis for presentations you might need to make to potential lenders, partners, or investors.

Framework for Getting Started

These are the key points to consider in writing a successful business plan:

- What is the purpose of the investment? That is, how does it fit into your long- or short-term overall financial goals and objectives?
- How are you going to increase the value of whatever it is you intend to buy?
- How do you intend to manage the property? Will it be a long-term holding period?

- How will you finance the property? Do you intend to get investors or will you finance it through a primary lender by yourself?
- How does the financial analysis look for the property? What are the projected fixed costs for refurbishment, the running costs for maintaining it, and the projected income to be generated from it?
- How does the investment timeline look for the property? When does it indicate that expenses will be incurred and income will be received?

You need the business plan to show your lender or investors the expectations for the project. To do that, it should include all the costs you estimate, including those for acquisition, refurbishment, holding, and financing. And it should give a project time frame, specifying, for example, how long you intend to hold the property. It should also give your potential lenders and investors some background information on how you arrived at your predictions. For instance, you could include project charts showing data for comparable rentals in the vicinity of the subject property.

Determining the Purpose of the Investment

Land banking (the holding of a property with the future intention of converting it to a more profitable use), is a good example of an extremely long-term investment (see Chapter 8 for a more detailed description). You'd be buying land, and the improvements on it, in the expectation that in time it will go up in value, perhaps because it's at a strategic location. Meanwhile, you'd pay the taxes on it, and that's your investment. But you don't intend to develop it yourself. You don't intend to build on it. Instead, you intend only to own it, letting it become more valuable as a result of appreciation and inflation.

In New York City, a good example of land banking would be acquiring an existing parking lot. Your intention is to continue running the property as a parking lot, but at some point in the future you will build a high-rise office building on the site. In another example, in Lansing, Michigan, you could buy a spacious two-story home situated on a large corner lot that's located in the path of future commercial growth. Meanwhile, you continue renting the house as a residence, and then at some time in the future convert the building into a higher use office rental. The reason: It's more profitable because commercial office space rents for about twice the rate of residential space.

You'll find that land banking works very well in an area or neighborhood that is in transition or looks like it's in transition. For example, you have a depressed area over here, while an area not far away is starting to flourish, is being rebuilt and rising in value. You could say, "Hey, I can buy here in this depressed area while it's cheap because sooner or later the growth nearby will come my way. And I want to be there when it happens. So I want to buy on the theory that there will be an uptick sometime in the future."

You can't really say how long it will take for that to happen. No one knows for sure. But you can be sure that the earlier you buy it, the cheaper the price will be. And conversely, the later you buy it—once the growth gets real close—the more expensive the price will be because the owner then says, "I can hold it myself, I don't need you!"

7. Meet and Negotiate with the Owner

When the time comes to meet and negotiate with the owner of the property you're interested in purchasing, keep in mind that the purpose of your visit is twofold. It is to not only make a good deal for yourself, but to also aid the troubled owner in his or her distressed situation. If everything goes according to plan, the troubled owner could receive cash for her equity (if applicable), and her credit will be salvaged while you acquire the property.

Prior to the visit you should refrain from using the telephone until an actual meeting with the property owner has been accomplished. This way you avoid the owner easily brushing you off over the phone. A personal visit is not only more businesslike, but will also give you the opportunity to look over the interior of the property.

Begin your approach by being friendly. You want the owner to feel "comfortable" in talking and dealing with you. This is essential. If people like you, they'll go all out to please you. Start with a simple introduction of who you are and why you're there, suggesting a mood of mutual assistance. While you're looking over the interior of the home, try to find a common ground to establish a good rapport. Find a common theme for discussion. Look around the home for photos and memorabilia. If the owner is interested in sports, talk sports. Look for family pictures and ask questions: "Is that your grandchild? You must be proud of her (or him)? How many grandchildren do you have? How many boys? Do you see them often?" The greater interest you show, the more you instill a "warm and cozy" feeling.

Portraying a good sense of humor is usually an excellent icebreaker, but be wary of anything that could be considered offensive.

You want to convince the distressed property owner of your sincerity and desire to reach a mutually amicable conclusion.

Once you've broken the ice, mention that you have discovered through your sources that his property might be for sale. If, in fact, the property is for sale, you can immediately get into the details of the transaction. However, should the troubled owner not currently have the property up for sale, a different approach has to be used.

Time is definitely of the essence in dealing with distressed property that is in the foreclosure process.

Time Element in Distressed Realty. It is important for you to understand that investment in foreclosed property is a very patient and timely business. To get results you have to exert the effort, which includes looking at a lot of potential investments, analysis of pertinent data, and persistent effort in order to keep abreast of available opportunities.

Remember that time is on the side of you, the investor. The pressure is on the distressed owner to remedy his precarious situation, or else he will lose the property in foreclosure, and his good credit rating. It is to your advantage to remind the distressed homeowner that you're interested in making a good deal for yourself, while at the same time helping him in realizing some cash (if applicable), and in salvaging his credit rating.

During these stressful periods that troubled homeowners face during foreclosure proceedings, it is important for you to also remember that they often tend to disguise the truth about certain matters. And understandably so, because the potential for loss of one's home is obviously a very stressful situation to deal with. Therefore, it's imperative that all details (the facts and related dollar amounts) of what the homeowner relates to you be verified. In other words, get him to show you the lender's paperwork that reveals the appropriate amounts in arrears and the exact dates of future events. And while you're in the homeowner's presence, keep the dialogue going to find out as much as possible about his financial condition and the property.

Should the distressed owner miraculously remedy his financial condition and bring the delinquent payments up to date, be happy for him. But at the same time continue to keep in touch, because now the homeowner is faced with an additional problem—how to keep up with the existing mortgage payments, plus paying back the additional funds he likely borrowed to remedy the initial crisis. Chances are, by continuing to keep in touch with him, the opportunity to make a deal on the property will arise once again.

Phrases to Stimulate Negotiations with a Troubled Owner. The following are suggested opening phrases you can use to stimulate negotiations with a troubled owner in foreclosure:

- "If you'll allow me to make a complete financial analysis of the property, I can be back in 24 hours with a firm offer that will remedy your present dilemma."
- "By assisting you during these troubled times, I can help myself at the same time."
- "I can function much faster than a real estate agent, plus you will save a costly sales commission."
- "I completely understand how you feel. By allowing me to acquire your property you can be assured that the lender, or anyone else, cannot profit from your hard luck."
- "My purpose in being here is to offer you cash for your equity, which you would unfortunately lose in a foreclosure sale. Therefore, by dealing with me you can salvage your good credit, drive away much better off, and start all over again."
- "Please allow me to see the documents on your home. Do you have the deed, the title policy, and the payment records?"
- "Be careful not to let other people know that we're negotiating a deal. If any realtors and lenders get involved, it could make our deal very messy."

It is important at the onset of negotiations that the owner is made aware that time is of the essence. Since he or she is in the midst of a foreclosure proceeding, care should be taken that the deal you're trying to negotiate is completed before it is too late.

Often, during initial stages of negotiating with the troubled owner, he might mention that he's trying to arrange new financing on the property in foreclosure. Somehow, he has the belief that the foreclosure can be remedied by acquiring additional funds. The important point for you to remember, as a foreclosure investor, is that when a property is in foreclosure, it's improbable that the owner will be able to acquire additional financing. It is unlikely any lender will underwrite an additional loan while the current loan is in default. Looking at the situation from a lender's point of view, if the troubled property owner cannot make payments on his current loan, why would anyone think he could make the payments on a new loan?

If, by some miracle, he is able to get a loan from someone, he's probably only postponing the inevitable foreclosure, because he now has to make additional loan payments on top of the loan on which he's already in default.

Should the distressed owner state that he's arranging another loan, advise him like this: "Okay, if you feel supplemental funds will remedy your precarious situation, then by all means do it. But if you cannot arrange the loan, or if you have problems later, please call me so I can present an offer for your property and assist in rectifying your credit."

The important point at this particular time is to leave the owner with a positive view of you as a foreclosure specialist who wants to help, so that if he gets into a distressed situation again, he knows who to call.

As a distressed property investor, you can act faster and offer better results to an owner in foreclosure than anyone else. The real estate agent who gets involved in the transaction requires the expense of a sizable commission, which is a needless expense when you—the private investor—purchase the property. And should government agencies get involved, they'll require expensive repairs and timely documents to be filled out before any money will be funded.

The Best Prospect in Town. A run-down shabby house will always be the best deal in town. In fact, as long as the building is structurally sound, the more run-down, the better. Each and every defect in the condition of the property presents opportunity to the shrewd distressed property investor. Every flaw can be turned into more profit for the investor.

Each defect with the property has to be noted, then you must do both a minimum and maximum cost estimate to correct each defect. These estimated costs are then added to your other estimated costs, such as the acquisition and financing costs. Then the deal with the distressed owner is made on the basis of the maximum cost estimate plus a reasonable profit for you, the investor. Once the property is acquired, maximum effort must be made to renovate the property at a price as close to the minimum overall cost estimate as possible.

Keep in mind that it's not important for you, the foreclosure investor, to be a jack-of-all-trades and have the ability to fix everything yourself, but it is essential that you're precise at discovering defects in the property and accurately know how much it will cost to repair each item. However, any of the handiwork you can do yourself will generate a lot of cost savings. Remember too that you should have a good idea of property values in your territory of operation so you can accurately determine what the renovated property will sell for. Obviously, it would be foolish to invest in a property if the total cost, including the cost of refurbishment, is greater than its market value after all renovations are complete.

If, like most of us, you're not a jack-of-all-trades, it would be a good idea to know a contractor who can walk through a run-down building with you and determine the soundness of key items such as the overall plumbing, electrical system, roof, and the foundation. The professional contractor cannot only point out problem areas you may have initially overlooked, but also give you a realistic cost estimate on doing the renovations. After the initial inspection, which is usually a casual first inspection, it's important that you are thorough in any follow-up examinations. After a time and a few walk-throughs with someone you hired to inspect, you will gain enough experience so you can make the same analysis yourself.

By thoroughly checking out the entire property, making a careful analysis, then honestly evaluating the potential sales price of the property once renovations are completed, you can rest assured that the risk has been minimized and a substantial profit will be realized.

If, by chance, after a careful analysis was made and the numbers simply did not work out, and the total costs of refurbishment are more than the projected resale value, don't entirely maroon the project. Go back to the troubled owner and reopen negotiations for a new deal. Point out that it's necessary for you to make a reasonable profit. If you're still unable to negotiate a deal, then it's time to look elsewhere for an investment. Chances are, if you keep in touch every three months or so, the same owner will be faced with financial difficulties again. Meanwhile, keep the information you've compiled filed away because the data you just attained might be useful in the future.

8. Estimate the Costs

Probably the least complicated way to acquire a property in foreclosure is to assume the existing loan in arrears, making up all the delinquent loan payments and penalties, purchasing the deed from the owner, and then taking possession of the property. Very neat and clean. But more often than not, distressed realty requires you to get involved with complicated matters, such as unpaid taxes or more than one loan in arrears.

In order to simplify these matters, we included a Cost Estimate Form (Figure 2-3) that takes into consideration all the items involved when

Figure 2-3. Cost Estimate Form

Address of Subject Property: _____

Costs to Acquire Property
Purchase the deed $_____
Delinquent taxes $_____
Bonds and assessments $_____

Delinquencies on First Loan
_____ months @ $ _____ = $_____
Total late charges and fees $_____
Advances $_____
Pay off second loan (include all
delinquencies, advances, and fees) $_____

Preliminary Cost Estimates
Title and escrow expenses $_____
Loan transfer or origination fee $_____
One month P&I and taxes and insurance $_____

Total Cash to Purchase:
$_____
Balance of all loans after purchase $_____
Other encumbrances $_____

Total Property Cost (Before Repairs):
$_____
Cost of repairs needed
   Paint $_____ Plumbing $_____ Roof $_____
   Electrical $_____ Termite $_____ Fencing $_____
   Landscape $_____ Floors $_____ Carpet $_____
   Wallpaper $_____ Fixtures $_____ Hardware $_____
Total Cost of Repairs
$_____
Total Property lost (after repairs)
$_____

investing in foreclosed property. By completely filling out this form, you'll become more aware of the total costs involved, which helps to eliminate potential errors.

Purchasing the Deed. Make certain that the owner (Grantor) of the subject property has the property vested in his or her name. To verify this, check the grant deed or the title insurance policy. If none of these are available, check the escrow documents when the owner purchased the property. If none of the three above items are available for verification, check the official records at the Country Recorder's Office.

You must know the difference between a *Grand Deed* and a *Quitclaim Deed*. When an owner of real property issues a Grand Deed, he is warranting that he has marketable title to the property. A Quitclaim Deed simply releases any interest the Grantor may have in the property. If the Grantor has no interest, he is not releasing anything. For example, assume you give me a Quitclaim Deed on the Brooklyn Bridge. Although you may not have any interest in the Brooklyn Bridge whatsoever, you are simply executing a statement to the fact saying, "I have no interest whatsoever in the Brooklyn Bridge." Obviously you have no interest in it, therefore, you are releasing nothing. When you receive a Quitclaim Deed it is important that the Grantor has an interest that is conveyed to you.

Real Estate Taxes. It's not uncommon for a foreclosed property to have delinquent property taxes assessed against it, and don't be surprised if up to three years of assessment have accumulated. This is often the case when the lender neglected to make provisions for an impound account covering the regular payment of taxes and hazard insurance. The purpose of an impound account is to allow the borrower to pay a prorated share of these expenses monthly into a trust account to which the lender pays when due. In the event you're dealing with properties that have FHA or VA loans on them, you can be assured that the property taxes are usually up to date because these types of government-backed loans make it mandatory for the lender to provide an impound account.

The best way of making sure the property taxes have been paid is to get information directly from the County Tax Collector. All that's required is a simple phone call if you can supply the tax collector with the complete legal description of the subject property. If that's not available, a personal visit to the County Tax Collector will be required.

Bonds and Assessments. Frequently, these items show up in less than fully developed areas of a city where sewers and sidewalks have not been completed. You have to be wary of these types of liens against real property because they do not always appear on the title report. These liens are recorded against real property and are set up to allow the homeowner to pay them off monthly over a period of years. In some cases, however, these bonds and assessments have to be fully paid off when the property is sold.

To verify if any of these type of liens are outstanding, or any other details about them, a phone call to the County Tax Department or the County Treasurer will resolve matters.

9. Gather All the Data and Close the Deal

At this point you have a particular property located that appears profitable; you have an appraisal (see Chapter 6, "Inspection and Appraisal of Foreclosed Real Estate"), and have arrived at an upper and lower price range that you're prepared to offer. What now?

You will now have to research all of the following and log it on the Property Information Form (Figure 2-2): names of the lender and Trustor or Mortgagor. Is it a first or second loan in foreclosure? When was it recorded and for how much? Is there a recorded second loan? If the second loan is in foreclosure, who holds the first? Can the first loan be easily assumed?

Other critical data you need to know is how much the loan or loans are in arrears. If the property taxes are delinquent, you need to know how much is owed. And are there any other recorded liens against the property?

Most of these questions can be answered in the office of the County Recorder where the subject property is located. All documentation involved with real property is kept open to the public in the County Recorder's Office.

The recording process dates back to before the Civil War. Now, as it did then, it provides to the public a notice of important documentation in regard to real property. When it comes time to develop data on a property in foreclosure, note that a first mortgage or Deed of Trust recorded first has priority over those liens that are recorded subsequently. In other words, the first in line is first in right to any claims on the property, should a default occur.

The actual recording process is done by the County Recorder. When a deed is recorded, the lender will submit a deed to the County Recorder, who files a copy of that deed in the official records.

Closing the Deal. In order for the distressed owner to be ready to make a deal during the default period, the following criteria must have been met before a transaction can take place.

The owner has to be convinced and feel confident that you, the foreclosure investor, are a knowledgeable specialist in the field of real estate. This will be accomplished during the first stage of negotiations, when you display your acquired knowledge about the foreclosure process, revealing to the owner precisely what will occur if the precarious condition is not remedied. As the investor, you also have to inform the troubled owner that time is of the essence, that it's too late to list the property with a realtor, or that it's too late to borrow additional funds. Further, that by selling the property to you now, the owner will relieve his distressed situation, salvage his good credit rating, and (if applicable) leave the burdensome property behind with some cash in hand. Otherwise, the foreclosing lender will ultimately sell the property and everything will be lost, including his credit rating and all his accumulated equity.

The distressed owner needs to feel that you appreciate his predicament, and that help is near at hand. He should also feel that he can speak openly with you, now that the limits of his financial difficulties are out in the open; that you're not intruding, so he doesn't have to disguise the facts about his troubled financial condition.

So now the troubled owner is informed and prepared to act. Time is running out and he has been alerted of the consequences of his precarious situation. He should realize that you can remedy the situation better than anyone else. He's ready to make a deal.

As Time Passes … the Lower the Price. Time is money. In no other field of business can this truism be more emphatically stated. During the typical 90-day span of a default period, in which the property can be reinstated, an offer to an owner during the first 30 days would be considerably higher than an offer made during the final days of redemption.

During the final days of the redemption period the offer would be at its absolute lowest.

By the time a property reaches the final days of the 90-day period of reinstatement, additional unpaid monthly installments have accumulated and more late charges have been added to the delinquent amount owed. The owner must be made aware of these facts, and that the quicker he acts to resolve this problem, the more he will get out of it.

Make Sure the Names are Correct. It is absolutely imperative that the seller's name on the deed is correct and all the information on the deed transferring the property is exactly the same as on the original deed the seller received when he or she purchased the property. If, for instance, the seller's true legal signature is Andrew J. McLean, it is necessary to transcribe the name exactly as it is shown, not Andy McLean or A. McLean. Errors frequently occur when information is copied from published information services. Therefore, always use the information gathered from the original grant deed.

First you must have the seller sign the Equity Purchase Agreement (see Figure 2-4), which will give you, the buyer, control of the subject property. This can be done after completing final negotiations and checking to see that, in fact, the property is actually transferable. Then the grant deed can be executed (see Figure 2-5), signed by the seller and properly notarized.

Once the seller signs over the grant deed, it is important that you immediately take it to the County Recorder's Office and have it recorded. After this is done, submit a copy of the grant deed to the title company. By immediately recording the grant deed, you can be assured that any liens recorded against your newly acquired property will be invalid, as long as they are recorded behind your name, and not before.

Again, I must remind you that local and state laws regarding the transfer of real property vary throughout the country, and for this reason it is difficult to cite precise guidelines about this important matter. Therefore, it will be to your benefit to discuss the basics of passing title with both a title officer from a local title company and with the County Recorder. Title companies will be happy to discuss local procedures, especially if you, in turn, give them your business.

Figure 2-4. Equity Purchase Agreement

Date: _____
Address of subject property: _____
Lot # _____ Block _____ Tract _____
Name of lender _____ Loan No. _____
Name of seller _____ Address _____
Name of buyer _____ Address _____

Buyer agrees to purchase and Seller agrees to sell the equity in the above described real property for the sum of _____ net to the Seller, receipt of which is hereby acknowledged by the Seller.

Buyer agrees to take title to the above described property subject only to existing liens and encumbrances not exceeding $_____.

It is also mutually agreed that: _____
_____
_____.

Seller is to deliver possession of subject property on or before _____20___.

If the property is not transferred to the Buyer by the above agreed date, all payments and further expenses incurred from that date forward shall be deducted from the net amount due the Seller.

Buyer will pay all escrow, title, loan transfer, and closing costs.

Monthly payments on the above loan including principal, interest, taxes, and insurance are $_____.

Impounds for taxes and insurance, if any, are to be assigned without charge to the Buyer. Any unforeseen shortage in the impound account will be deducted from the net amount due Seller at closing.

Seller will immediately execute a Grant Deed in favor of Buyer, which the Buyer has the right to record.

Seller will not remove any fixtures from the subject property, and will leave the property reasonably clean and in good condition.

Seller will allow Buyer access to subject property for any reason prior to date of possession of the Buyer.

Buyer will pay the balance of all funds due Seller at closing after checking title, loans, and liens, and the property is vacated.

Additions to this agreement: _____
_____
_____.

Buyer _____ Seller _____
Buyer _____ Seller _____

This agreement is to be filled out in triplicate, with a copy going to the seller, one copy for the buyer, and a copy for the buyer's file records.

10. What to Do Now that you Own the Property

In this final step, you want to be sure the deed is recorded, the utilities are turned on, and eviction procedures are initiated if unwanted tenants are

Figure 2-5. Sample Grant Deed

RECORDING REQUESTED BY

AND WHEN RECORDED MAIL THIS DEED AND UNLESS
OTHERWISE SHOWNBELOW MAIL TAX STATEMENTS TO

NAME

STREET
ADDRESS

CITY
STATE
ZIP

TITLE ORDER NO _____   ESCROW NO _____   SPACE ABOVE THIS LINE FOR RECORDER'S USE

GRANT DEED

THE UNDERSIGNED GRANTOR(s) DECLARE(s)

DOCUMENTARY TRANSFER TAX is $ _____
☐ computed on full value of property conveyed, or
☐ computed on full value less vlaue of liens or encumbrances remaining at time of sale, and

FOR A VALUEABLE CONSIDERATION, receipt of which is hereby acknowledged.

hereby GRANT(S) to

the following described real property in the

County of   State of California

Dated _____   _____

STATE OF CALIFORNIA   _____

COUNTY OF _____}SS
On _____ before me, the   _____

undersigned, a Notary Public in and for said State, personally appeared

_____   _____
_____
_____

_____ sworn to me
to be the person _____ whose name _____ subscribed to the
instrument and acknowledged that _____ executed the same
WITNESS my hand and official seal:

Signature _____

(This area for official notary seal)

occupying the property. At this time you should consider moving into your newly acquired property. Why? Because it's more efficient to work on the property you reside in than to live somewhere else. This way you don't have to constantly drive over to the property you're renovating. And when it's time to find a tenant, they can come to you instead of you driving over to the property to meet them.

It's Best to Think Long Term. Keep in mind that if you're thinking of renovating and then immediately selling the property, real estate is a better long-term investment than a short-term one. Over the long haul you'll make more money holding onto your realty investments rather than "flipping" them (selling them quickly), because if you sell them, you'll have to find another property to invest the proceeds from the sale. With this in mind, in Chapter 9 you'll find several profitable holding strategies in the disposition of your newly acquired investment. They include renting the property with a quality good-paying tenant, or renting it plus giving the tenant a buy option, land banking, or making a conversion to a higher rental usage.

Gaining Position of the Second Loan

Besides dealing with troubled owners, you also have the opportunity to acquire foreclosures before the auction by gaining position of any recorded junior financing on the distressed property.

You're likely aware that investing in foreclosures has become very popular among the public. Nowadays you can attend lectures, seminars, and purchase all kinds of training guides on how to buy foreclosed realty. Obviously, this increase in informed foreclosure investors will heighten the competition for available properties. But for the shrewd foreclosure specialist who wants to beat the competition to the punch, there's a very effective way of doing it—and that is to gain position of the junior financing. In other words, when the first loan is in foreclosure on a particular property, and you discover while doing a title search that junior financing, or a second loan, has been recorded against the property, then you want to buy the second loan at a discount and gain position.

Hard Money vs. a Purchase Money Loan

Typically, two types of secondary loans will exist on a given property. The first is a "purchase money" loan, which is initiated by a seller to facilitate the sale of a property by carrying back a second loan. In other words, the buyer of the property pays the seller on a second note until the second loan is paid off. For example, you sell a $100,000 house with $10,000 down, along with a first mortgage loan for $80,000 funded through a conventional lender, and the balance you carry back in the form of a second mortgage loan of $10,000.

The other type of secondary loan is the "hard money" second. For this type, the owner of a property takes out a second loan and receives actual cash dollars in return.

The differences between these two forms of secondary loans are crucial to you when it comes time to deal with the holders of these notes.

The "hard money" lender is usually a sophisticated lender who is in the business of lending money. He is both willing and able to protect his investment, and is prepared to take the property back through foreclosure, if necessary, to protect his vested interest in the property.

On the other hand, the purchase money note holder is usually not as sophisticated. He did not loan out actual dollars, as did the hard-money lender. He simply took back a note to facilitate the sale of his home. And since the sale, he has moved out of the neighborhood, perhaps to another state, and is unable to efficiently oversee his investment. It is unlikely he would foreclose on the property to protect his interest, and this makes him a likely candidate for you to purchase his note at a substantial discount. This is not so much because he lacks sophistication, but because he has moved away and does not want to be bothered, and probably has not received the last few payments due him.

Let's look at it from the purchase money note holder's point of view. He has carried back a note for $10,000 to facilitate the sale of his home and now lives out of state. Furthermore, he has not received payments on the note owed him in three months. Obviously concerned, he writes a memo to the delinquent note holder requesting the money past due. No response. So he telephones direct. But still no money. Then one day he receives a message from the first note holder that the borrower is three months past due on his loan payments, and that they have no other recourse than to begin foreclosure proceedings.

Now, in order to protect his second loan position, the purchase money note holder must make up all payments in arrears on the first loan and begin foreclosure proceedings under his second loan. This unforeseen situation was totally unexpected, yet it happens frequently, especially to sellers who move out of state. And should the purchase money note holder do absolutely nothing to resolve this precarious situation, the first note holder will continue with the foreclosure process, and if there's insufficient equity in the property (which is often the case), the second loan note holder will lose everything at the foreclosure sale.

Assume that the first note holder did in fact hold a foreclosure sale to recover his interest in the encumbered property. What actually happens? Since it is the first loan that is in foreclosure, then the sale eliminates any liens recorded after that lien which was recorded and foreclosed upon. If a property, for instance, had four loans recorded against it, and the first loan went to foreclosure, then all subsequent loans including the second, third, and fourth loans are eliminated. On the same property, if the second loan went to foreclosure, then the third and fourth loans would be wiped out, while the first would remain intact. The only time a lien is not entirely wiped out is when a property goes to foreclosure sale, and the proceeds from the sale are over and above that which is needed to cure the loan in foreclosure.

In effect, then, the foreclosure sale essentially wipes out any liens that were recorded after the particular recorded note that is being foreclosed upon. This includes abstracts of judgments. The foreclosure sale actually originates an entire new chain of title.

NOTEWORTHY

Sometimes federal tax liens and pending lawsuits are exempted from being wiped out in a foreclosure sale. If the Internal Revenue Service has a tax lien on the foreclosed property, they have 120 days to redeem the tax lien.

Locating the Second Note Holder

Assume that you have located a property in foreclosure and determined that it's the first loan that is being foreclosed upon. Now you have to find out if there's a second loan recorded against the property. This information is available at the County Hall of Records (County Recorder's Office). Look for a second trust deed or mortgage that has been recorded concurrently, recorded next, with the first loan of record.

A recorded document will usually have an attached address, which will give you a lead to the holder of the note. If the address is the same as the subject property, it means that at the date of recording, the note holder was still living on the property, and then moved away at a later date. If he or she has already moved to a new address after selling the property, then she'll be easier to find, because her new address will appear on the record.

If the address given in the recordation is current, you're in luck. But if the note holder has since moved away, you must find her before anyone else. This is often a most burdensome chore, but must be done in order to gain control. If you don't gain control of the second loan, then you'll have to assume the second at full value when negotiating with the first note holder. By negotiating with the second note holder, you'll have the opportunity to negotiate a substantial discount and earn a much better deal for yourself.

Okay, how do you find the second note holder if her present address is not recorded? If she still lives in the same city, she can be located by scanning the local phone book. If that doesn't prove fruitful, check the tax assessor rolls. If she owns any form of real property in that particular county, her name will appear along with her address or where the tax bills are sent.

If you're unsuccessful with the tax rolls, try the voters registry, which is available to the public. If the second note holder still can't be located, try mailing an urgent letter to the last known address, which is usually the address of the foreclosed property. Request that the letter be forwarded. In the contents of the letter, make mention to the holder of the note that she can receive cash for her interest and for her to contact you immediately.

While you're waiting for a return from your written request, try getting a forwarding address of the note holder at the post office.

If all other methods we mentioned failed to locate the second note holder, try making a personal visit to the subject property and inquire into her whereabouts. But be careful not to let the owners know of your true intentions, just that it's urgent that you contact the party who moved away.

Convincing the Note Holder to Discount

Convincing the note holder to discount the note owed him is tantamount to preparing a legal defense in a court of law. You must make him aware of what he will face if the distressed owner fails to make any further loan payments on the property. If the subject property progresses further into delinquency and the inevitable foreclosure sale occurs, the second note holder will likely lose everything. Should the second note holder decide to step in to salvage his position, he would bring the first loan in arrears up to date and assume control of the property. If he does this, he will essentially have to do the same things a specialty foreclosure investor would do—refurbish the property, then sell it or rent it.

On the other hand, if the second note holder made a reasonable settlement with you—the specialist investor—he would save time and effort, plus receive some cash for his remaining interest in the troubled property. Very few people want to go through the hassle of a foreclosure action. Once payments from the troubled owner become a few months delinquent, the typical second note holder usually begins thinking about how he can salvage something out of his precarious situation.

You must convince the note holder that you are in a better position to resolve this deteriorating situation. Make it clear that it would be advantageous to receive cash for his note, so that you—the investor specialist—can gain control. Otherwise, the note holder would be required to make up delinquent payments on the first note to make it current, then do costly repairs on the property, and devote a lot of time and attention to rent or sell the property once he gains control.

Keep in mind that once a distressed owner gets substantially delinquent in his payments to a second note holder, the holder of that note usually begins thinking of what the note is really worth. Most would welcome some form of relief to salvage something out of a failing business deal. Once a second note falls three or more months in arrears, most note holders would probably agree to accept a discount of 50 cents on the dollar, or less.

3

Guidelines to Buying at the Foreclosure Sale

Other than the default phase of foreclosure, you'll also have the opportunity to purchase foreclosed properties at a public auction, which is covered in this chapter. In the next chapter we will describe how to buy foreclosures after the auction.

Foreclosure auctions are either a Trustee Sale when the security instrument is a Deed of Trust, or a court-ordered sale when it's a mortgage instrument, where the lender can recapture losses by selling the property at public auction to the highest bidder. In this chapter we offer guidelines on how to profitably buy at a foreclosure auction, including how to determine a successful bid price. Also for your consideration, we included how to find foreclosure auctions.

What to Expect at a Typical Foreclosure Sale

Foreclosure sales are usually held on the front steps of a courthouse or in the corporate lobby of the foreclosing lender within the county of the property being sold. Essentially it's a public auction where the seller establishes a minimum bid that is the starting point for bidding on a particular property. The minimum bid is the *upset price*, which is the unpaid loan amount including all late fees and incidental costs associated with the foreclosure process. All bids must exceed the minimum bid, and the highest bidder is awarded the contract of sale.

Either the referee (mortgage foreclosure) or the Trustee (Deed of Trust foreclosure) begins the sale by explaining the bidding procedures to be followed, and then identifies the properties up for bid. Usually the property is first identified by its legal description and related tax map designations, followed by its street address and a general physical description; for example, three-bedroom two-bath detached single family residence with approximately 1,600 square feet of living space. Later, in Chapter 6, we include guidelines on how to inspect and evaluate a foreclosure before making a bid.

The typical foreclosure auction is not a flamboyant gathering of bidders standing around a fast-talking gavel-wielding auctioneer who yells out incoming bids. Instead, you will usually find that after the auctioneer describes the sale procedures and identifies the property up for sale, the verbal bidding is conducted in a conservative and orderly manner—with no fast-talking auctioneer banging a gavel.

Out of all the people in attendance, only a few are actually there to bid on available property. Some are there to become familiar with auction procedures so they can be better prepared in the future, when it's their time to actually bid on a property. And others go to auctions merely out of curiosity.

Landlord Tale: The 40 Thieves

While I was managing foreclosures in southern California during the 1970s, the local news media labeled a group of shrewd foreclosure investors "the 40 Thieves." You might be familiar with Ali Baba and his band of 40 thieves who, in the days of yore, roamed and pillaged the countryside of ancient Persia. To avoid capture from their pursuers, this clever roving band would hide out in a cave, concealed by a hinged cavern wall that would open on the command of "Open sesame."

The 40 thieves of modern California are not exactly the thieves of yesteryear, although their conspiring practices tend to be more like the "Carpetbaggers" of the Civil War era.

These so-called 40 thieves would show up at public foreclosure sales, appearing as individual investors unknown to each other. In reality, however, they were a band of investors with a prearranged scheme of action. Prior to the actual sale, they determined which member of the group was to bid on each particular property being auctioned. If anyone outside the group was present at the suction, the other members would buy off any apparent potential competition by paying them cash not to bid on the property. This, of course, would eliminate any competitive bidding, allowing the 40 thieves to purchase the property at the minimum upset price.

☞ **TIP**

If by chance there is more than one property being offered at the foreclosure sale, and there is just one other person interested in the bidding, consider doing the following: Before the sale begins, introduce yourself to the other person and find out what he or she is interested in. Perhaps you can work out a deal with them in which you avoid competing with each other on a particular property. For instance, you could say, "I will only bid on property A and you can bid on property B. This way you won't be competing with each other and you avoid bidding up the price.

Every State Has Different Auction Procedures

Please keep in mind that each state has statutory provisions that govern the auctioning of foreclosures. Some states, for example, require bidders to register before the auction, in order to provide proof that they have the financial resources required (typically 10 percent of the bid price) to pay the down payment. Other regulations require that the auction be conducted through verbal bidding, where each bidder calls out an offer for the property that he or she desires to purchase. Other states may use a different method of bidding on foreclosed property involving sealed written bids. These written offers are remitted to a designated authority, who opens them and declares the winning bid amount along with the person's name who offered it.

Before going to actually bid at a foreclosure auction, it's a good idea to attend a foreclosure sale in your local area to become familiar with the bidding procedure. This way you'll be better prepared and will know what to expect.

The Successful High Bidder

Normally, the successful high bidder at a bank foreclosure auction is awarded a Contract of Sale for the purchased property. Then he or she is expected to immediately remit the required down payment (usually 10 percent of the bid amount) in the form of a bank cashier's check, money order, or certified funds required by the holder of the auction. The successful high bidder is expected to pay the 90-percent balance owing usually within 30 days after the contract of sale is signed at the auction.

Conveying Title

In the United States, real property is conveyed either through a *deed* (Figure 3-1) or a *Torrens title* (Figure 3-2), also known as an "Owner's Duplicate Certificate of Title" (ODC). In both deeds and Torrens titles there is a legal description of the property on the front page. But unlike a deed, the Torrens title contains a history of all recordings on the property from its origins, including all legal instruments (Deeds of Trust, mortgages, liens, judgments, and satisfactions). It is worth noting that deeds and Torrens titles are *not* interchangeable documents—meaning one cannot be replaced with the other.

Regardless of which document is used to convey title, once it is recorded in the county where the property is located, the new property owner will be sent this important document (except in those states where a Deed of Trust is used as a security instrument, in which case the Trustee will be sent the deed or Torrens title). From then on, if a property owner loses a deed, it can be simply replaced by asking for a duplicate copy from county clerk. If, however, a property owner loses a Torrens title, usually a court order is required to replace it with another original Torrens title.

Foreclosure Sale vs. Traditional Purchase of Real Property

Buying real property at a foreclosure auction is considerably different from a traditional purchase between buyer and seller. Here are some distinguishing characteristics:

Figure 3.1 Deed

DEED

THIS INDENTURE, made the _____ day of _____ , two thousand and_____
BETWEEN

_____

party of the first part, and

_____

party of the second part,

    WITNESSETH, that the party of the first part, in consideration of 10 Dollars and other valuable consideration paid by the party of the second part, does hereby grant and release unto the party of the second part, the heirs or successors and assigns of the party of the second part forever.

    ALL, that certain plot, piece or parcel of land, with the buildings and improvements thereon erected, situate, lying and being in the

_____

    TOGETHER with all right, title and interest, if any, of the first part in and to any streets and roads abutting the above described premises to the center lines thereof; **TOGETHER** with the appurtenances and all the estate and right of the party of the first part in and to said premises; **TO HAVE AND TO HOLD** the premises herein granted unto the party of the second part, the heirs or successors and assigns of the party of the second part forever.

    AND the party of the first part covenants that the party of the first part has not done or suffered anything whereby the said premises have been encumbered in any way whatever, except as aforesaid.

    AND the party of the first part, in compliance with Section 13 of the Lien Law, covenants that the party of the first part will receive the consideration for this conveyance and will hold the right to receive such consideration as a trust fund to be applied first for the purpose of paying the cost of the improvement and will apply the same first to the payment of the cost of the improvement before using any part of the total of the same for any other purpose. The word "party" shall be construed as if it read "parties" whenever the sense of this indenture so requires.

    IN WITNESS WHEREOF, the party of the first part has duly executed this deed the day and year first above written.

    IN PRESENCE OF:

_____

Figure 3-2 Torrens Title

THE LAND TITLE REGISTRATION LAW
Owner's Duplicate Certificate of Tite

No. _____   FIRST REGISTERED_____

TRANSFER FROM   CERTIFICATE No._____

I, **LEROY J. URI**, Registrar of the County of _____, in the state of _____,
DO HEREBY CERTIFY THAT _____
of _____
Are the owners of an Estate in the following Land: ALL that certain plot, piece
or parcel of land, with the buildings and improvements thereon erected,
situated, lying and being in the Town of_____,
County of_____, State of New York, known and designated at a certain
map entitled _____

On this date_____as all by Lot No._____
And being described as follows: BEGINNING at a point on the easterly side
of Look Out Drive at a point 200 feet northerly as measured along the easterly
side of Look Out Drive from the corner formed by the intersection of its intersection with the northerly side of Mill Creek Road; running thence north
0 degrees 03 minutes and 12 seconds west along the easterly side of Look Out
Drive 60 feet; thence north 88 degrees 58 minutes 50 seconds east 179 feet;
thence south 0 degrees 3 minutes and 10 seconds east 60 feet; thence south 89
degrees 58 minutes 50 seconds west 179 feet to the easterly side of Look Out
Drive at the point or place of BEGINNING.

SUBJECT to the estates, easements, encumbrances and Charges
hereunder noted.
Charges hereunder noted.
WITNESS my hand and official seal at

_____

Registrar

You Buy Property "As Is" for Much Less Than Market Value. In
a traditional purchase of real property, you normally pay near market
value, or perhaps a little less. But when you buy at a foreclosure auction you end up paying a small fraction of what you would have paid in
a traditional purchase. That's because the bid price is typically based on
the loan balance and other costs to foreclose, not the market value of
the property being auctioned.

Another difference between a foreclosure purchase and a traditional
purchase entails representations about the condition of the property. A

foreclosure purchase is sold "as is," without any warranty whatsoever by the seller as to the property's condition. Typically, a property that has been foreclosed on has experienced months if not years of deferred maintenance. That's because distressed people going through foreclosure usually don't keep up with repairs and maintenance. (The usual attitude is, "Why should I maintain a property that someone else is going to get?") But in a traditional purchase you expect a roof without leaks, and that the plumbing, heating, air-conditioning, and electrical systems are in good working order. And unlike buying at a foreclosure sale, at the closing the sellers usually have to sign a disclosure that identifies any needed repairs or physical problems with the property.

No Refunds and No Contingencies. In a traditional purchase it's common for a buyer of real property to have a loan contingency clause written into the purchase contract, which entitles him or her to have the down payment refunded if they're unable to obtain financing from a lender. But when a foreclosed property is purchased at public auction, there are *no* loan contingency clauses permitting down payment refunds.

Landlord Tale: Timing Is Everything

When I was managing foreclosures in California, we sold a 16-unit apartment house in downtown Los Angeles for one-fifth of its value. It was in the spring of 1976, and this particular day we had foreclosed on the apartment house while it was pouring rain. At about noon one of the tenants of the building telephoned to tell me that water was gushing through her ceiling on the first floor. I told her I would take care of it. Meanwhile, a man—his name was Fred—walked into my office and inquired if we had any foreclosures for sale. We got to talking, and it turned out that, coincidently, Fred happened to own a roofing company. Later, I sent him over to the 16-unit property, and he informed me that he stopped the leak by masking a plastic tarp over the 12-inch-wide gap on the third floor roof. I ended up selling the building to him for $76,000, which approximated the cost we had in the property.

Fred's timing was perfect. He saved me a lot of work and we saved a realtor's sales commission. And I didn't have to secure the property or call someone else to do needed repairs. In return, I sold him a property at substantially below market value with great terms.

So if the buyer cannot come up with the required cash to close the deal within the required 30-day contractual period, she will likely forfeit the 10-percent down payment.

Burden of Evicting Occupants. In a traditional purchase, you can expect the property to be conveyed in vacant condition, without any occupants in the premises. However, when you purchase a foreclosed property at public auction, if any occupants still reside in the premises after the closing, then it's the buyer's (the successful high bidder's) responsibility to evict the occupants.

Delinquent Borrower's Right of Redemption. Another distinction about a foreclosure purchase is the delinquent borrower's right of redemption. It allows the delinquent borrower the right to reclaim his or her property by paying the entire balance owed the lender (the upset price) up until the foreclosure sale begins. Yet, in some states the delinquent borrower's right of redemption can be extended many months after the foreclosure auction by paying the upset price plus interest to the successful high bidder.

It would be a good idea for you to check into the right of redemption procedures, if any, that may apply in your particular state.

You May Be Responsible for Unforeseen Liens. In a traditional purchase of real property, you buy title insurance, which protects you from any unforeseen liens that may be attached to the property you're buying, and the insuring title company warrants that you have a clear and marketable title. However, when you purchase a foreclosure at auction, you may be responsible for unforeseen liens attached to the property. And the only way you can determine if any other liens are recorded against the foreclosed property is to pay a title company to do a title search.

First Loan vs. Second Loan Foreclosure

Let's look at two scenarios that illustrate the difference in how you would be affected, as a potential bidder at a foreclosure auction, when a first loan is foreclosing, compared to when a second loan is foreclosing. In both scenarios presume that the property's market value is $200,000, and there's a first loan balance of $80,000 and a second loan balance of $20,000.

Buying at the Foreclosure Sale

In the first scenario, only the first loan is delinquent, and that note holder is foreclosing. To initiate the bidding at the foreclosure sale, the upset price is announced at $81,100, which represents the unpaid first loan balance including incidental costs to foreclose. You bid one dollar over this amount, and since there are no other competing bids, you are awarded the contract at $81,101. Since the foreclosure action is on the first loan, you end up acquiring the property free and clear of any junior financing, such as any second or third loans. The end result is that you just earned $118,899 in equity because you purchased a property valued at $200,000 for $81,101.

Whenever the primary financing on real property, such as a first mortgage loan, forecloses, any subordinate or junior financing that was recorded subsequent to the first recorded loan is virtually wiped clear of the records. In other words, any junior note holders would lose their entire secured interest in the foreclosed property. In this scenario, the only way a second, third, etc., note holder can recover what is owed them from the delinquent borrower is to file an independent action for a judgment against him in an attempt to file liens against other assets the delinquent borrower might own in the county.

In the second scenario, the first loan is current but the second loan is severely delinquent, so the second note holder forecloses on the $20,000 loan. But in this particular situation, the successful high bidder acquires the foreclosed property "subject to" the first loan. The upset price is $21,000, which includes all incidental costs involved with the foreclosure. Again, you bid one dollar over the upset price, and since there are no other competing bids, you are awarded the contract at $21,001. You are the new owner of the foreclosed property *subject to* the first loan with an outstanding principal balance of $80,000. You can either assume the first loan balance, if the lender will permit assumption, or, if the lender accelerates the loan and demands payment in full, you would have to arrange enough financing to cover both the outstanding first loan balance and the upset price. Together they add up to $101,001. And since you were the successful high bidder on a second loan in foreclosure, you earned about $99,000 in equity by purchasing a $200,000 valued property for $101,001.

What happens when the high bid amount exceeds the upset price at a foreclosure auction? The surplus amount goes to pay off any junior note holders (second or third loans) or other creditors in order of their recordation. If there are no other recorded note holders or creditors, the overage goes to the property owner.

How to Determine if the First or Second Note Holder Is Foreclosing

How do you know which loan it is you are bidding on? Essentially, there are two ways for foreclosure specialists to distinguish whether the foreclosure action is on the first or second loan. One way is to do it yourself. If you have experience with real property documents and are familiar with the way things are done at the County Clerk's Office, you could search the appropriate public records to determine if more than one mortgage or Deed of Trust was recorded on the subject property. Typically, if more than one mortgage or Deed of Trust is recorded, the one recorded first is usually the first loan. The only exception is when a land subordination agreement is recorded.

The other way—especially recommended for inexperienced title professionals—is to use the services of a recommended title company to perform a search for you. But instead of a complete title search, simply ask for a "last owner search," also known as a "mortgage, lien, and judgment search." It is not as thorough, nor as costly, as a complete title search, yet it provides an accurate summary of the instruments recorded against the property. Moreover, it's the preferred and most cost effective way to make certain that you have in fact gathered accurate data about the position of the loan you're bidding on, whether it's a first, second, etc.

Notably, the last owner search is more appropriate as a preliminary report when you're interested in bidding on a foreclosed property and can use the acquired information to make an informed bid. But once you become the successful high bidder, you're better off paying the extra money and ordering a complete title report. Seek the advice of an attorney who specializes in foreclosures or a recommended title company for more information about a last owner search.

Guidelines to Bidding at a Foreclosure Auction

As mentioned earlier, before actually bidding at a foreclosure auction, it's a good idea to attend one in your local area to become familiar with the bidding procedure. That way you'll be better prepared and will know what to expect. But there are other preparations you can do before bidding at a foreclosure auction, which we'll go into.

Determining Bid Limits

The best strategy on bidding at an open foreclosure auction is to be totally prepared for it. You need to know in advance how much to bid, and never allow yourself to go over this predetermined price. Set a minimum and maximum price range that you'll be prepared to pay, such as, the property would be a great buy at $35,000 or less, but my upper limit price is $45,000, which I cannot, for whatever reason, exceed. This way, by setting predetermined price limits, you avoid getting caught up in the frenzy of competitive bidding and paying more for the property than you intended. Keep in mind too that you lose nothing if you don't buy at all.

Begin by inspecting the subject property, and then estimate its market value in renovated condition. Next, estimate the initial acquisition cost (the upset price). Estimate the costs for repairs and the time it will take to complete them. Determine monthly rental income. Fill out a Pre-Bid Cost Estimate Form (see Figure 3-3) using all the cost data you already gathered in the previous steps. And finally, determine your bid limits based on the calculated break-even price.

Your break-even point equals the market value of the property in renovated condition less the acquisition cost and all expenses and costs of repairs. Once the break-even price is established, you can determine profitable bid limits.

Let's go into determining bid limits in more detail.

Carefully Inspect the Subject Property. Carefully inspect the property and take photographs to help you identify it later. Unless you intend to demolish the structure completely and erect a new building, avoid foreclosures where you're unable to inspect the interior of the premises because it's inaccessible. Buying a foreclosed property without a careful inspection of the interior is tantamount to buying a used car without taking it for a test drive—you'll never know exactly what you're getting unless you carefully look it over and take it for a drive. You're better off bidding on a property that's accessible to a proper inspection.

(See Chapter 6 for guidelines on inspecting and appraising foreclosed property.)

Get a Written Estimate for Repair Costs. Bring a licensed contractor or property inspector to inspect the premises with you. That way, the two of you can detect structural problems and he can give you a written estimate of the cost of repairs, along with the amount of time it will take to complete them.

Estimate Costs to Acquire the Property. This includes the upset price you'll have to pay for the foreclosed property, the cost to evict the occupants, if any, the cost of title insurance, and the annual cost of hazard insurance.

Determine Market Value of the Property in Renovated Condition. You can pay for a professional appraisal or do your own evaluation with advice from realtors familiar with the area where the subject property is situated. If you plan to rent the property to tenants, you'll also have to determine what the subject property will rent for in order to calculate your monthly cash flow. (See Chapter 6 for more information on appraisal techniques.)

Determine the Property's Gross Rental Income, if Applicable. To determine the amount of rental income you can expect, talk to realtors who know the area where the subject property is situated, or check the "Houses for Rent" section in your local newspaper.

Your Bid Limits

Okay, now you should be prepared to determine your bid limits. Based on the break-even analysis in Figure 3-3, in order for you to earn a reasonable profit on this particular deal, your predetermined bid price limits would be range from a low of $45,600 (the upset price) to a maximum of about $90,000. So, even if you had to pay a maximum price of $90,000, you would still earn a reasonable profit of $50,430 (the break-even price of $140,430 less what you paid for the property at $90,000).

Use Figure 3-3 to estimate all your costs involved in acquiring a foreclosure at auction. Note that in the figure we first estimated the market value of the property after renovations were completed at $200,000.

Figure 3-3 Pre-Bid Cost Estimate Form

Estimated Market Value After Renovations	<u>$200,000</u>
Estimated Costs to Acquire:	
Upset price	$45,600
Evict tenants	$300
Mortgage loan cost	0
Insurance (one year)	<u>$1,800</u>
Total Estimated Costs to Acquire	$47,700
Estimated General Expenses:	
Property taxes (30 days)	120
Utilities (30 days)	150
Title insurance	450
Hazard insurance (30 days)	<u>150</u>
Total Estimated General Expenses	870
Estimated Repairs:	
New roof	$7,150
Paint	$2,200
Landscaping	$450
Carpeting	<u>$1,200</u>
Total Estimated Cost of Repairs	$11,000
Total Acquisition, Expenses, and Repair Costs	<u>$59,570</u>
Bid Price for a Break-Even Deal	$140,430
Bid-Limit Range: $45,600 to a maximum of $90,000.	

From that figure we deducted all the costs involved with the property, including the cost to acquire, repair, and maintain it. The total acquisition, expense, and repair cost is $59,570. When we deduct that figure from the estimated market value after renovations, the result is a break-even amount of $140,430.

Once the break-even price is determined, you can set your bid limits, which allows you a reasonable margin of profit. In this particular case, our Bid-Limit Range is set at a low of $45,600 to a maximum of $90,000.

By gathering all the pertinent data and then analyzing it, you can determine whether the acquisition of the foreclosed property is a worthwhile investment.

How to Find Foreclosure Auctions

Published lists of forthcoming foreclosure auctions are available from all different types of media, including the Internet, newspapers, magazines, subscription newsletters, etc.

The following are a small sampling taken from the Internet under "Foreclosure Publication Lists":

Profiles Publications, Inc.

Weekly Foreclosure Auction Schedules and Lis Pendens Filings (a.k.a. "Pre-Foreclosures") for Manhattan, Queens, Brooklyn, and the Bronx: www.nyforeclosures.com

FREE South Florida Weekly Foreclosure List

HUD-FHA. Bank REO's and other foreclosures. We are South Florida's Foreclosure Sales Experts. www.lesende.com

How to Make Huge Profits from Real Estate Foreclosure Properties

… Every Time You Buy Real Estate Foreclosure Properties. The highly … Nationwide Foreclosure Listings. Click on the map to select a … LOOKING FOR A FORECLOSURE? Subscribe today FREE Trial … www.foreclose.com

Free List of Foreclosure Homes, List of Foreclosure Properties, Buy Foreclosure Homes and Properties

… We Offer FREE LIST OF FORECLOSURE HOMES, Bank Owned Homes … keep scouring the local publications and costly websites to gather the information, or … www.vfindhomes.com

Pros and Cons of Buying at Public Auction

Compared to buying foreclosures in the other two phases, the overwhelming advantage of buying foreclosures at public auction is that the property can usually be purchased for a fraction of its market value, which amounts to the outstanding loan balance plus incidental costs incurred in the foreclosure process.

Unfortunately, buying foreclosures at auction has several disadvantages:

- The successful bidder may be responsible for unpaid liens recorded against the property.
- The successful bidder is responsible for evicting unwanted occupants in the premises.
- The delinquent borrower (the foreclosed owner) may have the right of redemption beyond the date of the foreclosure sale.
- The successful bidder has to pay all cash or arrange financing because the terms of the sales contract do not include a "mortgage contingency clause."

- The electrical, heating, and plumbing systems are sold in "as is" condition with no warranties from the seller.
- The buyer will likely have to compete against other bidders wanting to buy.

Most of the aforementioned shortcomings of buying at the foreclosure auction can easily be overcome when you purchase foreclosures in the third and final phase—after the auction, when the property failed to sell and becomes inventory of the foreclosing lender. In the next chapter you'll discover why purchasing foreclosures after the auction entails less risk and can be more profitable than buying foreclosed property in the other two phases.

4

Guidelines to Buying Foreclosures After the Auction

In this chapter you'll learn why the greatest opportunities for buying foreclosures are often found after the action—when they failed to sell and become inventory of the foreclosing lender. You'll also discover various other sources of foreclosure auctions, such as HUD repossessions, federal government auctions, and sheriff's sales, and how to successfully bid at them.

The Best Deals Are Often Found After the Auction

The third phase in the foreclosure process only occurs when the property fails to sell at auction. The foreclosed property was offered for sale to the public, and except for the foreclosing lender who usually opens the bidding at the upset price, there were no other bids. Therefore, the ownership of the property reverts to the foreclosing lender, and is placed on the books at a cost of the outstanding loan balance, plus all incidental costs associated with the foreclosure sale.

In most cases, especially when it's the first note holder who enacted the foreclosure, an institutional lender—such as a bank or savings and loan—becomes the new owner of the foreclosed property that failed to sell at public auction. If that's the case, then the newly acquired property is commonly referred to as real estate owned (REO), while others call it owned real estate (ORE), and some lenders simply call it "bank owned real estate."

Advantages of Buying a Lender's Real Estate Owned

REO, as mentioned above, is a lender's inventory of foreclosed real estate that failed to sell at public auction. It now belongs to the lender who funded the mortgage loan and encumbered the property as collateral against the loan. Compared to buying properties in the other two phases of foreclosure, purchasing a foreclosed property after the auction offers the foreclosure specialist many advantages:

- These properties are usually sold with great terms featuring a low down payment and below market interest rates that borrowers won't find anywhere else.
- Since the seller is also the lender, you can have them handle the closing and you can often negotiate to have them pay all the closing costs.
- The property is usually clear of any liens that may have been recorded against it. If any property taxes were outstanding at the time of foreclosure, the foreclosing lender usually brings them up to date.
- When a foreclosed property is purchased at auction, it's the new owner's responsibility to evict the occupants. On the other hand, when REO is purchased, it's the seller's responsibility to handle the eviction process.
- Buying in this phase is a lot less complicated, involves less risk (you get clear title), and you usually don't have to deal with competing bidders.

It is in this phase of the foreclosure process that offers the potential buyer a superior investment opportunity compared to buying in the other two phases. Why? Because unlike buying foreclosures in the other two phases, when you buy in the REO phase, with the exception of deferred maintenance, the foreclosed property will be free of all problems. That's because in the process of acquiring the property, the foreclosing lender will clear it of all outstanding liens, clear the title, and pay the back taxes. They own it free and clear. Which means when you buy the property, you'll be buying it with a clear and marketable title.

But there are other important advantages to buying foreclosed property after the auction. Other than getting a clear and marketable title, you can usually get the seller, who usually is a primary institutional lender, to finance the property with a small down payment at below market interest rates. Also, you can often negotiate for the seller to pay all the closing costs, mostly because institutional lenders usually have escrow facilities available in-house. Two other important considerations: You won't be competing with other bidders, as at a public auction, and it will be the bank's responsibility to evict any unauthorized tenants, not yours.

Compared to buying foreclosures in the other two phases, about the only disadvantage is that, because of the "dumping regulations" mentioned earlier, the asking price is usually closer to market value, whereas at public auction the asking price is usually based on the unpaid mortgage balance plus foreclosure costs incurred.

Giving a Deed in Lieu of Foreclosure

Instead of a delinquent borrower allowing his property to be foreclosed on, under certain circumstances he can work out an agreement with the lender that allows a full release of the remaining loan obligation in exchange for the deed (complete ownership). Usually, if the outstanding loan balance does not exceed the market value of the encumbered property, both the lender and the borrower can benefit by avoiding the time and expense that a foreclosure action requires. The lender benefits by avoiding all the unnecessary time and expense involved with going through the entire foreclosure process. The borrower benefits because he avoids the negative stigma of a foreclosure tainting his credit rating, and he eliminates the risk of a *deficiency judgment* should a foreclosure auction fail to earn sufficient money to pay off the outstanding loan balance. (Note that in states where instead of mortgages, Deeds of Trust are used as security instruments on real property, deficiency judgments may not be lawful.)

However, there is a significant disadvantage for a delinquent borrower when giving a deed in lieu of foreclosure: He forfeits the right to receive any surplus funds, which go to the lender, should the property sell for more than the outstanding loan balance.

Why Lenders Are Eager to Sell Their REO

Keep in mind that primary lenders are essentially in the business of taking in deposits and charging interest on the money they lend. When a real estate loan is funded, the lender isn't thinking that eventually he will have to foreclose on the property in order to recoup his money. Instead, the lender trusts the borrower and expects him or her to pay the loan off as contractually agreed upon. Foreclosure is merely a recourse to recover the borrowed funds the delinquent borrower failed to repay. Unfortunately, these lenders who had to foreclose have become reluctant property owners facing the unwanted task of securing, paying the taxes, buying insurance, managing, and eventually selling the foreclosed properties they now own.

The day an institutional lender becomes the unwilling new owner of a foreclosed property, the following scenario typically occurs: An employee of the lender is sent out to the foreclosed property to make an inspection and meet the marshal if an occupant needs to be evicted. Then, depending on the quality of the neighborhood, the employee orders a contractor to secure the property by boarding up all the windows and doors. And when he gets back to the office, insurance has to be purchased, to cover both liability and hazards. If the property taxes are in arrears, they have to be brought up to date. Then the property has to be evaluated to determine its current market value. Eventually, the property would be put up for sale by listing it with a local realtor, which means the added expense of paying a sales commission. Notably too, regulations require that money must be held in reserve to cover these nonperforming assets (the inventory of foreclosures)—money that could be better utilized as interest-earning mortgage loan funds.

Thus, the lender is responsible for all kinds of operational expenses with this newly acquired property, not to mention similar overhead expenses on the remainder of his REO inventory. All told, especially considering the added expense of REO employees to oversee these properties, it adds up to a huge overhead expense.

Why Don't Lenders Advertise Their REO?

You might be wondering why institutional lenders don't advertise lists of their REO in the local newspapers. Because advertising a supply of foreclosed property would be detrimental to the lender's public image in several ways. Potential borrowers would avoid applying for a home loan from that lender, fearing that if they fell behind in their loan payments the lender would publicize their addresses, which means the whole neighborhood would learn of their financial difficulties. And if the public became aware that a particular lending institution had a large supply of foreclosures, it could adversely affect the lender's financial image, causing people to think about depositing their money in a more secure institution elsewhere.

REO Buyers Get Great Terms

Federal law prohibits lenders from "dumping" their acquired REO in any particular area. Why? Because selling foreclosures at cut-rate bargain prices (or dumping for pennies on the dollar) would adversely affect the market value of other properties in the neighborhood. Based on the comparative sales approach to appraisal of improved property (see Chapter 6), the market value of a property is determined by comparing it to similar properties that recently sold.

So lenders do not advertise their REO, nor do they attempt to excessively underprice their inventory of foreclosed real estate. Instead, to attract people who are interested in purchasing from their inventory of REO, they offer great financial terms—extraordinary loan terms that investors won't find anywhere else!

When you buy foreclosures from a lender's inventories, you get loans with low down payment requirements at below market interest rates. Added to this attractive feature, you can usually negotiate for the lender to pay all the closing costs.

Guidelines to Buying a Lender's REO

Large multibranch institutional lenders usually manage their inventory of REO from their corporate headquarters location. During a typical business day the REO department receives numerous unsolicited telephone calls from the curious and ill-informed public inquiring if there's any foreclosure property available. And every day the person answering the phone gives a stock reply: "Sorry, nothing available." Except for making inquiries about the name of the realtor who handles the sale of their REO, you want to avoid phoning the REO department.

REO is usually sold through one or several local real estate brokers, and at times directly to known buyers with whom the REO manager has had previous dealings. The best way to learn about the availability of a lender's REO is to approach the REO department in person and to meet the manager. Establishing such a personal relationship at a lending institution is the only viable method of getting into the REO business.

Don't Be Shy About Your Intentions and Credit Rating

During your meeting with the REO manager, don't be afraid to mention that you intend to extensively renovate the property. Even better, support your intended renovations with a written business plan that specifies your renovations for the property. And don't forget that in most cases the seller of REO will also be the lender. So don't be shy about your excellent credit rating. Primary lenders love to do business with borrowers who show a past history of paying their debts on time. When they sell a property and simultaneously lend money on it to buyers with an outstanding credit rating, they don't have to worry that the property will again be foreclosed and return to its inventory. These attributes of good intentions and A-1 credit will be very helpful in persuading the REO manager to do business with you.

Preparing the Offer to Purchase REO

After you have inspected the subject property and are ready to make your written offer, you need to keep a few important things in mind. Even though list prices of a lender's REO are supposed to reflect market values, remember that you're dealing with an eager seller. Their inventory of foreclosures costs them a small fortune in overhead each month, not to mention the cost of holding money in reserve for these so-called "nonperforming assets." Therefore, even though there might be a suggestion that the list prices are "firm," never be afraid to negotiate a better price. (Guidelines to making an inspection are covered in Chapter 6, and instructions to preparing a bid/offer are covered in Chapter 3.)

Justify a Low Offer with Facts

Frequently a lender's REO can remain vacant and boarded up for years. And since the initial appraisal of a particular property was done, circumstances may have changed. For instance, when the property was initially placed in the lender's inventory, the aluminum siding and all the interior plumbing fixtures might have been in good condition. Since then, however, all the plumbing fixtures have been removed, some of the interior drywall is damaged, and much of the lower sections of aluminum siding were ripped off. As a result, the property's value has been substantially diminished, which the REO manager is likely not aware of.

When submitting a low offer, it's necessary to substantiate it with documented facts. Merely attaching a note to the offer stating that "the property requires extensive work" is not enough. You need to support your case with photographs of the damage, along with written cost estimates to repair the damage from a licensed contractor. This way, by supporting your offer with documented evidence, you make it easier for the REO manager to give good reason for accepting a low offer.

The written offer should be on a uniform purchase contract for real property that's appropriate for your state. The following are important key items that need to be included:

- *Address of the property being purchased.* Include the exact address, along with any identifying number or code the REO department may have assigned from its inventory of property.
- *Purchase price and down payment.* Include the amount you're offering to pay for the property, which is the total purchase price, along with the amount of cash you're applying toward that amount. A reasonable down payment should be in the range of 5 to 10 percent of the purchase price.
- *Deposit.* Submit a check for a good faith deposit, usually in the amount of $100 to $500, along with your written offer. If the offer is accepted, the seller will keep the deposit and apply it toward the purchase price. If your offer is not accepted, the deposit check will be returned to you.
- *Seller financing and closing costs.* If the seller is an institutional lender, you should expect exceptional financing terms. Be sure to

include the interest rate you intend to pay, along with the term of the loan. As a rule of thumb, you should negotiate for a rate of interest of 1 to 2 points below the going market rate for home loans, along with a term of at least 30 years. You should also negotiate for zero loan origination fees and for the seller pay all the closing costs.

- *Closing date.* Your offer should include a closing date, usually within 30 days, in which a clear and marketable title will be conveyed to you.
- *Contact information.* Include your name, address, and telephone number on the offer so the REO manager can contact you.

Finding REO

As mentioned earlier, an institutional lender's REO is usually managed from its corporate headquarters. Telephone a branch office to find out where the corporate office is located. Then you can make inquiries about the realtor who handles the listings of the lender's inventory of REO.

Visit Web Sites

Some of the larger multibranch lending institutions have Web sites that provide information about them to the public. If they handle the sale of their inventory of REO in-house, you can often find information about available property, such as list prices, a physical description, and how to access them. Or, if the inventory is sold through a realtor, contact information is posted.

Explore Neighborhoods

By simply driving through neighborhoods, you can often spot a lender's REO. Look for unattended, boarded-up properties with a posted sign noting who to contact. If no contact information is available, talk to the next door neighbors, who are usually a reliable source of finding the owner.

As a foreclosure specialist, it's your job to make a thorough search of the REO managers in your area and get a list of their inventory. You should also determine the realtors in your area who make it their business to list and sell a lender's REO.

HUD Repossessions

When FHA-insured borrowers fail to make their loan payments, the lender forecloses and places the property up for sale at public auction. If the property does not sell at the auction, the lender turns in an insurance claim to the Department of Housing and Urban Development. Then HUD reimburses the lender what is owed and takes over ownership of the foreclosed property. Finally, HUD puts the property—along with all the others it recently acquired through foreclosure—on the market for public sale.

HUD repos can be a great source of potential bargains for you as a foreclosure investor, but you have to consider two important drawbacks. First, HUD properties are sold "as is," without warranty. That means the buyer, not HUD, will have to correct all problems with the purchased property. The other drawback is that repossessed HUD properties, like almost all foreclosed property, have been seriously neglected over the years. When distressed property owners look to cut costs, they will usually defer maintenance first, before allowing their mortgage loan payments to become delinquent. Therefore, you can expect at least many months, if not several years, of deferred maintenance on most foreclosed properties.

However, even if a HUD property needs fixing up—and not all of them do—it can still be a great buy. For instance, HUD's asking price will usually reflect the fact that the buyer will have to make improvements. Also, HUD might offer special incentives, such as allowances to upgrade the property or to cover moving expenses, or a bonus for closing early. And on most sales, the buyer can request that HUD pay all or a portion of the closing costs. Your participating HUD realtor will have details. Be sure to have a HUD property professionally inspected before you make an offer so you'll know what repairs will be needed.

Finding HUD Properties

You can locate HUD property in several ways, including cruising the neighborhoods searching for HUD's For Sale signs, browsing the local newspaper for HUD's weekly ads, or visiting HUD's Web site at www.hud.gov.

Owner-Occupant Priority

HUD favors owner-occupants over investors in two ways: They have first choice, and they are offered FHA low or nothing-down insured financing.

Recently, the FHA has begun refusing to offer investors FHA insurance on HUD properties.

The Owner-Occupied Edge. During the first five days the property is on the market, HUD will accept bids only from buyers who intend to occupy the premises. If the property remains unsold, HUD will then allow anyone to bid for the next five days, but the owner-occupied bidders have the edge. The investor can win the bid only if no prospective owner-occupant submits an offer, even if the investor submits the highest bid. Only during the third selling round will HUD not give an advantage to buyer status.

Owner-Occupant Certification. HUD enforces stiff penalties to discourage investors from falsely claiming owner-occupant status. All owner-occupied buyers are required to sign a purchase contract addendum that certifies that they will occupy the property as their primary residence for a minimum of 12 months. Also, all realtors who submit owner-occupants' bids must sign a certification that they're not knowingly representing an investor. Penalties for false certification are as high as a $250,000 fine and two years in federal prison.

Purchasing HUD Property

Only HUD participating realtors are permitted to sell HUD property, and they must submit your bid for you. Usually, HUD properties are sold during an *offer period*. Upon expiration of this period, all offers are opened, and the highest reasonable bid is accepted. If a particular property goes unsold during the offer period, you can continue to submit bids until it's sold. Bids can be submitted any day of the week, including weekends and holidays. Bids are opened the next business day, and if your bid is accepted, your realtor will be notified with 48 hours.

Should HUD accept your bid, your realtor will help you through the paperwork process. HUD will issue a settlement date, usually within 30 to 60 days, by which time you need to arrange financing and close the sale. If you cannot close by then, you will forfeit your earnest-money deposit or pay for an extension of your sales contract.

For more detailed information, contact a participating HUD realtor, or check out HUD's Web site at www.hud.gov.

VA Repossessions

Similar to HUD repos, the Department of Veterans Affairs takes back unsold foreclosed properties from primary lenders with whom the VA guaranteed the loans. The properties are then offered for sale to the public.

Selling Procedures

Note that most VA rules and procedures are similar to those of HUD.

- Bidders are required to submit their bids through a VA-approved realtor. No negotiations directly with the VA are permitted.
- VA properties are sold through a sealed-bid process. Bidders can submit multiple bids either as owner-occupants or as investors.
- The VA sells all its properties strictly as-is, without any warranties whatsoever.
- The VA charges buyers who select its financing a 2.25 percent guarantee fee.
- The VA guarantees marketable title, and it allows buyers to obtain a title policy.
- The VA accepts bids only on VA forms and documents.
- The VA advertises its properties through a combination of broker lists, newspaper ads, and Internet Web sites such as www. va.gov.
- A 1 percent earnest-money deposit of the purchase price is required on all VA properties. All earnest-money deposits are made payable to and held by the realtor unless otherwise directed by the VA. If you're the successful bidder, the earnest money will be immediately deposited in the realtor's escrow account; otherwise, it will be directly refunded.
- The VA may decide to keep the earnest-money deposit if a bidder fails to close a successful bid for any reason other than failure to obtain financing.
- Similar to HUD purchase contracts, the VA does not allow a contingency for a property inspection after submitting a bid. However, bidders are allowed to inspect a VA property prior to making the bid.

- Buyers receive a vacant property at closing. The VA, when necessary, will evict homeowners or holdover tenants prior to listing a property for sale.

The VA Advantage for Investors

Although the VA and HUD have similar procedures, the VA has two distinct rules that favor investors:

- *Unlike HUD, VA owner-occupant bidders do not receive preferential treatment over investors.* The VA accepts the bid that results in the highest net proceeds regardless of the bidder's buying status.
- *Financing that the VA offers is very advantageous.* Usually a person can buy a VA property with less than 6 percent of the selling price total out-of-pocket cost. And the VA has qualifying standards that are more lenient than HUD's.

For an online listing of VA-repossessed property, see www.va.gov. Keep in mind that you do not need to be a veteran to purchase a VA repo, and that anyone is eligible to obtain VA financing on any property purchased.

Other than great financing with lenient terms, many investors find the VA repo program attractive for the following reasons:

- VA financing is assumable, which makes the property easier to sell because the buyer can take over the existing VA loan. During periods of tight credit (high mortgage interest), a low-interest assumable loan becomes very attractive.
- Since you'll have a small amount invested with corresponding high leverage, you should earn an accelerated return on investment as long as you paid a bargain price for the property.
- Even when you end up paying near market value for a VA repo, within a year such high-leveraged properties should rent for enough to provide at least a break-even cash flow situation.

Federal Deposit Insurance Corporation Sales

Besides insuring savings and checking account deposits in U.S. banks, the FDIC also functions in the role of its predecessor, the Resolution Trust

Corporation, as the receiver when an insured financial institution fails. As a government-owned foreclosure seller, the FDIC provides lists of available properties for potential buyers who are interested in purchasing residential and commercial realty as well as undeveloped land.

For an online listing of FDIC-owned foreclosures, see "Buying from and Selling to the FDIC" Web page on the FDIC.gov Web site.

You can also telephone your local FDIC Office and ask them about their list of available FDIC-owned foreclosures.

Federal Home Loan Mortgage Corporation Sales

Freddie Mac is a major player in the secondary mortgage market that buys residential mortgage loans from lending institutions. Real estate brokers in each state handle the management and sale of Freddie Mac owned properties. HomeSteps Asset Services handles the marketing for Freddie Mac foreclosed properties and also provide special financing for qualified buyers of Freddie Mac's inventory of foreclosed properties.

For an online listing of Freddie Mac-owned foreclosures, see the Home-Steps.com Web site.

You can also telephone your local Freddie Mac office and ask them about HomeSteps foreclosure listings.

Federal National Mortgage Association Sales

Fannie Mae is the largest player in the secondary mortgage market that buys residential mortgage loans from lending institutions. Sale of its foreclosed properties are handled by real estate brokers in each state. Special financing with incentives to qualified buyers is provided by Fannie Mae's staff at HomePath Specialists. Names of the servicing real estate brokers along with a list of foreclosed properties is available online or by telephone.

For an online listing of Fannie Mae foreclosures you can access its Web site at Fanniemae.com.

You can also telephone your local Fannie Mae Public Information Office and inquire about foreclosure listings.

Federal Government Auctions

Other than HUD and VA repossessions, each year the federal government auctions off all types of surplus and seized real estate, including homes, apartment buildings, office buildings, multiacre estates, and undeveloped land. The most active sellers at these auctions are the Internal Revenue Service, the Federal Deposit Insurance Corporation, and the General Services Administration.

Each of these organizations maintains a list of available properties, along with rules and procedures for buying them, at the following Web sites:

- Internal Revenue Service: www.gov.auctions/irs
- Federal Deposit Insurance Corporation: www.fdic.gov/buying/owned/real/index
- General Services Administration: www.propertydisposal.gsa.gov

Sheriff's Sales

A sheriff's sale, or *judicial sale,* is a legally forced sale that results from a foreclosure, property tax lien, a civil lawsuit, or a bankruptcy proceeding.

For example, if property owners go beyond a certain stage of delinquency on their mortgage loan, they are notified by the lender and the circuit court of the county that they can redeem their delinquency by remitting the overdue mortgage payments, along with any due penalties. If the owners do not pay, they are then considered in default of the loan, which will result in the mortgaged property going to a sheriff's sale. Conducted by order of the circuit court, these sales are usually held in a designated municipal building, or in a title company office.

Property sold at a sheriff's sale is sold strictly as is. Buyers are required to have a cashier's check for 10 percent of the sales price of the property being purchased. The balance owing has to be paid within 24 hours of the sale. Usually, the sale has to be confirmed in front of a circuit judge within four weeks of the sale, which allows the owners in default one last chance to redeem the property. This reprieve, of course, means that the buyer does not legally own it until the judge confirms the sale.

It's a good idea to attend at least one sheriff's sale before you become an active participant. That way, you get a feel for how they are conducted before bidding in a similar circumstance yourself. You have to be wary of assuming other obligations when you buy—such as delinquent property taxes or other liens attached to the property—so it's likely you'll need to do a title search before you buy at a sheriff's sale.

Private Auctions

During poor economic times sellers often decide to liquidate their properties through private auctions. During the early 1990s in California a large group of bankers pooled their REO properties and jointly auctioned off hundreds of properties at a time. And frequently, especially during typical slow periods of the year, housing developers will liquidate their closeout inventory with a public auction, so afterward they can devote their time and effort to the next housing project. At other times, a home builder in financial difficulty will use an auction to stimulate home sales in order to fend off his or her creditors.

Where to Find Auctions

Most auctioneers advertise the event in local newspapers, and you'll occasionally see large-scale auctions in national media, such as large display ads in the *Wall Street Journal*. Notably, part of their marketing strategy is to add the names of those who register to their mailing list. Auction companies strive not only to attract the maximum number of prospective buyers, but also to attract big crowds so they can instill a festive mood of excitement and anxious anticipation.

Also look for a list of local auctioneers in the yellow pages. Names of nationally known auction companies who hold large-scale local auctions include Hudson and Marshall, J.P. King, NRC Auctions, and Ross Dove and Company.

Auction Preparation

If you're interested in buying at an auction, it's advisable to first attend one just for the experience—not to buy. It's interesting to see how they operate—the professional auctioneers and bidders contending with each other.

To prepare for an auction:

- *Always have an established maximum bid price in mind*. Avoid getting caught up in the frenzied atmosphere that auctioneers like to create. Keep your established maximum bid price in mind, remembering that the further below your maximum the final buying price is, the better the bargain. Never allow the auctioneer's boosters bamboozle you into overbidding.

- *Before you bid, thoroughly inspect the property.* Prior to the actual sale, auctioneers schedule open houses for potential bidders to look over the inventory. Auction property will often sell at dirt-cheap prices because they're dilapidated old buildings waiting to be torn down. Or they may suffer from incurable defects. You or your inspector/contractor need to always thoroughly inspect property at an auction before you offer a bid.

- *Carefully appraise the property.* Compare the subject property to at least three similar comparables in the same neighborhood. Never rely on list prices. The only way you avoid overpaying is having knowledge of property values in your area of interest.

- *Study the related paperwork.* Prior to the auction, ask to see documents that pertain to the subject property—the lot survey, property tax assessment, legal description, and purchase contact you'll be required to sign.

- *Have an adequate deposit.* Eligible bidders are required to register before the auction begins and show proof of adequate funds (typically, a cashier's check for 10 percent of the successful bid price). Registrants are then issued bid cards making them authorized bidders. Unauthorized bids made by people without bid cards are not accepted.

- *Find out what type of deed you'll get.* Under a *warranty deed*, the seller guarantees clear title, subject to certain exceptions. Other kinds of deeds transfer fewer warranties. Before you accept a deed, be sure of its limitations, such as encroachments, easements, or recorded liens. Your best protection is to buy title insurance. And, if for any reason the property's title is uninsurable, get an opinion from a competent real estate lawyer.

- *Learn all the details of the sale.* Make inquiries about the financing available. Auction companies will often have prearranged financing on some or all of their properties. If so, get the details of the terms and what it takes to qualify. If you must provide the financing, find out how much time you're allowed to do so. Private auctions differ from government agency auctions in that payment in cash is not required. And inquire about whether the auction will be held under absolute terms or subject to a reserve price. There is no minimum bid requirement under absolute terms. With a reserve price, the highest bid must exceed a prearranged minimum price or the property is removed from sale.

Delinquent-Tax Auctions

In Sarasota, Florida, Manatee County has an annual *tax certificate auction* held on the tenth floor of the County Administration center in downtown Sarasota. On the first day the auction is held, it's not uncommon for the deputy tax collector and several other county employees to preside over the auction of more than 10,000 certificates for delinquent taxes on real estate. Here's how it works: When real estate owners don't pay taxes on their property, the county issues certificates for the amount of the unpaid taxes. The certificates are auctioned to investors for the amount of the unpaid taxes, plus a small processing fee. When property owners pay the taxes, they must also pay the certificate holder interest at a rate set at the auction, usually limited to a maximum of 18 percent.

If the property owners neglect to pay the taxes within two years, certificate holders can petition the county to sell the property at auction. Certificate holders recoup their investment, including interest, from the proceeds of the sale.

Some auction participants are hoping the taxes will be paid so they can collect the interest with minimum hassle. But other participants want the property, not the interest. If the taxes go unpaid for two years, the certificate holder can fill out the appropriate paperwork, pay about $200, and ask the county that the property be sold. If the taxes are still unpaid, the sale would be advertised and an auction held. The certificate holder will assume ownership if no one bids for the property.

Risks Involved

Such ventures can be risky if you don't do your homework before bidding. The certificates expire after seven years. This means certificate holders will lose their investment if they fail to petition the county to auction the property before the certificates expire.

Investors also risk holding certificates for property that's virtually worthless—such as platted lots in old subdivisions that were never developed. It's better to look for properties in developed subdivisions, particularly waterfront property.

Seek Other Bargain Opportunities

Besides all these great bargain potentials, there are other bargain opportunities lurking right around the corner—they're just not as obvious.

Great bargain opportunities can be found just by cruising the neighborhood. Get your camera and notebook out and start driving up and down the streets in your area, noting listed properties as well as FSBOs (For Sale By Owners). While you're at it, keep an eye out for property likely to be for sale but which has no For Sale sign. Telltale indications are unkempt vacant properties, boarded-up houses, and homes that are in dire need of care.

Once you have a substantial list, you can obtain ownership records from your local county courthouse or the property tax collector's office.

5

Key Ingredients to Making a Superior Realty Investment

Even a novice foreclosure investor—one who lacks experience and knowledge of the real estate marketplace—can expect to earn a small profit given an average rate of appreciation and enough time to overcome his or her shortcomings. Yet, to confidently purchase foreclosed property, paying a bargain price and converting it into a superior moneymaker that yields a great return, takes practiced skills and learned strategies. In order to make such a realization, you need proven know-how with established guidelines to lead you in the right direction. This way you minimize the risk and maximize the value of your investment. And that's what this chapter is all about: learning the six key ingredients that make up a superior realty investment. We also included three principles to maximize your investment and some time-tested general advice on residential investing, along with how to spot a real estate lemon.

Overview of the Six Key Ingredients

When you know precisely what to look for in a superior realty investment, along with what to avoid, you have a much better chance of being a

91

successful real estate investor. We will begin with a summary of the six key ingredients and then discuss each in detail.

1. *Specialize in detached single-family residences.* They are the wisest choice, especially for the newcomer to foreclosure investing. Avoid investing in vacant land or condominiums and cooperative apartments.

2. *Buy property that can be profitably improved.* When investing in property with minor defects that can easily be cured, you add value through cost-effective renovations.

3. *Buy improved property on a sizable piece of land.* Avoid speculation in vacant land and small parcels of real estate.

4. *Always finance your real estate with long-term fixed-rate loans.* Don't be foolishly enticed by lenders' offers of unpredictable and high-risk adjustable-rate mortgages or interest-only loans.

5. *Choose a good location in a thriving market.* You always want to avoid buying in a poor location with a declining market.

6. *Buy from motivated sellers.* Reason: You cannot bargain with an inflexible, unmotivated seller.

The Six Key Ingredients

1. Specialize in Detached Single-Family Residences

Specialization is crucial because one who specializes becomes efficient and is usually very good at what he or she does in a particular profession. Most medical doctors, for example, specialize in one particular field of medicine in order to gain expertise in a particular field of endeavor, rather than trying to be a so-called jack-of-all-trades, master of none. Most attorneys also specialize in one particular field of law, knowing that it's easier to be proficient in criminal law, for instance, or divorce law, instead of trying to be an expert in all facets of the law. It's more practical, and probably easier, to be an expert in one specific field than attempting to gain expertise in a broad range of subjects.

And why should you specialize in detached single-family residences? Because of the different types of housing—such as attached homes like condominiums and cooperative apartments—DSFRs have historically held their value better in weak markets and have appreciated more in strong, booming markets. Moreover, American homeowners have always had a deep-seated love affair with detached homes.

For the foreclosure investor, specializing in DSFRs is the wisest choice. There's a plentiful supply along with a strong demand for them created by first-time home buyers and other investors who know they're the best value available. Further, the attached home category represents less than 10 percent of the overall residential marketplace, and with such a limited supply and lack of demand for them, it makes any kind of attached housing *not* worth your while.

It also should be noted that cooperative apartments often have title problems that make them difficult to sell. And condominiums have expensive monthly association dues that increase every year, and they lack the demand appeal of a DSFR. Thus, we recommend that you do not invest in any type of attached home. About the only exception would be a condominium, but only if it has a superior location and can be purchased as a real bargain.

When you stick to learning as much as you can about DSFRs in your particular area of operation, values in the surrounding neighborhood, and the cost per square foot of detached homes, you'll have a very good chance of succeeding as a foreclosure investor.

Be a Specialist and Stay with What You Know or Do Best. Donald Trump's experience with the commercial airline business is a great example of why you should stay with what you do best. Because the minute you enter into an arena that's unfamiliar, it's easy to stumble and take a terrible fall.

In the fall of 2004, I was hired by the publisher, John Wiley & Sons, to coauthor a book with George Ross, Donald Trump's advisor and right-hand man, costar of *The Apprentice*. The book's title is *Trump Strategies for Real Estate*, and during the three months George and I worked together, he told me the following fascinating story about the Donald.

In 1989, in the midst of a prolonged aircraft mechanic's strike, after making billions successfully developing much of Manhattan's prime real estate, Donald Trump decided to purchase the Eastern Shuttle, which was originally part of the now-defunct Eastern Airlines. Financed through a consortium of 22 banks with a $380 million loan, Trump Air began on June 7 with hourly flights of Boeing 727 aircraft from New York's LaGuardia Airport to Boston's Logan International Airport and Washington's National Airport in Arlington, Virginia.

Trump pushed to make the new shuttle a luxury air service and a marketing vehicle for the Trump Organization. The aircraft were decorated with features such as maple wood veneer, gold lavatory fixtures, and chrome seat-belt latches. Trump Air also made advancements in certain technologies; it introduced the first passenger self-service kiosks at its LaGuardia base, and it offered rented laptop computers to passengers.

From its inception, Trump Air encountered financial problems. The shuttle's core passengers chose it for its convenience, not for its costly luxury features, and during the prolonged labor strike, many defected to the competing Pan Am shuttle or to Amtrak's Metroliner train service. To make matters worse, in 1989 the Northeast states entered an economic recession that depressed demand, and the August 1990 Iraqi invasion of Kuwait caused jet fuel prices to double.

Trump Air never turned a profit. The overextended debt load incurred at the company's creation unnerved Trump's creditors as his other high profile, highly leveraged casino interests showed signs of failing. In September 1990 the Trump shuttle defaulted on its loans, and the creditor banks took over ownership of the airline.

George Ross said that part of the reason Trump Air got into financial trouble was the lender's exuberance to lend Trump money. Up until the experience with Trump Air, everything Donald touched turned into gold; therefore, lenders were more than willing to lend him money for just about anything he wanted to do, even if the enterprise was not within his field of expertise.

The moral of this story is: Specialize in a business that you're knowledgeable in and do what you do best, instead of trying to be a jack-of-all trades (master of none). That way you will become very competent and knowledgeable in your own particular field.

2. Buy Property that Can Be Profitably Improved

Does the property you're thinking of buying have curable defects that can be fixed—without great expense or major effort—to enhance its value enough to earn a reasonable profit? One of the best ways to add value to your investment is to make selective, cost-effective renovations. Some of the simplest defects to correct are cosmetic. Often, especially with foreclosures, the past owners just never bothered to properly clean and maintain the property. Frequently, the only renovations needed are fresh paint, new carpeting, hardwood floor refinishing, and new landscaping. (See Chapter 8 for more details about renovating your acquisitions.)

Kitchens and Bathrooms Are Key. Every successful builder knows that the most important rooms in houses or apartments, as far as occupants are concerned, are kitchens and bathrooms. Extra dollars spent in these rooms will reap big rewards either in earned rent or selling price. If you're too thrifty with costs in remodeling your kitchen and bathrooms, it will be difficult to attract the upscale tenant or buyer. These two rooms are what sell houses and attract the high-end tenant. Not bedrooms. The first thing a prospective tenant or house buyer looks for are well-designed functional kitchens and bathrooms. With this in mind, there's an old proverb popular among realtors that goes like this: When a married couple is house hunting and thinking of buying a particular property, the first thing the woman considers is the appeal of the kitchen and the bathrooms; the man's first consideration is whether he can afford the monthly mortgage payment.

3. Buy Improved Property on a Sizable Parcel of Land

Sizable is key here because you're always better off with more land. Why? Because the more land you have, the more flexibility you have for expansion or usage. More land also makes the property more desirable (more spaciousness), which in turns makes it more valuable. In that regard, you have to understand that the improvements on the land—such as the house, garage, and other outbuildings—of course have value, but these improvements eventually wear down and become obsolete. It's the land itself that over the long haul endures and appreciates in value. Remember too that there's a limited, finite supply of habitable land. This means that the expanding population—mostly from immigration—will continue to put a lot of upward pressure on demand for habitable land, inevitably leading to even higher demand in the future.

Lack of sufficient land inhibits the growth potential of the property. Back in the early 1980s, when I first started to invest in Las Vegas, Nevada, I discovered that the best bargains were to be found investing in homes on large parcels of land. In particular, I began specializing in upper-middle-class homes built on lots that were at least a half acre in size. The reason was that I could get more for my money, particularly more land, and I found that the sellers of these half-acre properties usually overlooked the precise value of the land. In other words, frequently I could buy a 1,600- to 2,000-square-foot home on a half acre for about the same price as a similar tract home on one-fourth the amount of land. And when all was said and done, I had plenty of space to make additions to the house or do whatever, which I couldn't do without the added space of a large parcel of land.

Landlord Tale

In 1997, Rose and M.J. retired, sold their home in Texas, put their furniture in storage, and bought a two-year-old 34-foot Class A motor home. Along with their two miniature French poodles, they traveled full-time throughout the United States visiting friends and family. Eventually, Rose tired of all the travel, and they purchased a new home along the Mississippi Gulf Coast. They took all their stored furniture and moved it into the house, with the intention of selling the motor home. They put the recreational vehicle on an RV lot to sell on consignment, but it had no slide-outs (movable side walls that expand the RV's interior space). Then they discovered another problem: New RVs are financed with no money down, but used RVs require a down payment. And at the time, no one wanted a used RV without slide-outs. Then when they took the RV off the consignment lot, they had to pay fees to store it.

The problem was, they didn't have enough land at their residence to park their RV on. They ended up having to pay $75 a month to store it when they could have kept it on their property had they more land.

4. Finance Your Real Estate with Long-Term Fixed-Rate Loans

In you intend to finance your foreclosure acquisitions with traditional mortgage loans, you should avoid the risky types of financing, such as adjustable-rate mortgages (ARMs) or graduated loans and interest-only loans. It's more practical, safer, and in the long term more cost effective to stay with long-term fixed-rate mortgage loans. Don't be teased or induced into borrowing with an ARM, a graduated payment loan, or an interest-only loan just because the lender offers you a teaser interest rate that's lower than the rate on a similar fixed-rate loan. Over the full term of a long-term mortgage loan, you will inevitably pay much more for these riskier types of loans. (The advantages of fixed-rate loans are discussed in detail in Chapter 7.)

5. Choose a Good Location in a Thriving Market

Another key ingredient to making a superior realty investment is to buy property in a good location in a thriving market. Much has been said over the years about the importance of location as the prime consideration when investing in real estate. This is most certainly true when investing in a home for yourself, but it is not always the case when purchasing investment property.

An investment property should be a better-than-average moneymaker that appreciates in value. The subject property you're interested in may not be in the best part of town, but if it's a moneymaker, don't let the location stop you from making a sound investment. In other words, just because you wouldn't live there yourself, don't let the location detract from what otherwise would be a good investment.

Property in a District with Good Schools Is in a "Good Location". Whether you have school-age children or not, you always want to buy in a district with good-quality schools. Reason: When it comes time to rent or sell, you'll learn that strong school districts are a top priority among both renters and home buyers, which helps to increase rents and property values.

Location No-Nos. Instead of knowing what to look *for* in a location, sometimes it's better to be aware of what to *avoid*. Be wary of buying residential property in a neighborhood that has certain nuisances that may detract from the value. Before purchasing residential property, ask the following questions:

- Is it located in a floodplain and subject to floods?
- Is it located next to a commercial building, such as a warehouse or factory?

- Is it adjacent to a cemetery or an undertaker?
- Is it near an airport or under the flight path of incoming or departing aircraft?
- Does an unusual volume of vehicular traffic pass nearby that may prove to be a nuisance?
- Is it next to a school playground, where noisy children may interfere with the quiet enjoyment of the premises?

These characteristics of a location detract from the value of residential property. You can avoid these nuisances by carefully checking out the surrounding neighborhood before committing yourself to a long-term investment such as real estate.

Landlord Tale: Great Location in a Floodplain

I'll always remember a property owned by Wolverine Development of Lansing, Michigan, where I was employed as a property manager in 1972. Of the 200-plus properties owned by Wolverine, at the time it was the only one that did not have a tenant paying rent on it. Although it was situated at a key intersection, the site was, unfortunately, low-lying and subject to flooding, and no matter what incentives were offered, the site remained unoccupied for over 30 years and remained a burdensome expense.

A Thriving Market. Besides the location, you also have to be concerned with whether your subject property is situated within a "thriving market." Generally speaking, a thriving market is one that's not declining in population, employment, and real property values.

One example of a nonthriving market, or declining area, was the city of Houston, Texas, in the late 1980s. During that time, Houston experienced what economists call a "rolling recession." A glut of petroleum supplies in the world market caused oil prices to fall drastically. This resulted in oil companies severely cutting back on employment, with many related businesses failing as well. Like falling dominoes, many banks in the area also failed too during this time, primarily because of delinquent home loans that many unemployed borrowers living in Houston could no longer make payments on. The unfortunate result was an oversupply of housing and foreclosures, as many of the unemployed moved away to find work elsewhere. Eventually, real estate values in the Houston area dropped dramatically, and remained depressed for several years, because of this rolling recession.

You should also be wary of investing in smaller urban areas that depend primarily on one type of industry. If that particular employer experiences bad economic times or has to shut down operations, the surrounding area will inevitably become depressed. In contrast, areas that have diverse industries, such as Los Angeles or Boston, do not depend economically on one particular industry for employment. These diverse urban areas will thrive even if one major industry fails.

Always Consider the Logistics. The residential property you're interested in buying should be situated within a reasonable commute to and from the workplace. Consider too that residential property should always be in good proximity to shopping, restaurants, and entertainment. Potential tenants or buyers will be turned off by property that is poorly located in relation to these amenities.

Landlord Tale: Hurricane Katrina

When I first located to southern Mississippi in 1995, I always wanted to live along the picturesque Gulf Coast. Yet, better judgment, along with the high cost of flood insurance and the desire to protect our holdings from Mother Nature's wrath, told us to invest north of the Gulf of Mexico—to have a buffer between our real estate and the vulnerable Gulf. Beach Boulevard meanders along the Gulf, to the south, and what before Hurricane Katrina were once beautiful southern antebellum homes in the midst of thousands of live oak tress draped in Spanish moss is now a site of total devastation spanning 150 miles from Mobile, Alabama, to New Orleans.

On August 29, 2005, a 35-foot surge of seawater rolled ashore, and with it blew 150 mph winds that spawned deadly tornadoes. After eight hours of relentless blowing, Katrina's storm surge and devastating winds had totally destroyed 25 percent of the structures in southern Mississippi, mostly the low-lying properties situated close to the Gulf of Mexico. Even the lovely low-lying homes along the once scenic bayous received over 14 feet of flood surge.

When this terrible maelstrom was finally over, my wife Jenny and I were very fortunate. Of the three properties we own in Mississippi, we did not receive any water damage, and only our residence had any serious damage. We lost parts of our roof to a tornado, had ceiling damage in four rooms, the solarium blew into the adjacent woods, the backyard fence blew down, and the lovely live oak tree out front blew over. But because the house is built on high ground and situated nine miles north of the Gulf of Mexico, we were fortunate and did not get the full brunt of the storm, as so many others did that lived in vulnerable areas.

The moral of this story is: You need to protect yourself from the rages of nature. Avoid investing in vulnerable areas that are susceptible to devastating storms and flooding. Buy improved real estate on high ground buffered from coastal waters. Those who wish to live along the picturesque southern coasts of America will ultimately have to face the destructive forces of nature.

6. Buy from Motivated Sellers

You want to avoid dealing with inflexible or unmotivated sellers—people who, for whatever reason, are not motivated to sell. A motivated seller, on the other hand, is more inclined to be flexible with the selling price and terms of the deal. A motivated seller is someone who, because of certain circumstances, is prepared to sell below market value, and at favorable terms to the buyer. Such circumstances might include a pending divorce, death in the family, loss of employment, or other financial problems. If a seller is in any of these situations or a combination of them, he or she will often be extremely motivated and may be prepared to accept just about any reasonable offer.

In contrast, an unmotivated seller can put up serious obstacles to making a good deal. He or she may obstruct the making of a deal because there's nothing pushing them to sell. The seller may have a fixed price in mind, and come hell or high water, nobody will ever get the property for less.

With so many motivated sellers in the marketplace, especially those distressed owners in the midst of a foreclosure, there's no reason why you should have to deal with an unyielding seller.

If the property you're considering as an investment has this or any of the other five key ingredients, the probability is that it will be a very profitable realty investment. And consider too the following investment principles relevant to purchasing residential real estate.

Three Principles to Maximize Your Investment

You can maximize the investment yield on any property by following three fundamental principles in the selection of the detached single-family residence you purchase. As you read the following guidelines, bear in mind that they're not etched in stone—exceptions do occur.

The following three principles are excerpts taken from McLean's *Home Buyer's Advisor,* pages 77–78 (John Wiley & Sons, 2004).

Principle of Progression: Reason to Buy One of the Lesser-Priced Homes on the Block

This principle is based on the fact that in a particular neighborhood, the lower-priced homes tend to seek the value of the higher-priced homes. In other words, if you buy a modestly priced home in a higher-priced neighborhood, the more expensive homes in the neighborhood will eventually raise yours to a higher value. To that end, avoid the highest-priced house, or one that has been overimproved for the neighborhood.

For instance, suppose you're house-hunting in a neighborhood you like and you find a particular jewel. It's priced at $125,000 and is definitely the least expensive home in the neighborhood. The other homes are selling for $160,000 to $200,000—and now that you know this, you can't wait to make an offer.

But wait, you've got some investigating to do. You must find out why this house is so underpriced. If it has certain kinds of curable defects, which can be easily remedied, you may want to buy it. However, if it has incurable defects, find another property to invest in.

Curable Defects. Curable defects are flaws in a property that can easily be overcome without too great an expense. Suppose, for example, that the previous owners had poor taste—they painted the interior walls a hideous dark color, and to make matters worse, they covered the walls in the kitchen and bathrooms with dreadful-looking wallpaper. But these applications are merely a cosmetic defect, which could be overcome with a little elbow grease and a tasteful paint job.

Or, perhaps this jewel you found is the only two-bedroom one-bath home in the area, but both bedrooms are huge, allowing you to convert the two bedrooms into three, with an additional guest bath added on. If you can do the renovation for no more than $12,000, you'll have a total cost of $137,000 ($125,000 purchase price plus $12,000). Now you've created value, because you own a three-bedroom two-bath house in a $160,000 to $200,000 neighborhood.

You can add value to your investment by finding properties with curable defects that can be remedied inexpensively. Other relatively inexpensive remedies include a thorough cleaning, painting, modernizing a kitchen with ceramic tile floors and countertops, upgrading fixtures in a bathroom, and rewiring the electrical system with a higher-ampere system to accommodate modern appliances.

Incurable Defects. If a house has major deficiencies, it's not worth buying at any price. Would you want a house next to a junkyard or a bus depot? Or what about a downright ugly home? Just because the seller made a fortune in the deli business doesn't mean that you (or anyone else) would want to live in a house designed in the shape of a giant hoagie sandwich! And likewise there's no cure for a poorly located house.

These are major deficiencies, incurable defects, that cannot be remedied at an economically feasible price. It wouldn't even be feasible to pay $150,000 for the hoagie house, tear it down, and build a new home on the site (unless that's what comparable vacant residential lots sell for). If you did that, and spent another $125,000 building a new house, you'd likely have the dubious honor of owning the priciest house in the neighborhood. (See Chapter 8 for more information about making practical improvements to your investments.)

Principle of Regression: Reason Not to Buy the Costliest Home on the Block

This principle is the economic opposite of the principle of progression: The lesser-valued homes in the neighborhood bring down the values of the higher-valued homes. Or, put another way, if you buy the most expensive house on the block, the lower-valued houses around you bring down your house's value to that of the other houses.

In order to attain maximum value for your investment, the wisest choice is to purchase one of the less expensive houses in a desirable neighborhood.

Principle of Conformity: Reason Nonconformity Is Costly

In residential neighborhoods, conformity is good. Look for a house whose style fits in with the others. A southwestern adobe-style house with a tile roof—an architectural style that's common throughout Arizona and New Mexico—is hardly appropriate in the hills of Pennsylvania! A house that significantly stands out in a neighborhood might be great for you, but others may not share your taste for alternative design, and it could make the house difficult to rent or sell when the time comes.

Some Time-Tested Advice for Buying Residential Real Estate

The following basic advice is mostly fundamental to offer you a better overall perspective of investing in residential real estate. Some of these were included as common mistakes many novice investors make, to make you aware of them so you can avoid making similar mistakes,

Consider the Sale of Residential Realty Before You Buy It. When looking at prospective purchases, take into consideration the features and amenities of the property that other buyers would find appealing. In other words, pretend you're looking at the property's amenities through the eyes of other buyers. If you don't, it will be difficult to find a buyer or a quality tenant when it comes time to sell or rent the property.

Remember That Everything Is Negotiable. Shrewd foreclosure investors are fully informed of market conditions and neighborhood values. They also know when it's wise to make a lowball offer, and they realize that there are situations when it's best to make the initial offer the best offer they can afford.

Never Buy If You Can't Stay Put. If you cannot commit to remaining in one place for five years or more, then owning a home is probably not for you. The short-term costs of buying and selling are prohibitive over a very short term. And renting it out and maintaining the property as an absentee landlord is not recommended because it is too difficult to oversee from far away, and you lose direct control when you must hire a property management company to oversee it in your absence.

Never Be an Absentee Landlord. You never want to hand over the management responsibility of your realty holdings unless you can directly oversee the resident manager. And you cannot directly oversee a resident manager or a management company if you're an absentee landlord—someone who lives out of state or resides far enough away from the property that they cannot visit at least once a month. The reason is that there are too many ways unscrupulous people can take advantage of you. For instance, they could claim a unit is vacant when in fact it's occupied, while the manager pockets the rent. Or they can charge the absentee landlord for "invisible" repairs that are never done, while the owner pays for them and the manager, again, pockets the money. If you're not there to oversee all this criminal activity, how can you stop it or prove that it occurred?

Never Enter into a Bidding War. It's always better to buy from a motivated seller who will make concessions, instead of competing with other buyers who are trying to outbid each other. Remember the old saying, "There are always more fish in the sea," and likewise, there will always be more opportunities in the marketplace to buy bargain-priced foreclosures—you only need to spend the time to find them.

Real Estate Is a Better Long-Term Than Short-Term Investment. Over the long haul, you'll make more money holding onto your real estate investments than you will "flipping" them (selling them quickly). Here are several reasons why:

- After the sale you'll have to find another property to invest the proceeds in; otherwise you might be tempted to squander the gains.
- In certain situations, the tax law will require you to pay taxes on the gain. But there would be no tax liability if you didn't sell.
- The costs to procuring a sale can eat up your profits. Continuous selling of real estate, especially when you have to pay a realtor's sales commission, can get very costly.
- Frequently when you invest in real estate with a small down payment and then rent out the property, in the first year or two it's difficult to earn positive cash flow. Often you'll just break even or have a short period of negative cash flow. But as time passes you can increase rents and earn a much greater return.

- And most significant, you'll enjoy the benefit of growing equity through years of appreciation and loan pay-down, which would be lacking in a short-term sale.

Now that you have a grasp of the key ingredients to making a superior realty investment, and you've been given advice and apprised of how to avoid common mistakes when purchasing real estate, the next chapter looks at the inspection and appraisal of foreclosed real estate.

6

Inspection and Appraisal of Foreclosed Real Estate

Before you attend any auctions where you aim to bid or present any written offers on any foreclosed real estate, it's very important to carefully inspect and appraise the value of the properties you're interested in and to analyze the market conditions where the property is situated. These preliminary evaluations will be helpful in determining whether your potential acquisition is a desirable "diamond in the rough" or a dreaded "real estate lemon." This chapter will help guide you to inspecting and evaluating foreclosed real estate and how to spot a real estate "lemon."

Property Inspections

The purpose of the inspection is to determine whether the property is a worthwhile investment. And that decision will be based on the information gathered during the inspection. This includes pointing out problems and estimating the repair costs to correct them. You also have to judge whether the floor plan and architectural style of the building will appeal to potential renters or buyers.

When it comes to making an inspection of a foreclosed property, most often you'll find the property unoccupied, the utilities shut off, and the structure's doors and windows boarded up. Bring along a pencil and notepad to make observations about each property. Also take along a digital camera for taking pictures of each property, as a visual record is better than your memory, especially when you inspect five or more properties in one day. And since most properties will be boarded up with the utilities off, you need to bring along a flashlight or battery-operated lantern to give you a better view of the property's interior.

Once the photographs are developed, keep them along with your notes in a separate 9-by-12-inch manila envelope with the property's address noted on the front. Maintain a separate envelope for each property you inspect.

Gaining Access

If the property you need to inspect is a lender's REO, you have to contact the REO manager or the managing realtor to obtain an entry key. If the property will be sold at public auction, you need to contact the auction holder to find out how you can inspect the property.

When you arrive at the property, be wary that unauthorized persons could be inside the premises of a boarded-up foreclosed structure. It is not uncommon for homeless people, vagrants, criminals, or crack cocaine addicts to be hiding out in supposedly unoccupied structures. Before entering any foreclosed structure, especially if the doors and windows are boarded up, it's a good idea to make a cursory inspection of the exterior of the premises. Look for any damage that could reveal someone entered the building by breaking in.

It's also a good idea to avoid making the inspection alone. There's more security in numbers. Bring along your contractor or property inspector, who can help point out needed repairs and make an accurate written estimate of the renovation costs involved.

What to Look For

As you enter each room, start the inspection at the top—the ceiling—and work your way down the walls to the floor. Note the condition of the ceilings. Are there any damp spots or mildew that reveal telltale signs of a leaky roof? Do the ceilings need replacing? Are the ceiling fans or light fixtures missing? As you inspect the interior walls, look for mold or cracks. (Cracked walls usually indicate the foundation of the structure is settling.) If the floors are carpeted, look to see what's underneath. Perhaps the shabby carpeting covers hardwood floors that you can refinish, instead of recarpeting the entire house.

In the kitchen and bathrooms, look for missing fixtures that were removed, such as sinks, tubs, and toilets. Check the plumbing lines too; if they were made of copper, neighborhood thieves may have ripped them out. Also make sure the heating and air-conditioning unit is still in place, especially the compressor, which is usually located in the attic or in a centrally located closet.

If the property has been boarded up to protect against vandalism, check to see if the doors and windows were removed. If they were, where are they located? If they're unavailable, the new owner is responsible for replacing the doors and windows. Thus, you must include the cost of these items in your repair estimate.

If you're unable to inspect the property while the utilities are on, it's a good idea to assume the worst. To cover yourself for undetected damage, such as a central heating and air-conditioning unit you cannot turn on, you have to assume that it needs repair. Therefore, include such a repair cost in your estimate. If it turns out the unit is in fact operational, you'll be that much further ahead.

Property Inspection Checklist

Hiring a home inspector can ease many uncertainties by uncovering costly problems that could cost you thousands of dollars in repairs. A professional home inspector licensed by the American Society of Home Inspectors (ASHI)charges about $250 to $300, depending on location. The following are important items that need to be inspected:

- *Roof.* For shingled roofs, look for curled or missing shingles as evidence that a new roof is needed. Estimate $120/square (100 square feet) for a standard 20-year shingle roof, and $150/square for a 30-year architectural-style shingle roof. For asphalt roofs, if the granular composition surface is worn off or stains are evident on the underside of the overhang, it won't be long before the roof has to be replaced. Replacement of an asphalt roof on average-sized homes costs upward of $3,000 and will last about 20 years. The more expensive clay tile or wood shingle roofs start at about $5,000 and can last 40 years.

- *Electrical.* Modern homes are equipped with a 100 or 200 ampere service, which is adequate to handle today's appliances, such as Sub-Zero refrigerators, microwave ovens, and electric clothes dryers. Older homes frequently are equipped with a 60-ampere service, which could be adequate if the house is small and the clothes dryer, range, and furnace operate on gas. And keep in mind that rooms with only one electrical wall receptacle are underserved. Look to spend at least $1,200 for a modern 100-ampere service, plus at least $60 per additional receptacle.

- *Heating and air-conditioning.* Be sure each room has a heating register (the outlet). On the AC unit, check the compressor to see whether it's running smoothly. The large intake pipe should cool quickly after the unit is turned on. If it doesn't, you have a coolant leak.

- *Walls and windows.* In northern latitudes, look for storm windows. Cracked plaster is common in older homes; however, in newer homes it indicates the house is settling. Look for deteriorated caulking around windowsills and window frames; it allows heat loss.

- *Interior plumbing.* To check for good water pressure you need to turn on the water at a faucet. Meanwhile, you can also check for water leaks. Check in cabinets for drips underneath sinks, around toilets while flushing, and puddles in the basement. Older structures may have galvanized steel pipes (check by using a magnet; they are gray in color) or brass pipes, either of which will eventually have to be replaced. Newer plumbing systems shouldn't give you any trouble. The cost of replacing the old plumbing can be $2,500 or more, depending on the size of the house.

- *Termites.* These wood-chewing creatures are a particular problem in the southern latitudes, the Midwest, and California. Tunnels in the wood are a telltale indication of termites.

- *Foundations, basements, and underflooring.* Water stains on the basement wall and floor indicate previous water leaks or, even worse, flooding. Also look for white dust, which is the residue of salts washed out of the concrete. Due to the instability of the underlying earth, Florida homes should be checked to be sure the concrete slab is supported by pilings. Saggy or squeaky floors can be checked by examining the floor trusses underneath.

Also look for large cracks (one you can stick your finger into) in exterior retaining walls, foundation, interior walls, fireplace, chimney, concrete floors, and sidewalks.

Hiring a Professional Inspector

What's the best procedure for finding a competent property inspector? Two things you do not want to do: Never ask the seller for a recommendation, and never use the realtor's recommendation either. The reason you don't want a referral from a realtor is that even the most competent property inspector might avoid making too many waves, for fear that the sale will fall through. If the realtor loses a sale because the property inspector finds too many faults in a home, the realtor might never recommend the inspector again. Get referrals from friends or business associates who have recently used an inspector. Also check the yellow pages of your local phone book under "Building Inspection Services" or "Home Inspection Services."

Before you hire a property inspector, it is recommended that you first conduct a simple phone interview with several of them. Here are some pertinent questions to ask:

- Are you a full-time professional property inspector? The only acceptable answer to this question is yes.
- How many property inspections do you perform each year? An active full-time property inspector will make between 100 and 250 inspections a year. The inspector you hire should be familiar with the area where the property to be inspected is situated, to ensure that the inspector is familiar with local building regulations, local codes, and problems inherent to the area, such as floods, mud slides, hurricanes, tornadoes, or earthquakes.
- Are you certified or licensed? Qualified property inspectors typically have experience in a related field, such as engineering, construction,

or electrical work. Membership in ASHI or other professional organizations for property inspectors indicate some knowledge of property-inspection procedures.

- Do you carry insurance for errors or omissions? Errors-and-omissions insurance protects the homeowner should the property inspector make an error or overlook a problem.
- How thorough is the property inspection? Be sure that the inspection covers all the property's major mechanical and structural components, from the foundation to the roof. Never accept anything less.
- What kind of inspection do I get? The best type of inspection is a detailed written report with a description of the property's mechanical and structural condition. It should be written in plain English, and it must fully explain the implications of its inspection.

For the name of a property inspector in your area, contact:

American Society of Home Inspectors
Phone: 847.759.2820, or 800.743.ASHI
www.ashi.com

Questions to Ask Before Making an Offer

Before you submit a written offer or make a verbal bid at a foreclosure auction, there are certain important questions you need to ask the person responsible for the sale of foreclosed property, such as the REO manager, the managing realtor, or the auction seller.

Is the property boarded up? If so, where are the doors and windows? Usually, especially if the property is situated in a bad neighborhood, the foreclosing lender has the building boarded up to protect against vandalism. If this is the case, the entry doors and first-floor windows are often removed and replaced with plywood. Therefore, in order to do a proper inspection, you'll need a battery-powered lantern to see around the interior of the premises. (With the utilities off and the outside light blocked by the boarded-up windows, it will be very dark inside.) You also have to find out where the entry doors and windows are stored. If you have to pay for the cost of replacing them, you need to add this cost—along with the cost to remove all the plywood and install the entry doors and windows—to your repair cost estimate.

For the purpose of inspection, do interested buyers have access to the premises before bidding? Regarding foreclosures sold at auction, access information is usually available on the advertised Notice of Sale or from the foreclosing lender. For a lender's REO and government-owned foreclosures, contact the REO manager or the designated realtor who handles the sale of foreclosed property.

Have the utilities been turned on, or have the pipes been winterized (if applicable)? To do a thorough inspection you'll need to check the electrical and plumbing systems. But if the plumbing has been winterized—antifreeze added to the pipes in northern climates—the seller will have to clear the system before the water can be turned on.

What will be the status of the foreclosed owner's "right of redemption" after the sale? If the security instrument was a Deed of Trust in the foreclosure sale, then this issue is not applicable because the foreclosed owner does not have the right of redemption. However, if the security instrument was a mortgage and the property was sold under a court-ordered auction, then the foreclosed owner's "right of redemption" is an issue. In some states the foreclosed owner's right of redemption is lost once the auction begins. In other states the foreclosed owner can redeem the property for a limited period after the auction if he pays the winning bidder the full upset price, plus interest. Check with a real estate attorney or realtor knowledgeable in foreclosures regarding a previous owner's right of redemption that may apply in your particular state.

What are the terms of the sale? You need to know the required amount of down payment and the form it must be in. Usually, the seller will require a cashier's check or money order, and in some situations will accept cash. You also need to know the closing date, which is commonly 30 days after the offer was accepted.

Is the sales contract assignable? Sales contracts are usually always assignable unless there's a stipulation written into the contract that prohibits it. Thus, if you're bidding at a public auction, where there is no contingency for financing, you'll find that sales contracts are commonly assignable. However, when you're buying a lender's REO, and he's providing the financing and the loan is contingent upon your credit rating, then the sales contract is usually not assignable.

Are there occupants presently residing in the property? When you're the successful high bidder at a foreclosure auction, it will be your responsibility to evict any unwanted occupants residing in the premises. When you buy a lender's REO, it will be their responsibility.

Are there any restrictive covenants, easements, or public zoning restrictions that could adversely affect the future use of the premises? The following are common deed restrictions that certain neighborhoods, governments, or other entities enact that can adversely affect the use of your acquired property:

- A restrictive covenant or zoning restriction that prohibits parking of recreational or commercial vehicles on the property.
- A restrictive covenant that prohibits certain colors to be painted on the exterior of houses within a designated community.
- You would have a serious problem renting your acquired property to tenants if the community has a moratorium on issuing rental permits.
- If the property you purchased has a structure that has been designated a historical landmark, there could be restrictions regarding any alterations of the exterior.
- The deed may have a private easement permitting your landlocked neighbor access to and from his residence.

Are there any outstanding liens or judgments attached to the property? This is a very important question to ask when you're bidding for foreclosures at public auction. The only way you can be sure you're getting a clear and marketable title is to buy title insurance or make a thorough search of the public records in the County Clerk's Office. However, when you're buying from a foreclosing lender's inventory of REO, usually the seller has already taken care of any outstanding liens or judgments.

Besides the property inspection and estimating the cost of needed repairs, you will also need to determine the property's market value in renovated condition. You can begin by going out and getting a feel for property values in the territory you intend to operate in. On weekends visit open houses and talk to realtors. Find out what an average size residential lot is selling for; and ask about the selling price per square foot of living area. A competent, full-time realtor will be your best source of market information.

You could, of course, hire a professional appraiser and pay $300 or more to evaluate each property you're interested in. Or you can save money and learn how to do your own appraisals, which we go into below.

The Comparable Sales Approach to Appraisal

Also commonly referred to as the "market data approach to appraising improved real property," the comparable sales approach is appropriate for evaluating detached single-family residences, condominiums, cooperative apartments, and small apartment houses (up to four units) when a number of similar properties are available for comparison. Thus, this technique would not be appropriate for evaluating a unique 4,200-square-foot custom-built home because it would be difficult to find similar comparables in the same area.

Start by finding three comparable properties that have recently sold (within six months) in the same area and that closely match the subject property. The comparables should match in approximate size, age, condition, amenities, quality of construction, floor plan, and room count.

Now look at the following two different appraisal techniques: The first is a quick appraisal based only on square footage of living area, and the second looks at both square footage and the features of the properties. Both appraisals take into consideration the price per square foot of living area, but the second is more precise because it also compares the subject property to the comparables on a feature-by-feature basis.

Quick Appraisal Based Only on Square Footage

Say, for instance, you have located three comparables (comps) for the subject property. Comp A has 1,620 square feet, Comp B has 1,730 square feet, and Comp C has 1,885 square feet. Each of these homes have sold within the last four months for the respective prices of $115,020, $111,325, and $130,442. To determine the selling price per square foot of living area, you

Figure 6-1.   Appraisals Based on Square Footage

    Comp A: $115,020 = $71 per square foot
                    1,620 square feet

    Comp B: $111,325 = $64.35 per square foot
                    1,730 square feet

    Comp C: $130,442 = $69.20 per square foot
                    1,885 square feet

Average price per square foot of Comps A through C = $68.18

divide the square footage of each home into the selling price, as can be seen in Figure 6-1.

If the subject property you're appraising has 1,810 square feet of living area, then based on comparable square-footage cost, calculated from an average of the three comparables of $68.18, you can quickly determine that its estimated market value is approximately 1,810 x 68.18 = $123,400.

Estimating market value based only on the square footage of comparable sales will suffice when you need a quick, off-the-cuff appraisal. However, to make a more precise evaluation, you also need to compare the subject property to the comparables on a feature-to-feature basis.

Precise Appraisal Based on Features and Square Footage

Once you have three comparables that are similar to the subject property, you have to adjust for differences in features and amenities between them and the subject property. You accomplish this by adding or subtracting the value of features to and from each comparable to make them equivalent to the subject property. In other words, you want to know what the comparable would have sold for had it been precisely (with the same features) like the subject property.

For instance, looking at Figure 6-2, consider the –$4,000 adjustment to Comp B for sales concessions. The $111,325 sales price in the deal included the seller's custom-made draperies. Since draperies are not usually included in a real property sale, the sales price had to be adjusted down to make it equal in value to that of the subject property, whose sale does not include this particular item.

Appraisal of Foreclosed Real Estate

Figure 6-2. Adjustment Process

Item	Comp A	Comp B	Comp C
Sales Price	$115,020	$111,325	$130,442
Features:			
Sales concessions	0	−4,000	0
Financing concessions	−4,000	0	0
Date of sale	0	2,000	0
Location	0	0	−10,000
Floor plan	0	3,000	0
Garage	5,000	0	8,000
Pool, deck, patio	−4,000	0	6,000
Indicated value of subject	112,020	112,325	122,442

Following are explanations for several adjustments listed in Figure 6-2:

- *Comp A, financing concessions at −$4,000.* This comparable had valuable seller financing in the form of a low-interest purchase-money loan at 7.5 percent with only 5 percent down. Since at the time of the sale the market interest rates were 8.5 percent with 20 percent down, the value of favorable owner financing must be deducted from the sales price.
- *Comp A, garage at +$5,000.* The subject property has an attached two-car garage, while Comp A has only a single-car garage. To equalize the difference, you have to add $5,000 to Comp A's sales price; that is, if Comp A had been constructed with a two-car garage, it would presently be worth $5,000 more.
- *Comp C, location at −$10,000.* Unlike the subject property, Comp C has a great location at the end of a cul-de-sac with a wonderful view of a nearby lake. Thus, the added value of a great location with a view has to be deducted from the comparable to equalize the value of the subject property.

At this point you might be wondering how I arrived at an exact dollar amount for each of these features. There is no easy answer. However, as you gain expertise at evaluating real estate, you begin to get a feel for what certain things are worth. Meanwhile, when you're out prospecting for bargains, don't be afraid to ask a lot of questions. Ask your realtor about construction costs and residential lot values. In particular, keep informed about costs per square foot of living area, based on different qualities of construction. As you're viewing different properties, make a list of features that make a difference. Ask the realtor or a building contractor what he or she thinks the added feature is worth. Then weigh their evaluations against your judgment to arrive at a value for a particular feature.

☞ TIP

It's always a good idea to know the year the building you're evaluating was constructed. To determine this, lift the lid of the bathroom's water closet (the toilet); you'll find the manufacturer's date embossed on the inside. The date you see is a good indication of the year the structure was built. The only exception is if a new toilet was installed to replace the original.

Spotting a Real Estate Lemon

You've probably heard the horror stories. A couple of naive home buyers, after committing to a huge mortgage loan and putting their life savings into a down payment, move into what promises to be their ultimate dream home—only to spend their free time battling against a leaky roof, a faulty electrical system, pet odor, and a cracked foundation. Unfortunately for them, they've got a real estate lemon.

Problems, of course, vary from lemon to lemon, and the property inspector—who we recommend you use before buying any foreclosure—will usually alert you to trouble before you buy. But unfortunately, more and more home buyers are walking into bottomless money pits without a careful inspection.

Richard Collier, the CEO of Choice Point, which issues CLUE reports, says, "People fall in love with homes, but don't get the facts about them. It's like a blind date. They have no idea what they'll get."

Perfect dream house or not, you might consider buying another house if the inspection report flags problems with the house's structure or foundation, roof, mold, or pet odor.

Here's what it can cost you:

Leaky Roof

A roof replacement could cost between $5,000 and $20,000, depending on its size and the quality of the material. (Replacing our roof in September 2005, after Hurricane Katrina, cost $8,000 on a 2,300-square-foot home using high-grade architectural shingles.) When you make an inspection, keep an eye out for signs of leaks. Make inquiries about the age of the roof. And have your house inspector tell you the roof's life expectancy.

The inspector should check the shingles for wear and tear, says Richard Matzen, president of the American Society of Home Inspectors. If water or snow can pool on the roof, for example, you may need a replacement sooner than you think. Each type of roofing comes with its own wear cycle. Cedar shake or shingle roofs, for example, often have a shorter life cycle than other types of roofing and can be maintenance-intensive if the wood is a cheap grade.

The Cracked Slab

You might be unaware of what a cracked slab is, but you know it can't be anything good. It isn't: A cracked slab is a fracture in the foundation of the building, and ignoring it could lead to eventual collapse.

Cracks in the foundation come from unstable soil beneath the slab, Richard Matzen explained. Soils may be unstable for different reasons: Along the Pacific Rim, houses may have seismic problems; in the northern and northeastern states, frost and frost heaves can lift frozen soil like an ice cube in a tray—and can break a weak foundation in the process.

Moldy Walls

Mold has been around for thousands of years. Yet, according to the Insurance Information Institute, public concern about mold contamination—and mold claims submitted to home insurers—have skyrocketed over the past few years.

Jim Hastings, a realtor in Las Vegas, Nevada, says, "Wall mold is common on the West Coast, and in desert states like Arizona and Nevada.

"Years ago, we'd see mold in a house from a water leak, in the corner of a shower, and it was no big deal. But now there are molds that cause health problems—allergies or dizzy spells.

"Detected early," Hastings says, "mold can often be removed with bleach and water. However, if the home is not maintained and the mold becomes hazardous, it must be removed professionally, or *remediated*," to avoid health risks. Depending on the severity of the problem, it could cost $500 to $15,000 to remedy the situation.

If your inspection reveals any discoloration on the walls, the inspector will order a mold test, which costs about $300. That will confirm whether you need professional mold removal.

Pet Odors

"Buyers often underestimate the odor that pets leave in homes, even very clean homes," says Rhonda Richardson, a realtor in northern Virginia. "New owners may need to have carpets replaced and floorboards bleached to remove odors, especially if cats lived in the home years before you."

Richardson goes on to say that "any realtor worth his salt will have sellers clean their carpets professionally before putting a home up for sale, and that often will temporarily overshadow the smell. Then they move out, and you move in. After some moisture and closed-house conditions—say, a few days of rain—the odor could resurface with a vengeance."

The cost to replace carpeting and flooring can run up to $8,000.

It's Better to Avoid the Auction and Buy REO

As you can see, there's a lot of questions to ask and a lot of potential problems to overcome with foreclosed property. But remember, as mentioned earlier, when you purchase a lender's REO you avoid many of the problems foreclosure investors have to face when purchasing in the other two phases of the foreclosure process. For instance, you don't have to compete with other bidders, you don't have to worry about judgments and liens attached to the property, you don't have to arrange outside financing because the seller can give you a great loan, you don't have the responsibility of evicting the occupants, and you don't have to worry about the foreclosed owner's right of redemption.

Learn as Much as You Can About the Local Real Estate Market

When you become familiar with a particular area, such as your designated territory of operation, you gain knowledge. Knowledge becomes power that you can use to make better deals because you become an informed investor. In time, you become more efficient because you no longer need to research—you already know the answer. When you know values such as replacement costs per square foot, rental rates, the value of residential building lots, and so on, it's easier to spot a bargain or to quickly determine whether a property deserves further attention. Moreover, if you know what it costs to make certain renovations and repairs, or if you have knowledge about certain changes coming to a particular area, such as new interstate highways or regional shopping centers, you can capitalize on the coming changes.

7

Financing Foreclosed Real Estate

This chapter aims to save you some money and to keep you informed about all the necessary how-to's of borrowing money to purchase foreclosed real estate. You'll discover why the financing is so crucial to the profitability of your realty investment, along with the principle of leverage. You'll also learn how to take advantage of the full range of today's real estate financing methods, including the "no verification loan," originating FHA and VA loans, and other alternative financing methods.

Not Long Ago, You Had No Choices

Once upon a time there were no alternatives to choose from when taking out a loan to buy real estate. You only had one type available, and it was a straight term interest-only loan. You paid just the interest on the loan and periodically the lender renewed it, basically perpetuating the principal owing into the future

But nowadays you can choose from a wide variety of mortgage loans with all kinds of repayment plans—some start out small and gradually increase, and some are even convertible from one type to another. You have fixed and variable-rate loans where the rate of interest can remain unchanged or vary, depending on market interest rates. You also have a variety of payment plans that can graduate, or increase, as the loan matures. And once the home is acquired and you gain substantial equity in it, you can take out a reverse mortgage that pays you a regular monthly payment over the life of the loan. And of course, you have a variety of government-backed loan programs that either insure or guarantee lenders against default by the borrower.

The Financing Is Crucial

Borrowing money to invest in real estate is one of the most crucial elements in any real estate transaction. Arranging the wrong type of long-term financing can cost the borrower thousands of extra dollars over the life of a mortgage loan.

The use of borrowed money to purchase real estate serves several purposes: It gives you more leverage, which enables you to purchase much more, often 20 or 30 times, than what you could buy otherwise for cash; it reduces your equity exposure; and your interest payments on the loan serve as a great tax reduction.

But there's more to successfully financing real estate than just shopping for a better interest rate. You also should know how to determine how much to borrow, how to save on loan origination fees, and how to decide between using a fixed- or adjustable-rate loan.

Most of the Cost Is in the Financing

Perhaps the costliest thing you will ever purchase is, remarkably, not the house or other real estate you might buy; it's the mortgage loan you borrowed to acquire that real estate. That's right. If you borrow to buy real estate, as most of us do, then it's the mortgage loan that costs the most—depending on the rate of interest, perhaps two or three times as much as the property you purchased with that borrowed money.

Since many realty investors tend to focus primarily on the monthly payment, little attention is paid to the aggregate interest costs of the mortgage loan. You need to look into the various costs involved with financing real estate because the financing is often crucial to whether your investment is ultimately profitable.

Financing Foreclosed Real Estate

Suppose, for example, you buy a $100,000 house and borrow $80,000 at 10.5 percent for 30 years. That mortgage loan, if paid off over the entire 30-year term, will cost you $183,448 in interest—more than double the amount you borrowed, and almost double the price of the house. And that's not even counting the $80,000 in principal that you have to pay back. In other words, in a period of 30 years you actually paid $283,448 for a $100,000 house!

When you learn how to take full advantage of today's financing methods, you can save tens of thousands of dollars on a long-term mortgage loan. By following the guidelines set forth in this chapter, you can avoid the costliest mistake many realty investors make—paying too much for the wrong financing.

A 1 Percent Differential Can Save You Tens of Thousands

In Table 7-1, look at how much you can save in interest charges between paying 8 and 7 percent on a $110,000 loan over 30 years. Over a 30-year term, during which the borrower makes 360 equal monthly payments, the differential is $75.31 per month, and when that figure is multiplied by 360, the result is a savings of $27,112.

Save on Loan Fees Too

Besides shopping for a better rate of interest, there are savings to be earned on the amount of fees lenders charge to originate a mortgage loan. The loan origination fee—usually from one-quarter of 1 percent to 2 percent of the loan amount—is the most significant fee the borrower has to pay. You need to shop around to learn how much lenders in your area charge to originate

Table 7-1
Savings Earned on a 1-Point Differential in Interest on a $110,000 Loan

| | Lender | |
Factor	A	B
Rate of interest the borrower pays	77%	8%
Monthly payment of P&I	731.83	807.14

Difference in payment between A and B = $75.31 × 360 = $27,112 a mortgage loan. For instance, on a $160,000 loan, a savings of just 1 point in the origination fee can save you $1,600 when the loan is funded.

And if you take out a conventional loan with at least a 20 percent down payment, you won't have to pay for primate mortgage insurance (PMI). Anything less will cost you an additional $40 to $100 per month in PMI, depending on the amount of the loan. (A more thorough discussion of conventional loans and PMI follows.)

Loan Alternatives

Real estate loans can be classified in several different ways. One means of classification is according to the plan of repayment of the loan that the borrower and the lender agree upon. The basic repayment plans available are:

- Interest-only (straight-term) loans
- Adjustable-rate loans
- Fixed-Rate Amortized loans
- Convertible loans

Interest-Only Loans

Also referred to as the "straight term" or "balloon" loan, this particular type requires the payment of interest-only and no payment of principal during the term of the loan. At maturity the entire principal is due and payable in one final balloon payment.

Prior to the Great Depression that began in 1929, the interest-only loan was the most common payment method for real estate financing. But as the economic depression worsened and the entire world economy failed, most lenders who held real estate loans were unable to "roll over" or perpetuate these interest-only loans. The results were devastating. Lenders began calling these loans, requiring the borrowers to pay the entire principal amount owing, which they did not have. Then the lenders began foreclosing on these loans throughout the entire country.

The Great Depression made almost everyone—especially those in the financial industry—aware of the inherent dangers in this type of financing. A more practical form of real estate loan soon materialized in the amortized loan.

During stable periods of economic growth when inflation is not excessive, long-term lenders have no problems with funding long-term fixed-rate loans. But beginning in the early 1980s excessive inflation became a problem for the world economy. Along with it came rising interest rates for mortgage loans. In the meantime, lenders were stuck with low fixed rates of interest on their loans that they were unable to adjust. Thus the emergence of the adjustable-rate mortgage, which allowed lenders to adjust periodically to represent current market rates.

Adjustable-Rate Loans

Adjustable-rate mortgages (ARMs) were conceived by long-term lenders to protect them from radical changes in market interest rates. Lenders prefer them over fixed-rate loans because the loan can *adjust* to market conditions over the term of the loan.

The initial rate offered the borrower is often called the "teaser rate," because it is usually set lower than a comparable fixed interest rate. (The borrower is induced, or "teased," into choosing the ARM because of its attractive initial rate, and because of the lower rate, the borrower can qualify to borrow more.) The initial rate is allowed to fluctuate (along with your monthly payment) every one, three, or five years, over the term of the loan. The period from one rate change to the next is referred to as the *adjustment period*. Thus, an adjustable-rate loan with an adjustment period of one year is called a *one-year ARM*.

Most ARMs are based on a formula that includes an *index* and a *margin* (amount of profit). When the index rate moves up or down, so does your adjustable interest rate, along with your monthly payment. The amount the rate of interest is allowed to change is usually set at 2 percent during each adjustment period, and an overall cap (usually at 5 percent) is placed on the overall increase over the term of the loan. The *term cap* is the maximum amount the rate of interest can go up or down during each adjustment period. The *life cap* is the maximum rate interest can go up or down during the life of the loan.

Primary lenders use indexes tied to some easily monitored rate, such as the U.S. Treasuries security rate. Then the lender applies a margin to the index used. The interest rate a lender quotes you on the ARM is equal to the index rate plus the lender's margin.

Now look what happens to an adjustable-rate loan that's allowed to adjust upward 2 percent every two years with an overall cap increase of

5 percent. Let's say the loan is for $100,000 over a term of 30 years with an initial rate of interest of 6 percent. The adjustable-rate loan starts out with monthly P&I of $600 at 6 percent, then at 8 percent it increases to $734, and after four years it increases again, to 10 percent with a monthly payment of $878, and it's finally capped out at 11 percent with a monthly payment of $952. So, in five years it's possible for an adjustable-rate loan to adjust upward from 6 to 11 percent, with your monthly loan payment increasing accordingly from $600 to $952, or a $352 increase in five years.

Given all this, one might wonder why anyone would consider taking out an adjustable-rate loan for 30 years. The answer is that many borrowers tend to stretch their budgets and force themselves into accepting ARMs. They're actually lured by the ARM's initial lower interest rate because it appears cheaper, and such a mortgage enables the borrower to qualify for a higher loan amount. But if interest rates increase over the years—which they're likely to do—the borrower will be faced with increased loan payments, which they may or may not be able to pay.

The only time I would recommend taking out an ARM to finance real estate is when you intend to borrow short term—three years or less. Compared to a fixed-rate loan, a short-term ARM could be practical and cost effective because of the initial below-market-interest rate, which would save you money. The savings on lower interest shares for most ARMs come in the first one to three years, and these loans are usually lower in total cost than a comparable fixed-rate loan.

But if you expect to pay on the mortgage loan for more than three years, a fixed-rate loan would be more sensible, especially when you're not in the position to endure the uncertainty associated with adjustable loans.

Convertible Loans

Another alternative for real estate borrowers is a convertible loan that starts out as an adjustable loan but can be converted to a fixed-rate loan usually about three to five years after being funded. It gives you the best of both worlds—the lower initial rates of the ARM, and the option to lock in a fixed rate at some future time.

The features of the convertible loan:

- The rate of interest fluctuates; however, the borrower can lock in a fixed rate when the time of convertibility is right.
- There is a slightly higher interest rate than an ARM, plus a conversion fee. (You pay for a valuable option.)
- When you convert to a fixed rate on your adjustment period anniversary date, the rate is usually 0.25 points higher than the going rate of your lender's fixed rate loan.
- The convertible ARM is ideal for those who (1) like to take advantage of lower initial interest rates and fear the results of future rising interest rates, and (2) are likely to be selling the newly financed real estate within three years.

Unlike the nonconvertible ARM, the convertible ARM brings a certain measure of predictability to mortgage loan needs. A typical convertible loan permits the borrower to switch from an adjustable rate to a fixed rate of interest on the anniversary dates of the loan closing, usually limited to a three- to five-year conversion period. The converted fixed rate will remain unchanged until loan maturity. If the convertible option is not used, the loan stays as a typical ARM with the usual caps on increases, restricted to an overall 5-point increase over the term of the loan. The cost of having the convertible option varies, but is usually on a range of $250 to $750. That's a substantial savings when compared to the cost of refinancing on a comparable new loan, which could cost upward of $3,000.

Conventional and Nonconventional Loans

Besides a variety of repayment plans to choose from, real estate loans are divided into two categories: loans insured or guaranteed by the federal government (and in some cases the state government) and loans that are not. The most common government-backed loans are sponsored by the Veterans Administration (VA) or the Federal Housing Administration (FHA). Home loans made without government sponsorship are termed *conventional loans.*

Conventional Loans

Compared to the guaranteed VA loan and the insured FHA loan, the conventional loan usually has more stringent qualification standards, frequently has a prepayment penalty, and is often not assumable.

The special features of a typical conventional loan:

- The minimum down payment required is between 5 and 20 percent.
- If the down payment is less than 20 percent, the lender requires the borrower to pay private mortgage insurance (PMI), which costs about $40 to $100 each month.
- The loan is usually not assumable and often has a prepayment penalty.
- There is not as much red tape, and it can be funded faster than nonconventional loans.

Private Mortgage Insurance

Before a conventional loan is funded with less than a 20 percent down payment, the lender requires the borrower to buy insurance that protects the lender against default. Private mortgage insurance (PMI) costs about half a point of the loan amount and adds about $40 to $100 to the borrower's required monthly payment.

☞ TIP

After you've paid on a conventional mortgage for a few years and your equity in the home is at least 20 percent, you're entitled to cancel the PMI policy and pocket the savings. Note that you must initiate the cancellation.

FHA-Insured Loans

The FHA assists borrowers who might not be able to meet the higher down payment requirements and qualifying standards used for conventional loans. The FHA works through local lending institutions to provide federal mortgage insurance for the purchase, rehabilitation, or improvement of affordable housing.

Any borrower with a reasonable credit history is eligible for an FHA loan. The minimum down payment requirement is 3 percent, and the borrower is permitted to finance the closing costs and the required mortgage insurance premium, which are added to the monthly payment. They are not restricted to veterans, but are available to anyone who meets the requirements of the FHA and has a minimum 3 percent down payment. FHA loans are insured against default by the borrower, and therefore the lender is able to grant the borrower more lenient terms and a smaller down payment than conventional financing. Eligible properties are one- to four-unit residential structures.

The features of FHA-insured loans:

- You can borrow with as little as 3 percent down.
- The credit qualification standards are not as stringent as they are for conventional financing.
- There is no prepayment penalty.
- The loan is assumable, with qualifications.

☞ TIP

Similar to the cancellation of PMI on a conventional loan, after you've paid on the FHA-insured loan for a few years and your equity in the property is at least 20 percent, you're entitled to cancel the mortgage insurance policy and pocket the savings. Note that you must initiate the cancellation. (Many homeowners are not aware of this entitlement, or the PMI entitlement, and needlessly continue paying the premiums over the life of the loan.)

VA-Guaranteed Loans

VA loans are underwritten and processed by conventional lenders, but a portion of the loan is guaranteed by the Veterans Administration against default. The VA loan is extended to qualified veterans, entitling them to borrow money for homes, mobile homes, and farms, with the benefit of no money down and favorable closing costs. Ease of qualification and the no down payment requirement are the hallmarks of this great benefit extended to those men and women who have served honorably in the U.S. military. All you need is your form DD-214 (Proof of Discharge). Send it to the VA, and you get back a Certificate of Eligibility. Submit your certificate to a lender that makes VA loans and get reproved. The local VA office can provide more details.

Features of the VA loan:

- Currently you can borrow up to $203,000 with no money down.
- There's no prepayment penalty.
- PMI is not required.
- There's a limit on closing costs charged the borrower.
- The loan is assumable, with qualifications.

Both FHA and VA loans offer the foreclosure investor much more latitude than do conventional loans. This is because these loans can usually be assumed with qualification by the new buyer while the existing interest rate is maintained, rather than paying higher market interest rates for a new loan that may reflect market conditions. Furthermore, these government-backed loans usually do not have a provision for a prepayment penalty if the loan is at least two years old.

NOTEWORTHY

Since 1986, existing FHA and VA loans are assumable with qualification of the new borrower. It should be noted that FHA and VA loans underwritten prior to 1986 can be easily assumed without qualification.

The No-Verification Loan

A new type of loan recently emerged for those who have a good credit history called a "no verification" loan. They're designed for borrowers who have difficulty in verifying income or assets.

Normally, before the appearance of this kind of loan, mortgage lenders required all kinds of documentation from the loan applicant. This included proof of income, tax returns, W2s, bank statements, and job verification. But under this streamlined program for no-verification loans, the applicant simply states the amount of income he or she earns.

However, the lender will usually require one form of verification; in my particular case in 2003, I was required to submit a letter from my accountant stating that he prepared my federal income taxes for the last two years.

The loan interest rate is determined by the loan-to-value position in the property and the credit score of the borrower. Also, there are different levels of no-verification loans. There are *stated income, no income,* and *no job* (essentially no named source of income). The difference among these levels is the type of income verification the borrower provides. Usually, the less verification, the greater the rate and/or down payment required.

15-Year or 30-Year Term?

Besides choosing which type of financing program best suited to your needs, you must decide which term you favor—15 years or 30 years. Table 7-2 compares the two.

When you borrow $110,000 at 9 percent interest, the monthly loan payments are as follows:

15-year term =	$1,115.69
30-year term =	$ 804.62
	$ 311.07

The differential in the monthly payment between the 15- and 30-year loan in this case, as can be seen, is $311.07.

As Table 7-2 indicates, the 15-year term is ideal for those who can afford the higher monthly payments, and compared to the 30-year term, it saves the borrower over $89,000 in interest payments, and notably, lenders usually charge a half-point lower rate of interest than for a 30-year term. But for tax purposes, the 30-year term gives the borrower a higher tax deduction for the interest paid. The shorter term loan, of course, costs you $311.07 more each month, but you'll enjoy the satisfaction of owning your own home, free and clear, in half the time it takes with the 30-year loan.

Therefore, if you want the monthly savings and the greater tax deduction, the 30-year term could be the most sensible choice for you.

Table 7-2

Comparison of Accrued Equity and Interest Paid on 15-Year and 30-Year Fixed-Rate Loans

| | Loan Amount = $110,000 at 9% Fixed Rate | | | |
| | 15-Year Accrued | | 30-Year Accrued | |
Time	Interest Paid	Equity Earned	Interest Paid	Equity Earned
After 5 years	$45.051	$21,890	$43,767	$4,510
After 15 years	90,824	110,000	122,061	22,770
After 30 years	–	–	179,663	110,000

Tables 7-3 and 7-4 illustrate monthly payments (principal and interest) at selected interest rates required to amortize 15-year and 30-year fixed-rate loans. To calculate your monthly loan payment, at the top of the table row select the appropriate rate of interest. The entry in that column where your interest rate and the loan amount intersect is the computed monthly payment (rounded to the nearest dollar) for principal and interest that you will pay to fully amortize the loan. Note that if your particular loan amount is not illustrated, you can simply add smaller amounts to calculate the amount you need. For example, with a loan amount of $110,000, add the payments for a $60,000 loan and a $50,000 loan.

The Best Alternative: A Long-Term Fixed-Rate Amortized Loan

The best alternative to the interest-only loan and the unpredictable graduated loan or an adjustable loan is the long-term amortized loan that comes with a fixed rate of interest, featuring predictable (unchanging) equal monthly payments over the loan's term and a zero balance owing at maturity.

A fixed-rate amortized loan features equal monthly payments of both interest and principal until the loan is completely amortized (paid off). The best feature, though, is that it comes with a fixed rate of interest that remains unchanged over the life of the loan. This means you don't have to deal with feelings of anxiety or uncertainty about future changes in your

Table 7-3
15-Year Fixed Monthly Payment (P&I) at Selected Interest Rates

Interest Rate(%)/Interest($)

Payment Amount	5.0	5.5	6.0	6.5	7.0	7.5	8.0	8.5	9.0	10.0
$50,000	$395	$409	422	436	448	464	478	492	507	537
60,000	474	490	506	523	539	556	573	591	609	645
70,000	554	572	591	610	629	649	669	689	710	752
80,000	632	654	675	697	719	742	765	788	811	860
90,000	712	735	759	784	809	834	860	886	913	967
100,000	791	817	844	871	899	927	956	985	1,014	1,075

Table 7-4
30-Year Fixed Monthly Payment (P&I) at Selected Interest Rates

Payment Amount ($)	Interest Rate (%) / Interest Amount ($)									
	5.0	5.5	6.0	6.5	7.0	7.5	8.0	8.5	9.0	10.0
50,000	268	284	300	316	333	350	367	384	402	439
60,000	322	341	360	379	399	420	440	461	483	527
70,000	376	397	420	442	466	489	514	538	563	614
80,000	429	454	480	506	532	559	587	615	644	702
90,000	483	511	540	569	599	629	660	692	724	790
100,000	537	568	600	632	665	699	734	769	805	878

interest rate, which would inevitably lead to changes (usually a significant increase) in your monthly loan payments. And, since it's fully amortized, you don't have a balloon owing at the end of the loan's term.

The problem with the non-fixed-type loans, such as graduated and adjustable-rate loans, is that they're too unpredictable. You could be faced with substantial periodic increases in your monthly loan payment should market rates increase. Lenders often try to entice borrowers to apply for an adjustable loan with the so-called "teaser rate" we referred to earlier, which is an attractive low interest rate that initiates the loan. But as time passes the initial teaser rate adjusts upward, and within a few years the borrower is paying an excessive rate of interest compared to a comparable fixed-rate loan. Naive borrowers may be lured by the adjustable-rate loan not only for its attractive interest rate (usually 1 or 2 points lower than a comparable fixed-rate loan), but also because a borrower can qualify to borrow more due to the lower initial rate.

Long-term lenders love adjustable-rate loans because if market rates go up, they can raise the rates they charge borrowers, which takes much of the risk out of lending money over the long term. On the other hand, fixed-rate mortgages favor the borrower because they're predictable—the borrower knows what to expect over the entire term of the loan.

Take, for example, an adjustable-rate mortgage that starts out at 5 percent. The ARM is allowed to increase to a maximum of 10 percent with annual increases capped at 2 percent a year. After the initial funding of the loan, the credit market tightens, which causes mortgage interest rates to be raised. So, within three years the lender has increased the interest rate on the loan from 5 to 7 to 9 and then capped at 10 percent in the third year. On a $120,000 loan amortized over 30 years, the monthly payment at 5 percent starts at $644. By the third year the borrower is paying a whopping 10 percent interest and the monthly payment has increased to $1,054, an increase of $410 per month. Many people are simply not prepared to handle the added financial burden of a situation like this.

Compared to the interest-only loan, a fully amortized loan commonly has a term of either 15 or 30 years, although some borrowers prefer a 20-year or 40-year term.

Initial monthly payments on the amortized loan consist mostly of interest. But as the loan matures, more of each payment is applied toward the principal, since interest on an amortized loan is figured on the loan's outstanding principal balance. After each payment is made, the principal balance is reduced, which results in a smaller interest portion and a larger principal portion of the overall payment.

Table 7-5 is an example of an amortization schedule on a $15,000 loan at 6 percent with equal monthly payments of $126.58 that fully pay off the loan in 15 years. Note how the interest portion of the payment starts at $75 for Payment 1, then is reduced in Payment 2 to $74.74. Note also that as the interest portion of the payment is reduced, the principal portion of the payment increases each month. The principal payment increased 26 cents in Payment 2. Eventually, as the loan nears maturity, most of the payment will go toward the principal balance owing and less will go toward interest because there's substantially less owing after making almost 15 years of payments.

Partially Amortized Loans

This loan is similar to the fully amortized loan, except it has a significant balloon payment due at the end of the term. The partially amortized loan allows the borrower a smaller monthly payment and to pay down some of the principal owing.

As an example, a partially amortized loan could have the following terms: $80,000 loan at 10 percent interest amortized over 30 years at $702.06 per month, but payable in 20 years. Thus, at the end to the 20 years

Table 7-5
Amortization Schedule on $15,000 Loan at 6 Percent for a 15-Year Term with a Monthly Loan Payment of $126.58

Payment No.	Due Date	Remaining Principal ($)	Monthly Payment ($)	Principal Payment ($)	Interest Payment ($)
1	2/1/05	14,948.42	126.58	51.58	75.00
2	3/1/05	14,896.58	126.58	51.84	74.74
3	4/1/05	14,844.48	126.58	52.10	74.48
4	5/1/05	14,792.12	126.58	52.36	74.22

the borrower would owe a balloon payment of approximately $53,000. If the loan was payable in 30 years, it would be fully amortized with no balloon owing, but such a fully amortized loan would require a higher monthly payment of $772.02. Comparing the two monthly payments, the borrower saves $69.96 per month with the partially amortized loan; however, a substantial balloon will be owing at the end of the term.

The Principle of Leverage

To use leverage in real estate means to invest a small amount of cash (a down payment) to acquire a significantly greater value in property, instead of investing all cash. As an example, a purchase that is 90 percent leveraged would combine a 10 percent down payment with 90 percent financing. Zero leverage would be a full-cash purchase with no financing involved. Due to the influence of inflation and the ever-growing demand for a finite supply of habitable real estate—which, among other factors, causes appreciation—you can achieve the greatest yield on your invested dollars by getting as much leverage as possible when investing in improved real estate.

To see the advantage of using leverage, let's look at buying one property using two different techniques. In the leveraged investment we use 90 percent financing along with a 10 percent down payment, as opposed to purchasing the same property with zero leverage (an all-cash purchase). If you purchase the property for $100,000 with a $10,000 down payment and finance the balance owing, and a year later you realize an increase in value of $10,000. Because you only put $10,000 down on the property and it appreciated $10,000 in a year, you realized a 100 percent return on investment ($10,000 return divided by $10,000 invested = 100 percent).

Now suppose you could purchase the same property with $100,000 cash (zero leverage), and a year later that property also increased to $110,000. In this scenario your investment is $100,000, the appreciation is still $10,000, but the return (yield) on investment is only 10 percent ($10,000 return divided by $100,000 investment = 10 percent). From this example it's easy to see that the use of leverage to invest in real estate produces a much higher yield—the yield using leverage was 10 times the rate of return of the zero leverage scenario.

Keep in mind that even giant blue-chip corporations such as General Electric and IBM, which have a surplus of cash on hand and can easily pay cash, instead use leverage to finance their real estate purchases to increase their return on investment.

This principle of leverage in realty investing stimulates another important point about financing: Large amounts of income-producing mortgage debt—not consumer debt (such as owing money on car leases, furniture loans, and credit cards)—can actually be a good wealth-building tool.

Guidelines for Borrowing Money

The wise use of credit is crucial to successful realty investing. Think of it as forming a sort of hypothetical partnership with your lender, but unlike a true partnership, you don't have to pay your partner a share of the profits—just interest on the money borrowed from him or her.

Incur Mortgage Debt but Avoid Consumer Debt

When it comes to real estate, mortgage debt is good because it's usually associated with high leverage and often with generating income (rent), which pays off the mortgage debt. Conversely, consumer debt—credit cards, etc.—is a liability that usually does not generate income, and it therefore becomes a serious financial burden to the debtor.

A person who has high mortgage debt is usually a debtor who owns plenty of income-producing real estate that pays down the mortgage loans with the income it generates. For example, let's say you buy a four-unit apartment building for $160,000 with a $16,000 down payment, and you take out a mortgage loan for the balance owing of $144,000. The debt service, property taxes, and insurance add up to $1,350 a month, but each of the units rents for $500 a month. Therefore, your monthly gross income is $2,000. Deduct your basic fixed expenses and debt service ($1,350), and you have a gross operating income of $650 per month. So the income you're collecting pays off the mortgage loan. In other words, you're paying of the debt with other people's money.

Borrow as Much as You Can for as Long as You Can

It makes good business sense to borrow as much as you can for as long as you can when investing in real estate. Why? Because if the credit market loosens and interest rates go down, and you have the right of prepayment without penalty, you can effectively refinance at a lower rate of interest and save money. And if the credit market tightens and interest rates go up, you don't have to worry about refinancing because the rate you're paying is probably lower than the prevailing market rate of interest.

But that's only part of being a sensible realty investor. Three other factors to consider are that (1) loan proceeds are not treated as taxable income, (2) interest paid on real estate loans is deductible from taxable income, and (3) you reduce your equity exposure.

Reducing Your Equity Exposure

Borrowing as much as you can for as long as you can does not necessarily mean that you should apply for a loan in excess of the value of the asset you're encumbering (using as collateral). Yet, if you think about that, it's not a bad idea. If you could mortgage a property for more than your investment in it, you end up with a built-in profit whether or not you pay off the mortgage loan. Of course, failure to pay the mortgage loan at maturity will inevitably cause foreclosure, which means loss of the property and any equity you may have in it. However, if the value of your mortgaged real estate has gone down substantially since you financed it, allowing a loss by foreclosure could be a better financial decision than continuing to pump money into protecting your investment when the likelihood of recovery is not good. This is why the less equity you have in a mortgaged property at that time, the better it is for you financially.

Timing Your Purchase

The principle of borrowing as much as you can for as long as you can also has a lot to do with timing your purchase. Many indecisive people may be inclined to wait for interest rates to come down, thinking if they wait long enough, they can get a better deal on a loan. Meanwhile, the property they were interested in buying is snapped up by someone else, and an opportunity is lost. You must realize that it's very difficult to predict which direction interest rates are headed. You're better off borrowing as much as you can for as long as you can, and then allowing the market to take care of itself. Remember, if the credit market eases, you can always refinance; and if it tightens, then you can feel good about already having a rate that's below the prevailing interest rate.

How Much Can You Borrow?

For a quick estimate, many mortgage lenders traditionally use the *gross income multiplier*. A conservative lender would typically take your gross annual income and multiply it by 2.5 to arrive at an amount you can borrow, while a more liberal lender might go as high as three times. So if you earn a gross income of, say, $40,000, using the 2.5 multiplier, you could borrow $100,000, and using the three multiplier, you could borrow $120,000. Keep in mind that these quick estimates do not take into consideration the borrower's other monthly debt obligations, and that mortgage lenders want to be careful that your home loan—including the monthly cost of homeowner's insurance and property taxes—is not greater than you can reasonably afford.

To derive a more precise *affordable* home loan, most primary lenders permit a total debt-to-income ratio of no more than 36 percent. Total debt payments include all monthly payments toward any kind of consumer debt, such as car loans and credit cards, plus the mortgage loan payment that covers the added cost of homeowner's insurance and property taxes. The guidelines assume a housing payment-to-income ratio of 28 percent for a conservative estimate (the limit you'd expect from a conventional lender), and 29 percent for the liberal lender (the limit allowed on FHA-insured loans). Table 7-6 lists the 29 percent ratio for different annual and monthly gross income levels.

Avoid Balloon Payments

Certain types of loans, such as interest-only and partially amortized loans, will have a balance owing at the end of a loan's term. This lump sum or *balloon payment* is essentially a promise to pay an additional amount of cash at some future time. If the promise isn't kept, it most certainly will cause a foreclosure. You want to avoid burdening yourself with any kind of balloon payment because, more likely than not, when the time comes to make the balloon payment, it always seems like it's the worst time—when you don't have the money.

If you must obligate yourself to a balloon payment, try to minimize its effects by keeping it small and extending the term as far into the future as

Table 7-6
Loan Qualification Guidelines

Annual Gross Income ($)	Monthly Gross Income ($)	29 Percent of Gross Income ($)
15,000	1,250	363
20,000	1,667	483
25,000	2,083	604
30,000	2,500	725
35,000	2,917	846
40,000	3,333	967
45,000	3,750	1,088
50,000	4,167	1,208

Source: U.S. Department of Housing and Urban Development

possible. This makes the balloon payment easier to live with because you'll have more time to prepare for the payoff.

Avoid Prepayment Penalties

Many conventional mortgage loan contracts have a clause written into them that entitle the lender to charge the borrower a penalty for premature payoff of the loan. The penalty is typically six to 12 months interest on the principal balance owing. (On a $150,000 loan at 7 percent, you'd be paying a penalty in excess of $10,000.) Make sure the mortgage loan you arrange *does not* have a prepayment penalty written into your contract—otherwise, you could be penalized thousands of dollars if, for whatever reason, you decide to prepay or refinance the loan before it matures.

Both the balloon payment and the prepayment penalty are hindrances to what normally should be a carefree and profitable real estate investment. These nuisances can also inhibit the sale of your property under a loan assumption agreement, because then the buyer (who would be assuming the existing loan) would be responsible for the lump-sum payoff on the balloon payment and the prepayment penalty.

Maximize Leverage with Special Loan Programs for Owner-Occupants

Below, we list various high-leverage loan programs available to assist low-money-down investors. But first, keep the following in mind: In order to qualify for owner-occupied financing, you have to honor the lender's occupancy requirement, which means you must intend to live in the mortgaged property for at least one year. With that stipulation, you can begin making acquisitions by selecting a high loan-to-value (LTV) loan program that's most appropriate for you.

Invest in a one- to four-family property, move into it for one year, then rent it out and repeat the strategy again. Even after you move out, the owner-occupied financing remains with the property.

Eight No-Down- or Low-Down-Payment Possibilities

Here's a list of eight programs that provide realty investors with all kinds of no-down or low-down-payment possibilities:

1. *FHA 203(b)* is the most popular program available through the Federal Housing Administration (FHA), which insures real estate loans funded by conventional lenders. Cash-short buyers can finance one to four units with as little as 3 percent down. Interest rates are usually slightly higher than market rates, but qualifying standards are more lenient than conventional loans. Loan applicants who show steady income and good faith in paying their bills usually qualify. And in many cases, closing costs can be wrapped into the mortgage loan. Maximum loan limits vary in each state, but the highest limits are currently $333,700 on single units, $427,150 on two-family units, $516,300 on three-family units, and $641,650 on four-family units.

2. *FHA/VA 204(v)* is similar to the 203(b) except that it's offered only to qualified veterans and the down payment requirement is lower.

3. *FHA 203(k)* is ideal for home buyers who want to renovate, rehab, or add more value to the property. This two-in-one program allows borrowers to combine a home's purchase price and renovation costs all in one mortgage loan.

4. *FHA qualifying assumptions.* When market interest rates are high, look for sellers with FHA loans that originated when rates were lower.

Pay the sellers for their equity (or whatever amount you negotiate) and then assume the seller's FHA loan. Qualifying for this type of loan is a lot less complicated than originating a new loan, and you gain the benefits of acquiring an existing loan at below market interest rates.

5. *FHA/VA no qualifying assumptions.* Millions of these loans were originated prior to 1986, when the FHA and the VA stopped making them. Though most of them have been repaid, a few sellers have retained them. The no qualifying assumable loan is the easiest and least costly loan you can get because there are no questions asked of the borrower, and all that's required is payment of a small assumption fee.

6. *HUD homes.* When FHA borrowers fail to make their loan payments, the Department of Housing and Urban Development, the parent of the FHA, takes over ownership of these properties. HUD properties can be purchased with as little as 3 percent down. For more details, ask a HUD-registered realtor or see the HUD Web site at www.hud.gov.

7. *VA loans.* If you're an eligible veteran, you can borrow up to $240,000 with no money down to buy a home. To start the ball rolling, remit your discharge papers to the VA to get your Certificate of Eligibility. No cash to close and ease of qualifying are two more of the benefits given to those who served honorably in the U.S. military.

8. *VA qualifying assumptions.* Existing VA loans can easily be assumed by veterans or nonveterans. When market interest rates are high, look for sellers with VA loans that originated when rates were lower. And similar to FHA no-qualifying assumptions, the VA loan is easy to qualify for and costs less than originating a new loan.

Loan Sources for Those with Tarnished Credit

If you lack an A-one credit rating and you're having difficulty finding a lender, there are other sources that have less stringent qualifying requirements than the usual conventional and nonconventional lenders:

- *Mortgage brokers,* because they're independent agents who often represent primary lenders nationwide, are likely to know of lenders who arrange real estate loans for buyers with less than perfect credit histories.

- *Nonqualifying assumable loans,* along with seller financing, are a great method of acquiring real estate, especially since it's likely the seller won't be as concerned as a banker about your credit history.
- *Cosigned loans.* With a cosigner on your mortgage loan, you have a better chance of qualifying for a loan with a primary lender. This method, however, makes the cosigner responsible for payment of the loan should you default.

Shopping for a Mortgage Loan

We already discussed the all-important interest rate—how you save thousands of dollars on a long-term loan just by reducing the rate of interest 1 percent. You can increase your savings even more by becoming familiar with points and other fees that mortgage lenders charge, including how to compare loan offerings and where to shop for the best mortgage loan.

Where to Start

Most long-term residential loans are funded by savings and loan associations, banks, credit unions, and mortgage bankers. If you're already a customer of any of these, start there. Established customers often get preferred rates and terms.

Although they do not directly fund real estate loans, mortgage brokers can be very helpful. As independent agents that represent many lenders, they can shop among them looking for the best loan deal. And if your credit history is tarnished and you're finding it difficult to qualify for a loan, a good mortgage broker can direct you to special lenders who may be willing to fund you a mortgage loan.

Points and Fees

When arranging a mortgage loan, you usually have the option of paying up front additional points—a portion of the interest that you pay at closing—in exchange for a lower fixed rate of interest over the loan's term. If you own the mortgaged property over a long term—say, five years or more—it's usually better to pay the points, because the lower interest rate you get will save more in the long run.

Alternatively, if you want to pay less in points at the funding of the loan (perhaps due to cash constraints), you can pay a higher rate of interest on the loan. The shorter the term of the loan, the more cost effective it would be to pay less up front and more later on.

Consider this example concerning the points versus interest rate trade-off. Suppose you need to borrow $150,000. Lender A quotes you 7.0 percent on a 30-year fixed-rate loan with a 1-point origination fee. Lender B quotes 7.5 percent with no points. Which offer is better? The answer depends entirely on how long you intend to pay on the loan.

The Lender A loan at 7.0 percent costs $998 per month plus 1 point, which is $1,500.

The Lender B loan at 7.5 percent costs $1,049 per month.

You save $51 per month with the Lender A loan, but have to pay $1,500 to get it.

To compute which loan is more cost effective, divide the cost of the points by the monthly savings, or $1,500 divided by $51, which comes to 29.4. It will take 29.4 months to recover the $1,500 cost of the points. So, if you expect to pay on the loan for less than approximately 29 months, you would choose the no-points loan from Lender B. But if you expect to pay on the loan for more than 29 months, selecting the Lender A 7.0 loan plus the 1 point will save you money.

Annual Percentage Rate

When it comes time to compare the overall costs of loan offerings between lenders, the comparison of APRs is the bottom line. Comparing APRs puts all the competitors on a level playing field.

The APR is the true cost of credit offered to the consumer in percentage terms. It is the annual rate charged for borrowing expressed as a single percentage number that represents the actual yearly cost of funds over the term of a loan. It includes any fees or additional costs, such as the loan origination fee, associated with the transaction.

Borrow Against Built-Up Equity

If you have a substantial amount of equity built up in your home or other realty holdings, you can borrow against the equity and use the cash proceeds to invest in foreclosures. When you go to borrow and already have an existing mortgage loan on the property, you have two options: You can either refinance or take out a home-equity loan.

Refinance or Take Out a Home-Equity Loan?

This decision depends entirely on the current market rate for mortgage loans and the rate you're paying on your existing first mortgage loan. If the current market rate for mortgage loans is lower than the rate you're now paying, it's better to refinance. By refinancing you replace your existing mortgage loan with a more cost effective loan that has a lower rate of interest.

But if the current market rate for mortgage loans is higher than the rate you're now paying, arranging a home equity loan is more sensible. This way the existing low-interest-rate first mortgage remains intact.

Primary lenders will usually allow you to borrow up to 80 percent of the equity in the property being mortgaged. (Equity = current market value less the remaining loan balance.) So, if the property you intend to refinance is valued at $150,000, and you owe $50,000 on it, you then have $100,000 equity in the property. Since the lender will give you a loan for up to 80 percent of the equity in the property, your maximum loan amount would be $80,000.

Rule of thumb: Refinance your existing mortgage loan when the market rate for new mortgage loans is at least 2 points below the rate on your existing loan.

Seller Financing to Purchase REOs, Including FHA and VA Repossessions

As mentioned in Chapter 4, lenders who have an inventory of REO will usually give the buyer a preferred loan with great terms, and often will handle all closing costs involved in the transaction. When buying REO from a lender's inventory, you can expect to get financing from the seller at bargain rates not found anywhere else. You can often negotiate for an interest rate 1 to 2 points below the going market rate for fixed-rate loans with no origination fee. The down payment can also be between 5 and 10 percent, which will give you a greater return. Additionally, you can often negotiate for the seller to pay all the closing costs.

The federal government's REOs—such as foreclosed property owned by HUD, the VA, and the FDIC—are extremely motivated to offer very favorable terms to potential buyers. They, of course, are in the business of lending money on real estate—not managing and selling real estate. They would prefer lending money at preferred interest rates with great terms rather than spending a small fortune managing their inventories of foreclosed real estate.

Buy for Cash, then Get Financing

If you have a lot of built-up equity in your home, you could refinance the existing loan and use the cash proceeds to buy foreclosures at auction. That way you could work more efficiently, using some of the funds for repairs. Then, when the property is completely renovated, take out a mortgage loan on it and use the money to buy more foreclosures. Every time you complete the renovations on additional acquisitions, take out a new loan and do the same thing over again.

It's more efficient because you don't have to worry about the lender refusing you a loan when the property is run-down and in need of repair. A lender is more likely to approve a loan when looking at a completely renovated property.

Chapter Lessons

- When financing real estate, always choose long-term fixed-rate loans, unless you intend to hold the property for less than three years, in which case the choice of an adjustable-rate loan would be more cost effective.
- Refinance any existing mortgage loans when market interest rates are at least two points below the rate you're already paying.
- Remember the principle of leverage—that the more leverage you use investing in real estate, the more it increases the return on your investment.
- To be a successful real estate investor, you have to view the financing of real estate as sort of a joint venture with your lenders. However, as the owner/investor, you don't have to share with the lender the profits realized—you're required to pay only the interest on your use of their money.

- Be wary of overextending yourself and having big expectations of excessive appreciation in the short term. We know of a man in Florida who, expecting 15 percent annual appreciation, bought a four-unit apartment building for $250,000 with a $25,000 down payment. Two years later, because the real estate market became overbuilt and tanked, he ended up losing his down payment plus 15 months of subsidizing his negative cash flow. The lessons here are as follows:

1. Never expect the value of the property purchased to appreciate excessively, especially during the short term.
2. Be wary of negative cash flows.
3. Don't overpay for a property because you expect excessive short-term appreciation.
4. Never overextend yourself; that is, do not borrow more money than you can feasibly pay back.

8

Making Improvements to the Fixer-Upper

In this chapter we offer important guidelines on what to look for in a profitable foreclosed fixer-upper. We also discuss improvements that pay and those that don't. You'll also learn why kitchens and bathrooms are so important in a realty investment, along with how to hire a contractor and control repair costs. Then, in the next chapter, you'll discover several profitable holding strategies for your renovated fixer-upper.

What to Look for in a Fixer-Upper

Anyone can buy an old dumpy-looking property and spend a fortune fixing it up. But that's not very profitable, because you can't make any money overspending on repairs and renovations. You want to keep an eye out for ways to improve a particular property without expending too much money and effort.

The savvy real estate investor is someone who can see through the imperfections and has the vision and the courage to assemble the financial resources to make the correct practical improvements that will do the most to substantially increase the value of the property. And he or she creates this increase in value by adding "sweat equity," which is doing most of the renovations yourself, instead of paying someone else to do it. These renovations can include patching drywall, interior and exterior painting, landscaping, and doing a thorough cleaning of the premises inside and out. If you believe you fit that mold, here's what you can expect to achieve after renovating your fixer into a desirable home:

- You will own a home or rental property for a lot less than you could otherwise have afforded to buy.
- You will have redesigned and decorated a home the way you like it, instead of having it reflect someone else's perception of taste and style.
- By creating sweat equity, you will have significantly increased the property's value much more than the cost to make the renovations.

Landlord Tale: The Las Vegas House

A good example of what to look for in a fixer-upper can be demonstrated from a property we purchased on the southwest side of Las Vegas, Nevada, in 1986. Although it was a custom-built 2,200-square-foot home, it had a plain look to it and poor curb appeal. It had a drab stucco exterior, with no trim around the windows. On the positive side, it had an attractive tile roof, a three-car garage, and was situated in a nice neighborhood on a half acre of horse-zoned real estate.

The home was in great shape; it just needed a few decorative touches to make it more appealing. For example, one of the biggest turnoffs was the sunken living room. When entering the home from the front door, you dropped down about eight inches into a sunken living room that was covered with a dreadful looking carpet. And instead of wood baseboards, that same dreadful carpeting extended up the walls eight inches. My wife and I decided right away that the living room carpet, including the carpeted baseboards, had to go.

The remainder of the house, except for a huge kitchen with solid oak cabinets throughout, was very plain and lacked any character whatsoever. All the walls were painted off-white, and except for the kitchen, there was no wood trim or wallpaper anywhere in the house.

The first renovation we did was to pull out the living room carpet, the pad underneath it, and the eight inches of carpeted baseboard. Then we laid in beautiful tongue-and-groove golden-oak flooring with a moisture-proof pad over the concrete slab. When we finished the floor, we attached eight-inch strips of tongue-and-groove oak laid at a 45-degree angle on the two walls in the living room near the entry. Next we stained the oak wall trim to match the tone of the golden-oak flooring. For the finishing touch, we encased both archways in the living room and adjacent dining room with oak trim molding, which were also stained golden oak. Finally, we applied two coats of satin gloss polyurethane to the oak trim and archway moldings. Wow! It looked great. The oak floors and trim made a great first impression when you came in the entry to what was once a very plain home.

Next we made some minor changes to the exterior; something special to make the so-called "curb appeal" more appealing. I purchased three sets of wood dormers at Home Depot, painted them reddish-brown to match the tile roof, and secured them around the windows that faced the street. What a difference a little window trim made.

We did the entire project—including adhesive, oak flooring, the oak trim, and the dormers—ourselves. We not only found the entire project to be a true pleasure to work on and see materialize, but notably, it cost less than $1,000 in materials. Our neighbors were impressed with the changes, and our friends loved all the new woodwork. Yet the final satisfaction came when we leased the house, giving the tenants an option to buy it, and earned a huge profit. I truly believe that we would not have earned as much profit, nor received such a positive response from neighbors and friends, had we not added that finished woodwork to that once very plain and common-looking house.

Developing a Market-Sensitive Fix-Up Strategy

At this point you might inquire about the rules for creating value when purchasing a foreclosed fixer-upper. Other than creating value through sweat equity, there are none! Features that one person likes, another hates. What's popular in a Phoenix, Arizona, stucco ranch with a tile roof may be out of place in an upper-east-side Manhattan flat. Likewise, amenities admired in the New England states would be inappropriate in South Florida. And certain home features that appeal to you may not suit the tastes and lifestyles of most people. Money spent to remodel a kitchen in Detroit might return a profitable two dollars for each dollar invested, while in Phoenix, returns for a similar renovation might be a losing proposition, with a scant return of 50 cents for every dollar invested.

So, how does someone go about satisfying the lifestyles and tastes of potential buyers or renters who will look over your property? Put your own personal tastes aside and obey the guidelines of today's successful home builders. Then carefully research the market to determine precisely what today's home buyers want.

You can do your own research by asking local realtors what buyers are looking for in a home. Also, you can visit new home developments, taking special note of their decorating themes, floor plans, floor covering materials, and countertops. While you're touring the models, make inquiries about what amenities and features are in most demand and which ones are rarely chosen.

Visit open houses too, seeking ways other property owners have improved and decorated their homes. You can also browse through some of the major home improvement outlets in your vicinity to see what they have, such as Home Depot and Lowe's, and talk to associates who work there. And while you're there, take a look at some of the how-to books on home improvement.

Improvements that Create Value and Those That Don't

What improvements to a home create value? Unfortunately, there are no absolute rules etched in stone. There are, however, some practical guidelines to determining whether a property is a candidate for renovation and which improvements are sensible and worthwhile doing.

When you're out seeking potential properties to purchase, there's a certain way you have to look at them. You have to disregard your first impressions and enthusiasm. Instead, determine what's wrong with the properties—why you find them unappealing—then try to arrive at practical solutions. Looking at them this way will help you narrow down your list of possible investments. Ask yourself: Which of these properties could I decorate and improve in such a way that it would be more appealing to prospective tenants or buyers than it is now, and therefore would be likely to substantially increase its market value?

Here's an example of a common problem area you'll often come across when looking at houses that lack appeal. You find a house that at first seems very nice, but it's a five-bedroom two-bath dwelling with only 1,700 square feet of living area. The problem is that the bedrooms are too small, which is the reason it does not appeal to most potential buyers and tenants. Meanwhile, in deciding whether to buy this house, you determine that you'll need to knock out some walls and convert this five-bedroom dwelling into a more practical house with three large bedrooms. Now the question put before you is: Would the converted house's value and appeal be worth the capital investment and effort you have to make? To answer that question, consider the following two-for-one rule.

The Two-for-One Rule

The two-for-one rule is a basic guideline saying that every dollar invested in house renovation should yield at least two dollars in increased market value. In other words, property renovations that cost $5,000 in material and labor should realize at least $10,000 in market value gain.

Frequently, many of the properties you'll look at will appear neglected and given little care and attention. Commonly you'll see overgrown bushes and shrubs, an unmowed, weed-infested lawn with trash strewn about, an exterior that needs paint, and a few broken windows. Nevertheless, if the house is structurally sound and everything else checks out—such as the heating and air-conditioning, the electrical, and plumbing systems—all the neglect and disrepair presents a great profit opportunity for the investor with foresight. And the greatest profit will be earned by investors who can economically spruce up the property and make the practical renovations themselves, through sweat equity, instead of paying someone else to do it.

To figure out whether this property is indeed a good investment, all you have to do is estimate what it will cost to spruce up the landscaping, to thoroughly clean up inside and out, paint, and repair the windows. Now double that total cost figure (the two-for-one rule) to see how much the improvements would add to the value of the property. Add that double cost figure to the total price you'll have to pay for the property. Then ask yourself: Will I be able to sell the renovated property at a price that will earn a worthwhile profit?

Put another way, after renovations and cleanup are completed, will the property be worth at least what you paid for it, plus double the cost of cleaning and renovating it? If you answered yes, then it's likely to be a shrewd investment and a prime candidate for a profitable renovation.

Improvements Most Likely to Increase Property Value

The following are practical improvements that will usually make a property more appealing to potential buyers and tenants, and thereby increase its market value:

- Improve curb appeal.
- Make the interior decor more appealing and add pizzazz by updating fixtures.
- Thoroughly clean the entire property inside and out.
- Pay attention to the most important rooms—the kitchen and the bathrooms (not the bedrooms).
- Create more usable space.
- Reduce excessive noise.

Improve Curb Appeal. Most home buyers and renters decide whether to look inside a house based on its "curb appeal"—that is, what they see when they drive by or arrive at a house for a showing. Good curb appeal attracts people, makes them pull over to the curb, get out of the car, and look closer at what you have to offer. At the very least, you want them to stop long enough and have sufficient interest to take down your address and phone number and come back again. You improve the property's curb appeal by dressing up its exterior appearance.

One way of improving curb appeal is to enhance the landscaping at the front of the property. For example, instead of arbitrarily planting three or four nondescript bushes along the front elevation of the house, carefully conceive a planning scheme that will look appropriate and can be easily maintained. For example, you could select plants that are not fast growers and are therefore not apt to become overgrown too quickly.

Also, consider using the services of a landscape designer. Most are not expensive, and the good ones know how to enhance curb appeal. Together, you and your designer can create an impressive landscape, with the landscaper recommending plantings to augment the topography as well as the size and shape of the site. They can also utilize certain plantings to emphasize or deemphasize a site's buildings to attract attention to those features you want noticed.

The entire concept of curb appeal is meant to be visual. It is perceived value. It doesn't have to be expensive, but it has to be *perceived* as valuable. It can be achieved by the choice of colors, the types of plantings, and so on, so that prospects say, "This looks like a wonderful place to live." They "perceive" value through your well-conceived plantings, tasteful use of color on the house exterior, and lovely landscaped site, which blend together to portray your property as a desirable place to live.

Other features to make the property appear desirable could be the shiny brass hardware on the front door, or the stylish front door itself, perhaps made of stained wood. Or it could be the window treatments, a beautiful Japanese maple growing on the front lawn, or a curved walkway bordered by tall, majestic Italian cypress trees that lead up to the garden.

All of these enhancements, and many others, can change a drab or plain-looking property into a desirable one. These improvements are not necessarily expensive. Rather, they add value by blending certain things together to create a perception of value.

Make the Interior More Appealing and Update the Fixtures. When it comes to a home's appealing features and tastefully appointed home decor, it's usually the little things that count the most. For instance, add lightly stained wood trim to a plain room. Paint over gaudy dark-colored walls with light earth tones to make the rooms appear brighter and more spacious. Or remove gaudy wallpaper and paint with appealing light colors to achieve the same bright and spacious appearance. Adding polished granite or ceramic tile to an entry or kitchen floor can add pizzazz to what would otherwise be a plain-looking home. The addition of special moldings too, such as a stained chair rail and baseboard in the dining room or kitchen, or crown molding in the living room or master bedroom, can create a special ambience. And you can replace older, drab-looking light fixtures with modern decorative ones.

Remember to keep it simple but tasteful. Too much of anything can become garish. By adding just the right amount of flair and creative design touches, you can make what was once commonplace very interesting and desirable.

Clean the Entire Property, Inside and Out. Whether you intend to sell or rent the property, it's important that it be thoroughly cleaned before you show it to any prospects. Why? Because a spotlessly clean property will not only rent or sell faster than a dirty one, but will appeal to a more reliable, clean-living tenant who can pay a higher rent, or a more affluent buyer who can afford a higher-priced property.

With rental properties, many lackadaisical landlords take the position, "Why should I go to the trouble of giving a spotlessly clean unit to tenants when they'll only leave it dirty whey they move out?" This attitude only begets poor results. Quality buyers and renters are repulsed by filth, and they will choose to live elsewhere. The kind of people who accept rental units with grime-encrusted stoves, soiled carpets, and filthy windows are the same kind who won't care for your property.

Cleanliness is especially important in the kitchen and bathrooms. Make an extra effort to remove dirt and stains on countertops, bathtubs, sinks, toilet bowls, and mirrors.

When you demonstrate cleanliness in your available units, you'll achieve four positive things: (1) You attract a better grade of tenant, (2) earn a higher rental rate, (3) display the level of cleanliness you expect, and (4) you'll get a better price when you do sell. Investors will pay more for properties with better tenants because better clientele will mean to them—as it does to you—less trouble, lower risk, and more reliable rental income.

Focus Your Attention on the Kitchen and Bathroom. When it comes to the interior of the house, focus your renovation efforts on the kitchen and bathrooms. If you hold off on making improvements in the kitchen and bath areas, you'll have a problem attracting the luxury customer. What appeals to most house-hunting people more than anything else are the features and spaciousness of the kitchen and bathrooms—not the bedrooms. When prospecting for a new home, the first thing the woman of the house looks for is practical and appealing kitchen and bathrooms.

When considering remodeling a kitchen, think about installing countertops of granite or solid surface material such as Avonite or Corian, rather than common laminates. These materials cost more, but they're eye-catching and will help create the perceived value you're trying to achieve.

Making Improvements to the Fixer-Upper

Don't be a miser when it comes to the kitchen. Install great-looking cabinets, build lots of storage space and a large pantry, along with a center island work place. Also, go the extra mile and use first-line appliances. For the luxury tenant, install a Sub-Zero model refrigerator with an ice maker. Make sure the kitchen is well-designed for convenience and has lots of usable space. Great features and amenities make a house more appealing. Your objective should be to get the prospect to think, "Wow, this kitchen is gorgeous, and it's got everything I need."

With the bathrooms, think spaciousness. Upscale buyers or tenants are seeking more usable space, so offer them as much as conditions allow. Put extra money in top-of-the line vanities, countertops, and light fixtures. Install a whirlpool tub instead of a plain bathtub, and in the stall shower, have the added appeal of a steam unit. Lots of storage space and soothing color combinations, such as a tasteful blend of earth tones, are also appealing.

Outside the bathroom you can add other attractive features, such as spacious closets with built-in shelving and shoe racks.

When you're thinking of renovations, you should be asking yourself, "Where can I effectively spend my remodeling dollars to make the greatest visual impact?" The reply most often is in the kitchen and bathrooms.

Create More Usable Space. How does one go about creating additional living space economically, which in turn substantially increases the market value of the property? First and foremost is to forget about converting the garage into a living area. Why? Because it is already a functional storage place for cars and other things not suitable for storage in the house. People who convert their garages into living areas are making a terrible mistake because the lack of a garage seriously hampers the marketability of the house. People prefer a garage because it provides storage space for vehicles, lawn equipment, tools, and other miscellaneous items.

Consider converting an attic or basement into a living area. Or perhaps you can enclose a patio or porch. You could also add a second story "mother-in-law" quarters, or construct a guest apartment off the back of the house. What about combining small rooms to make larger rooms (such as converting five small bedrooms into a more appealing scheme of three large bedrooms, as discussed earlier)?

Reduce Excessive Noise. To residential property owners, excessive noise is a big nuisance that costs money. In multiunit buildings especially, excessive noise will cause too much turnover among tenants, which equates into vacancies and lost rent. When you're considering the purchase of an attached home, such as a condominium or cooperative apartment, or a multiunit building, check the soundproofing between the units. If you put your ear up to the wall and can hear a television, a toilet flush, or people talking in the adjacent unit, be wary. Unless you can correct the noise problem, you'll be faced with a never-ending stream of tenant complaints and high level of tenant turnover.

You should also take account of noise when considering the purchase of detached structures. If you discover a noise problem, then before you make your initial offer to buy a particular property, consider ways to reduce the noise. Can you solve the problem by adding more wall insulation, soundproofing some or all of the windows, building a block wall, constructing an earth berm, or planting trees or shrubs?

Remember that most upscale homeowners and tenants will pay a premium for peace and quiet, and many won't tolerate too much noise.

No-No Improvements

Foremost among the no-no improvements, as mentioned earlier, is converting the garage to a living area. The reason is because you'll no longer have a great place to store and protect many of your valued personal items, such as vehicles, lawn and garden equipment, and tools. It's also a great place to have a useful workbench. If you need more living area, build something new attached to the existing living area of the house instead of eliminating functional garage space that's already useful. Most house-hunting prospects require a garage as a valuable storage facility.

Another no-no improvement is the installation of an in-ground swimming pool. You'll never recoup the huge investment, and only a small segment of the market will be interested in buying or renting a house with a pool, which means you have virtually written off most house-hunting prospects, because most of them are not interested in having a pool.

Converting large rooms into more, smaller ones is another no-no. You always have to keep in mind that house-hunters, especially those trading up, are looking for more space, not less.

Making Improvements to the Fixer-Upper

Landlord Tale: A House and a Converted Cabinet Shop

In January 2005 we purchased a great property situated on 3.2 acres of the prettiest real estate in all of southern Mississippi. It was an all-brick 2,400-square-foot ranch home with a 1,600-square-foot cabinet shop nearby. Right away we thought of converting the cabinet shop into a guest house or a rental, but there were several problems to overcome. Although it sat on a concrete slab and had four solid exterior walls with adequate windows and entry doors, it didn't have a water supply, a bathroom, a sewer to hook to, heating or air-conditionting, and it had only 40 amps of electrical power coming off the main house.

The first thing we did was bring out a home builder in order to get some ideas for plans and how much it would cost to implement them. We decided on building out a two-bedroom one-bath unit with the following features and amenities: a new 100-ampere electrical service; a Series 12 Carrier heat pump installed in the attic; white ceilings throughout, with a light popcorn application; four ceiling fans with remote controls; interior walls with an orange peal texture, painted a flat lemon yellow; staining the window trim and baseboards in Early American style; installing golden oak cabinets with a built-in microwave over the GE range in the kitchen, plus ceramic tile countertops and ceramic tile on the kitchen floor, the hallway, and the bathroom. The remaining floors were covered with a high-grade beige-colored Berber carpet over a thick pad. The five closet doors were also covered in Early American stain to match the trim. And we installed an underground septic tank with an adjoining septic field. In the bathroom, we built a raised floor so we could enclose the plumbing, instead of chopping up the concrete slab. Also, we enclosed the kitchen and bath plumbing along the common interior wall connected to the septic tank.

All told, I hired three professional craftsmen on an hourly basis to assist me, and the entire project took us two months and about $18,000 in labor and materials to complete. It turned out fantastic, and instead of a cabinet shop we now have an extra house on the property that rents for $960 a month.

The moral of this landlord tale is: You need to look for ways to create value when you buy real estate. We took an old cabinet shop, and along with $18,000 in cash and four guys working on the property, and turned it into a good-size two-bedroom house valued today at about $150,000. That's an increase in market value of $120,000, since the bank appraiser valued the cabinet shop at $12,000 back when we purchased the property.

You also want to avoid decorating the interior walls in dark color schemes. It makes the rooms appear small and dreary. When it comes to interior color schemes, think light and airy. It will make your rooms appear more spacious.

Finding Opportunity in Problems

When it comes to renovating a fixer-upper, keep in mind that almost anyone can do the simple things—like the painting, patching drywall, and cleaning up around the property. Yet, it's the more difficult tasks that create the greatest opportunities for earning big profits. That said, you need to look for those special fixer properties with problems that at first seem difficult but not impossible to solve. Many realty investors lack imagination, and the minute they walk through the door and see things they don't like, they say, "No way. Let's look for something else to buy." If you can look at a problem area and try to imagine how to overcome it and make the property more appealing, you'll come out way ahead of other investors who lack this problem-solving ability.

Problems that can usually be overcome include the design and use of the living-area space (as we described in the conversion of a small five-bedroom house into a more desirable home with three spacious bedrooms) and poorly designed or equipped kitchens and bathrooms. When you're looking at a problem property, you should always be thinking, "What can I do to overcome the defects and improve the appeal?" And then, keeping in mind the two-for-one guideline, ask yourself, "Will those improvements add enough value to make the investment worthwhile?"

Necessary Repairs and Improvements

Property owners who skimp on repairs and defer regular maintenance will inevitably have disastrous results. This is especially true for rental units, because as the property gradually deteriorates from lack of proper care, quality upscale tenants will find somewhere else to live. The loss of good clientele means lower rent levels, which in turn results in reduced cash flow for the property owner. As the property gradually loses its appeal, it deteriorates further, until the run-down property has to be sold at a reduced price. This bad scenario is likely to be a real life experience for owners with the misconception that they can save money by avoiding necessary repairs and deferring maintenance on their properties.

To optimize rental income and keep your properties at their highest market value, it's absolutely necessary to always maintain them in A-one condition. This means *at all times*—not just the day you're showing them to prospective tenants or buyers. All systems have to be in working order at all times, and the property must be thoroughly clean inside and out, showing no signs of wear or abuse. This is crucial because any prospects viewing the property will discount from the value of the property anything in disrepair or that is dirty. Or even worse, your prospects might become repulsed and just stop in their tracks, having no desire to see anything more, and head out the door to look for something else more appealing.

The following items deserve special attention in the regular maintenance of any property:

Landscaping

Regular maintenance of the landscaping makes your property appear more desirable, which enhances its curb appeal. If potential occupants drive up and have a negative first impression, they will likely go on to look at another property instead of getting out of the car to look further at your property. To lure more prospects out of the car and into the premises, properly maintain your landscaping. Keep the lawn mowed, trim all the trees and shrubs, and remove any dead or unattractive bushes.

Electrical System

For a property to appear in A-one condition, all the lightbulbs should be working properly. Replace any fluorescent bulbs that flicker or that are slow to light. Inspect wall outlets and their covers. Replace any charred or broken ones. Electrical wall outlets should never have numerous adapters or extension cords plugged into them. Such a condition is a fire hazard, and it's evidence that there are insufficient electrical wall outlets. Also check the building's fuse or breaker box to determine the amperage coming into the property. Nowadays the typical three-bedroom two-bath home requires at least 100 amperes. Anything less will probably require an upgrade.

Plumbing System

Check all faucets for leaks and drips. A dripping faucet requires installation of a new washer. Check the drainage flow from sinks and bathtub drains to see if they empty quickly: If they don't, the traps need cleaning out. Inspect the float valve in toilet tanks to be sure that it automatically shuts off the fill valve. Replace any toilet seats that are stained or in disrepair. Check for leaks around the bathtub perimeter and shower stalls. Apply caulking to repair cracks or seal leaks. In the northern latitudes, make sure all water pipes exposed to the weather are well insulated to keep them from bursting in subzero weather.

Appliances

If you provide appliances in your rental properties, be sure to keep them spotlessly clean. Also, keep the appliance owner's manuals in a convenient place where the tenants have access to them.

Doors and Locks

All doors on the premises should close properly, without squeaking or being overly tight. Lubricate any squeaky hinges. Doors that are too snug need to be planed down. Replace any damaged screening on screen doors. And for security purposes, it would be wise to replace any broken or worn-out door locks

Windows and Screens

Repair any windows that, for whatever reason, won't open. Replace all cracked glass, and repair all damaged frames and inoperable pulleys, including damaged weather stripping. Replace all broken or torn screens.

Walls and Ceilings

As we mentioned earlier, you want to avoid dark colors on walls and ceilings. For the interior of your dwellings, use light earth tones and neutral colors that will blend with people's furnishings. Light earth tones are also more appealing because they make the rooms appear bright and airy, which makes them seem more spacious. Repair cracks in plaster and drywall with spackling, sand the areas smooth, and then paint. Try to maintain a bright, cheerful ambience throughout the home or rental.

Heating and Air-Conditioning

Dirty, grime-laden heat ducts and registers are one of the biggest turnoffs among prospective occupants. They're the result of a dirty intake filter. Should the prospects find a dirty filter, they could rightfully assume that it was never changed regularly, and they would therefore suspect that the system itself could be damaged. It's important to replace the furnace and air-conditioning intake filters monthly (and instruct your tenants to do the same), and be sure that the registers and ducts are clean and the systems are operating at maximum efficiency.

Storage Areas

The basement and garage areas should be cleaned and tidied up to give them a more spacious look. Old things you don't need or want anymore can be given away or liquidated at a garage sale (think of the extra space you'll gain, along with the money you might earn).

Hiring a Contractor and Controlling Costs

Whether you hire a contractor to make the renovations and repairs depends on whether you have sufficient fix-up funds and how much work you're capable of doing yourself, and thereby earning "sweat equity." If you're in a big hurry and have plenty of cash to invest in more real estate, you can get more accomplished by hiring contractors to do the work. But it's more profitable to do most of the work yourself. Personally, I enjoy doing much of the work. I hire contractors only for the work I'm not capable of doing, such as laying carpet and doing some of the more sophisticated electrical work. Over the years when I had to hire contractors, I watched carefully and asked many questions, and afterward was often capable of doing the job myself.

When you hire a contractor, follow these guidelines:

- Be sure to get references on the quality of their work. The better contractors build their business on their reputations, and their satisfied customers will be your best references.
- Make inquiries with at least two contractors, and get written bids for the work you expect to be completed.
- Get at least three references from each contractor, then check them out. Telephone each reference and ask if there were any problems

with the job. If there were, did the contractor correct them? Check also on whether the contractor assessed any extra charges on top of the original estimates, and ask if the job was completed on time.

• Draw up a preliminary plan that you can show the contractor. A floor plan drawn to scale with certain specifications would give the contractor something substantial to work with.

When it comes to handling construction and renovations, you need to learn as much as possible about every aspect of the real estate business. The more knowledge you gain about prices, costs, options, materials, real estate services, and so on, the more opportunities you'll have to reduce costs and increase profits.

9

Profitable Holding Strategies After the Acquisition

Now that the foreclosed fixer-upper is renovated, you have several alternative holding strategies to consider. Of course, you could move in and make it your family's residence. You can also rent it to tenants, and there are several ways of accomplishing that. If the circumstances are right, you could make the home a furnished boardinghouse for college students. Or you could simply rent it unfurnished to a family. You could also rent the home and give the tenant an option to buy it, which earns additional income through option fees. Additionally, you have the choice of later converting the house to higher earning office space. And finally, you could fix and flip the property, selling it outright for cash or on a long-term installment sale.

In the next chapter you'll learn how to manage your real estate holdings efficiently, without many of the hassles inexperienced landlords have to endure.

A Buy and Hold Strategy Is Best

Before the profitable holding strategies are discussed, I want to stress an important point discussed throughout this book. I bring it up again because it is so crucial, and hopefully you can learn from some of my past mistakes.

Over the 37 years that I've been involved with real estate investing, the only significant regret I have is that I wish I'd held on and never sold many of the properties I once owned. Why? Because good real estate investments are difficult to find, and when you're constantly selling them, you're forever trying to reinvest the proceeds to replace them. This is especially true when owning rental property, because over the long term it is more profitable and efficient than constantly buying and selling real estate over short-term periods.

Over the long term, your costs will remain relatively stable, while rents will always be increasing. In contrast, if you sell your real estate after owing it for just a short time, you not only have to pay taxes on the earned gains, but also have to invest in another property, and rather quickly so that you don't squander your gains. And don't forget all the costs involved in selling the property, such as a realtor's sales commission and other closing costs.

What's more, you can feel confident in holding properties over the long haul. That's because of one of real estate's unique characteristics—its limited supply. Land has supreme value because of its finite supply. In other words, they're just not making any more of it. And for that reason alone, land that's well located will always be in demand and will always increase in value.

Experienced, savvy realty investors, like Donald Trump, seldom liquidate their holdings outright because they know if they do, they will have to incur selling costs and pay taxes on the gain. They also know that they'll have to reinvest the proceeds quickly, and they know how difficult it is to find another profitable investment. That's why they maintain a long-term strategy of buy and hold for their real estate investments.

Renting to Tenants

After you've moved into a house and finish certain renovations to make the property more appealing, it could be a worthwhile strategy to find another house to renovate and use for your primary residence and rent out the home you now live in. This strategy is very efficient because you're working on the house you reside in, instead of working on a house you constantly have to drive to. And when it's time to rent the property, you can direct tenant applicants to meet you at your home, rather than having to drive to the rental to show it every time an interested applicant wants to see the property.

Renting a Portion of Your Home

The objective with this strategy is to purchase a larger house than you actually need, then make part of it your residence and the other part a rental unit. For example, purchase a large two-story house with, say, 1,500 square feet of living area upstairs and similar square footage downstairs. (You could also buy a large single-story ranch house with an area attached that could be made into an independent mother-in-law quarters.) The rental unit should have a separate entrance, with a kitchen and at least one bathroom, and a bedroom or two. When the rental unit has its own entrance and kitchen, it's less likely the tenant will be a nuisance.

This type of rental arrangement has several benefits. Because you're earning rental income, you can afford to purchase a larger and more expensive property. Under federal tax law, you can depreciate part of your residence (the rental unit) and deduct it against rental income. And you also have the benefit of having someone to look after your property when you're away, and perhaps feed the dog and gather your mail.

Landlord Tale: A Perfect Country Home, But ...

In the spring of 2004, Mike and Barbara thought they found the perfect country home, situated in Biloxi, just ten miles north of Mississippi's picturesque Gulf Coast. It was a lovely two-story custom brick home featuring four bedrooms and three baths, with 2,000 square feet of living area downstairs and 1,200 upstairs, a huge three-car garage, and all of it situated on a beautiful three-acre site with a white picket fence overlooking a tree-lined lake. But unfortunately this great house was only perfect in Mike and Barbara's dreams—not only was it too pricey for their housing budget, it was much too big for what they actually needed, especially since the kids were grown and had moved away from the nest.

Knowing that they just had to have this house, they got creative. The upstairs already had adequate living space for one or two people. If it had an independent entrance and kitchen, they could rent it out. And the rent they earned would solve the affordability problem.

In the end they bought the house for $220,000, spent an additional $8,000 to build a stairway entrance, and added a small kitchen upstairs. They made a $40,000 down payment and took out a 30-year fixed-rate loan at 6 percent on the $180,000 balance owed. The monthly payment on the principal and interest was $1,079, but after renovations were completed, they rented out the upstairs for $900 per month, which meant Mike and Barbara's monthly P&I housing expense was only $179. Adding $210 a month for property taxes and homeowner's insurance, their total monthly housing expense turned out to be only $389 per month. Not bad for a three-acre country home that in the beginning seemed unattainable.

A Furnished Boardinghouse for College Students

If you live in a college town, consider buying a big house near the campus with lots of bedrooms, then convert it into a furnished boardinghouse and rent out the bedrooms to several college students. The larger bedrooms could accommodate two students, while others would pay more for their private rooms. This type of rental is very lucrative, because you can earn twice the amount of rent compared to renting to an individual family.

Location of the property is crucial for student housing. If the property is near the campus, you can accommodate students willing to walk or ride a bike to class. If your potential boardinghouse is situated more than a few miles from campus, you're restricted to tenants who have a motorized vehicle.

Landlord Tale: My Boardinghouse

In 1972, when I was a senior at Michigan State University, I used a $5,000 inheritance as a down payment to purchase a large six-bedroom home on a half-acre site five miles from the MSU campus. I filled it up with furniture, rented out five of the bedrooms to college students, and used one of the bedrooms for my own residence. When all was said and done, I managed to earn $150 over and above all my monthly expenses, which included living rent free.

Meanwhile, my friend, Jim Van Debunte, who at the time practiced criminal law in Lansing, also owned 19 houses situated around the campus, which he rented to college students. One day he told me that his rental properties were so lucrative that they earned him four times more than his law practice.

Of course, you would need to furnish the boardinghouse, and you'd have to require substantial deposits to cover potential damage.

Simply renting out your property is a worthwhile strategy to realize a reasonable yield on your investment. There is, however, another strategy that offers greater returns and fewer landlord hassles than simply renting to tenants: Give the tenant a buy-option.

Giving the Tenant an Option to Buy

If the available unit is *not* part of an apartment complex but instead a detached single-family dwelling or a condominium, a profitable alternative to renting is to give your tenant an *option to buy*. So, instead of just a standard leasehold agreement, you make a special arrangement giving your tenant an option to buy the property, and you charge them a monthly *option fee* that applies toward the specified purchase price.

For instance, say you rent a house to a tenant for $950 a month and you also give the tenant the option to buy the house. Thus, in addition to the payment of monthly rent, the tenant pays you $250 a month for the option that applies toward the purchase price. So instead of collecting just $950 a month in rent, you collect an additional $250, or a total of $1,200 a month. If the tenant does not exercise the option to buy, he or she loses all the applied option fees.

The option to buy is a separate part of the rental agreement, and it specifies the price and terms of the purchase agreement. Under a typical option agreement, the owner (optionor) of the property gives the tenant (optionee) the right to purchase the rented property at a specified price and terms within a designated period of time.

Buy-Option Example

Let's say that you have a nice three-bedroom, two-bath home you can rent for $950 a month. But instead of just renting the house, why not earn a bigger profit by giving the tenant an option to buy the house for $145,000 and charge them a monthly option fee during the first year of the rental agreement?

Here's how the numbers work : The tenant pays rent at $950 a month plus $250 a month in option fees, which apply toward the purchase price of the property being optioned. If, at the end of the year, the tenant wants to exercise the option to buy, he or she has to come up with a down payment of $5,000. He already has applied $3,000 ($250 monthly option fee x 12 months = $3,000), so in addition he needs $2,000 in cash to meet the down payment requirement. (We'll go into this in more detail below.)

The terms of the purchase can be an "installment sale on a land contract," whereby the owner continues paying on the mortgage loan but the tenant-buyer pays the owner on a land contract at a negotiated rate of interest, preferably higher than the rate the owner is already paying on the existing loan. The tenant-buyer does not get title to the property until all the terms of the land contract are fulfilled. Furthermore, the tenant-buyer forfeits all monies already paid if he or she defaults on the terms written in the land contract.

Buy-option strategies can be very lucrative tools in real estate investing. They're attractive because they have a broad market appeal to potential tenant-buyers who lack the capacity to purchase a home using traditional methods. Some people who want to buy their rented home lack the required down payment, or they like the idea of making their down payment on the installment plan (paying monthly option fees that apply toward the down payment).

There's another advantage to utilizing this strategy: Buy-option tenants tend to take better care of the rented property than ordinary tenants, and that's because they know someday they'll own the property. So they're more inclined to making improvements to the property, even prior to exercising the option to purchase.

Let's go into it in more detail, returning to the sample home you purchased, above, for $120,000. You have a $100,000 loan at 6 percent over 30 years with monthly payments of P&I of $1,013. And as noted earlier, you have a tenant who pays $950 a month in rent plus $250 in option fees. The agreed option price of the house is $145,000.

After a year of renting, your tenant exercises the buy-option for $145,000 with a $5,000 down payment, and you finance the balance of $140,000 on a land contract at 8 percent for 30 years, or amortized monthly payments of $1,338 P&I. Note that because of the spread in interest rates between what you're paying and what's being paid you ($1,013 versus $1,338), you earn the differential of $325 per month.

Buy-Option Terms Must Be Specified in Writing

The precise terms of the buy-option agreement must be spelled out in a written contract. That way there will be no doubt or further negotiation between the parties involved. The landlord and the tenant-buyer will know exactly who is responsible for what, and for how much.

Figure 9-1 is a sample of the wording for an Option to Buy Agreement on the home we just discussed.

A buy-option agreement can be as creative as you want it to be: However, it should remain relatively simple in context to avoid any misunderstandings. For instance, should your tenant-buyer require a longer term on the option, there are essentially two methods of determining the future selling price for an extended term (longer than one year). After one year,

Figure 9-1. Option to Buy Agreement

This option to purchase is made and entered into this 1st day of April, 2005, by and between Andy Seller, hereinafter called Landlord (owner) and Fred Buyer, hereinafter called Tenant.

Subject property is a detached single-family dwelling located at 3750 Arby, Las Vegas, Nevada, 89107.

Landlord hereby agrees to grant an option to purchase to Tenant based on the following terms and conditions: Provided the Tenant shall not then be in default of leased property, Tenant to have the option to purchase subject property at a price of $145,000 for one year beginning April 1, 2005, and expiring March 31, 2006.

Tenant agrees to pay a monthly option fee of $250 during the term of the option, which will be applied toward the purchase price. Tenant further agrees to pay a down payment, including paid option fees, of $5,000 to exercise this option.

Tenant agrees to finance the balance owing of $140,000 on a land contract in favor of the Landlord at 8 percent per annum for 30 years at $1,338 principal and interest per month.

After the option is exercised, Tenant agrees further to pay all taxes, insurance, and loan payments into a trust account for disbursement to all parties concerned and pay for such a trust account.

Tenant also (when the option to buy is exercised) agrees to purchase subject property in "as is" condition.

Landlord agrees to have all loans, taxes, and insurance current at the time of execution of this Option to Buy Agreement.

Landlord further agrees to apply all security deposits and cleaning fees under the lease agreement toward the down payment upon execution of this agreement.

The parties hereto have executed this option on this date first above written:

By _____ Landlord

By _____ Tenant/Buyer

you could set the option price at the one-year price plus 1.5 times the consumer price index (CPI). Then, if the CPI is, say, 4 percent, the selling price after two years would be 1.5 times the 4 percent CPI, or 6 percent higher than the established selling price after one year.

The other alternative is to arbitrarily fix a selling price at which the tenant-buyer can purchase the property during a specific term, such as $155,000 after two years, and $170,000 after three years.

Structuring the Setup of the Option Agreement

The buy-option agreement also needs to spell out any special arrangements between the parties concerned. These may include the disposition of any prepaid deposits (cleaning, pet, and security) and appliances (washer, dryer, refrigerator) the landlord furnished. The cleaning, security, and pet deposits that have been prepaid by the tenant, for example, can be applied toward the down payment. And if the landlord has furnished any appliances for the tenant's use with the rented property, their exact disposition has to be written into the option agreement. If they are to be included in the selling price, say so in the buy-option agreement; otherwise, spell out the price you require for such items.

When it's time for the buy-option to be exercised, you can open an escrow so that you'll have a neutral third party carrying out the provisions of the buy-option agreement according to procedures common in your state. Once the escrow is completed, however, it's important to open a trust account for the protection of both you and the buyer. Most title companies will also function as a neutral trust to disburse funds.

The purpose of setting up the trust is to have a neutral third party that will take in the buyer's funds, make all disbursements (loans, taxes, and insurance), then send you a check for what is left over. This assures you and the buyer that everything is taken care of under terms of the contract. You don't have to worry about the taxes and insurance being paid, and the buyer doesn't have to worry about the existing underlying loans being paid.

Land Banking

This holding strategy involves investing in a property you intend to hold and generate income from, but at some time in the future convert it to a different, more profitable use. An example of this strategy can be illustrated by a parking lot investment in Manhattan, in New York City. After the property is purchased, you continue to operate the parking lot, but your long-term intention is to build a high-rise office building on the land at some time in the future when demand is high for office space. Meanwhile, you continue to operate the parking lot until the time is right to construct the office building—perhaps when office space in the area is scarce and construction money is available at a low or reasonable interest rate.

Another example would be the construction and operation of storage rental units on a site that, because of future growth, you believe will be strategic. It might be a future site for an interstate ramp exit, or an intersection on the outskirts of a city or town in the path of future growth. Meanwhile, you rent out the storage units with the intention of someday tearing them down and building something more profitable on the site, such as a shopping mall or an office complex. Or you could buy a house on a large corner lot in the path of future outward city growth, keeping it rented until, after five years or so, you can convert it to a corner minimart or strip mall with lots of tenants paying commercial rents. This strategy has a huge advantage over investing in similarly located unimproved land—with no structures built on it—because the rented dwelling generates income until growth makes the conversion to commercial use feasible. If you owned vacant land, you would have to pay the loan and taxes without the benefit of income. More important, because there would be no improvements on the land, you would have no tax relief because there would be no building to depreciate.

Converting Properties to Other Uses

Converting property to commercial usage can be very profitable because commercial space, on average, rents for twice the rate of residential space. Prime examples can be seen all over a thriving metropolis: Near downtown areas you'll see buildings that were once large, older homes converted to commercial office space; what was once a 40-acre farm on the outskirts of town is now a sprawling regional shopping mall. And in residential areas you'll see former apartments now serving as condominiums. These are good examples of conversions in which both land and improvements were adapted to a more profitable and higher usage as the region grew and changed.

The purpose of doing conversions is to upgrade the usage of improved real estate so you can earn more profits. And, given that commercial space typically rents for twice residential space, it's wise to always be on the look-out for residential properties that can be converted to commercial usage. The following are profitable types of conversions accomplished by innovative investors:

- Apartments to condominiums
- Apartments to office space
- A house to office space

Apartments to Condominiums

In order for this type of endeavor to be profitable, ideally you need to acquire the apartments cheaply enough so that when you sell each unit as a condominium, the money you receive will be substantially more than the average price paid for each unit.

All the costs involved in the conversion, such as legal procedures and other incidental expenses, as well as the value of your own time and effort, are usually figured in a two-to-one ratio—meaning that the sales price of each converted condo unit should be at least twice that of the average purchase price for the unit when it was part of the apartment building. For example, if the purchase price of the apartment building is an average cost per unit of $30,000, then the sales price of each individual condo will have to be at least two times that figure, or a minimum selling price of $60,000. This two-to-one markup guideline is necessary to absorb the incidental costs incurred, plus the time and effort to make the conversion.

The legal costs of converting apartments to condos begin with the city where the property is situated, which has to approve the change in property usage. They will require you to submit plans explaining exactly how you intend to make the conversion. Should the city consider your plan adequate, it will approve. If not, the city will probably not turn down your request completely, but make its approval contingent upon you making certain changes they will specify, such as adding bathrooms or more parking.

Before you decide to do a condo conversion, analyze the local area to determine what comparable condos are selling for—units similar in size, quality, and features to what you intend to build. The information gathered will help you make the decision whether it will be feasible to purchase, renovate, and sell the converted units at the two-to-one ratio.

Apartments to Office Space

If there's a shortage of available office space in the area in which you're interested, then converting apartments to office space could be very lucrative. But before you go proceed, consider the following:

- Is the property you wish to convert within a commercial zone? If not, can the zoning be easily changed?
- What is the present vacancy rate for office space in the area of the subject property? If too much space is already available, it would be unwise to convert.
- Does the property have adequate parking for office space? Typically, the city will require one parking space for every 500 square feet of rentable office space.
- How much will it cost to convert? Could you borrow the money to finance such a conversion?
- And finally, will the incidental costs, legal procedures, and time and effort be worth the eventual profit you will realize?

Analyze the situation carefully. Thoroughly study the finances of the projected conversion, keeping in mind the two-to-one rule. Then, if you think you can purchase the property at a reasonable cost and do a conversion and realize a big enough profit, by all means go ahead with your plans.

A House to Office Space

Again, based on the fact that commercial rent is usually twice that of residential, converting a house to commercial usage can be very profitable. Examples of profitable conversions are a large house transformed into a law office or medical clinic. Of course, not every house is appropriate for such a conversion. The ideal property should be located on a busy street with enough square footage and available land to accommodate a thriving business and the customer parking to go with it. Also, bear in mind that in order to make this type of conversion you'll likely need a change in zoning from residential to commercial use.

The following is a good example of converting a house to office space.

On the west side of Las Vegas, Nevada, along Jones Boulevard, there are a number of luxurious single-story ranch homes situated on half-acre lots. In 1986, Jones Boulevard was expanded from a two-lane road to a six-lane boulevard. This change, which added more traffic to the once quiet neighborhood, caused homeowners along the boulevard to become disenchanted with their location. All of a sudden their homes no longer had a distance buffer from the street, and, along with it, were affected by the noise from the construction and added traffic. As a result, many properties along Jones started going up for sale.

A shrewd investor then decided to buy one of these lovely ranch homes and convert it to a family dentistry center. This investor made a huge profit because the situation was ideal for conversion: property owners unhappy to find their homes facing a busy boulevard, plus a large good-quality structure on a busy location.

As this example illustrates, you can profit by being alert for certain changes occurring in your area. The widening of roads, new interstate highways, or other such changes can present opportunity for the shrewd investor who has the ability and foresight to make profitable conversions.

Purchase a Large Site and Build Another House

If you recall, a key ingredient to making a superior realty investment, as discussed in Chapter 5, was to *buy improved property on a sizable parcel of land*. The reason this is so important is that the more land you have, the more flexibility for expansion or usage you have as well. With this in mind, the strategy of purchasing a large site and building another house can be a lucrative method of investing in real estate.

For instance, you could buy a house on the outskirts of the city on a large parcel of land. Meanwhile, you live in the house with the intention of building another house on the property for your own residence, and renting out the old house. But before you sign on the dotted line, be sure that zoning laws allow you to build another house.

How It Works

Dave and Sherri spent more than a year trying to find the ideal home in a great country location on the outskirts of Biloxi, Mississippi. Finally, they found the perfect house, but Dave didn't like the location. Then he found the perfect parcel of land, a picturesque 10 acres that overlooked a tree-lined lake, but Sherri didn't care for the house that was on it. The solution: Even though Sherri didn't like the house, they purchased the perfect parcel of land anyway, because Dave promised Sherri that he would build their dream house on it. They would only live in the existing house temporarily, and when the dream house was finished, they would move into it and rent out the other house.

This strategy has several benefits to it. In most cases you can build a house on preowned land for a lot less than it costs to buy a new house; therefore, you have built-in equity when the new house is constructed. And you can usually get 100 percent financing on the construction loan.

Get the advice of a competent lawyer skilled in real estate before you actually attempt such a strategy. Keep in mind that your lender will want to hold the only mortgage on the property. In other words, you'll usually need to take out a construction loan to build the house, then get a new mortgage loan to pay off both the construction loan and the original mortgage loan.

Advantages to Building Another House on a Large Site

Besides the benefits of great leverage with 100 percent financing and built-in value, this investment strategy has the following advantages:

- Since the property qualifies as an owner-occupied dwelling, you get better financing. (The lender will give you a preferred interest rate and require a lower down payment because the property won't be classified as an investment purchase.)
- Having the rental house virtually next door makes it more convenient to show to prospective tenants, and it will be easy to maintain and look after.
- You'll have a built-in profit, because the new house, when finished, will likely be worth substantially more than the cost to build it.
- Should you go away for an extended period, your on-site tenant can look after your house.

Fix and Flip a Short-Term Investment

Although this book recommends long-term holding strategies for your realty investments, some of you might find this short-term method more in line with your objectives. We call this technique "fix and flip" because it involves paying cash for a property, quickly fixing it up, then reselling (or flipping) it at a profit. It's ideal for the investor with access to $50,000 to $100,000 in ready cash. Such capital can be generated from your own funds, a partnership, or borrowed from an institutional lender. The motivating principle behind this strategy is the fact that a cash purchase commands a bargain price, especially when the seller is motivated to sell.

Properties that best qualify are those that have a substantial amount of equity and a seller unwilling to carry back a note; they require renovation, yet are sound in structure and overall construction. A large amount of equity means that, in most cases, the seller has owned the property for an extended period. Since the seller purchased the property for substantially less many years ago and is unwilling to carry a note or renovate the property, he or she will be inclined to sell at a bargain price quickly to cash out of the property.

To illustrate this technique, let's say that you've located a particular property that can be purchased for $67,000 cash and, if renovated, can be sold within six months for $110,000. And let us assume that you have a lender that will lend you $72,000 for six months. Such an unsecured short-term loan would probably cost you about 10 percent, plus 2 points. So, you borrow $72,000, of which $67,000 represents the acquisition cost, while $5,000 is the cost to renovate the property. Interest on the loan for six months is $3,600, plus 2 points at a cost of $1,440, for a cost to finance of $5,040, plus repayment of the principal—the $72,000 you borrowed.

Although the cost to finance this short-term investment may seem excessive at first glance, this investment strategy supports a high finance cost because of realizing such a substantial net profit, especially considering that this strategy is so highly leveraged, using no funds of your own.

Granted, were you fortunate enough to possess the ready cash to purchase, quickly renovate, and sell the property without borrowing the required funds, you'd obviously be that much further ahead, because you would save $5,040 in finance charges.

Figure 9-2 illustrates how the numbers work in the fix and flip strategy.

Note that the realtor's sales commission is another variable cost that's included in this analysis. Due to the short period of time involved with this strategy, we usually pay a commission to effect a quick sale. However, if

Figure 9-2 Example of Fix and Flip Short-Term Purchase

Acquisition cost	$67,000	
Cost to acquire and renovate:		
Closing costs	500	
Cost to renovate	5,000	
Cost to finance loan of $72,000	5,040	
Tax and insurance (six months)	300	
Utilities (six months)	<u>200</u>	
Total expenses 11,040		
Total acquisition cost and expenses	78,040	
Property selling price	110,000	
Less the following selling expenses:		
Realtor's sales commission (6 percent)	6,000	
Closing costs	500	
Total acquisition cost and expenses	<u>78,040</u>	
Total overall cost	84,540	<u>84,540</u>
Net profit before taxes	<u>$25,460</u>	

you can procure a sale without the services of a realtor, you would earn an additional $6,000.

How the Fix and Flip Strategy Works

The key to making this strategy work—assuming you borrow the needed working capital—is to have made tentative arrangements with a lender. In other words, you should already have an unsecured line of credit of $50,000 to $100,000 set up prior to making a purchase. Then, as soon as you find a suitable property, you make an offer contingent on acquiring sufficient financing. If your offer is accepted, it is then analyzed by your lender. Should the lender agree, you have a deal. If not, your offer is void based on the financing contingency.

To ensure that you earn a reasonable profit from this technique, use the following rule of thumb: If you can buy a property for no more than two-thirds of its selling price after it's renovated, then it's likely you've found a suitable property. In the example given in Figure 9-2, the purchase price was $67,000, which is less than two-thirds of the selling price of $110,000. If you purchased a house for $80,000, the selling price would have to be at least $120,000 to incorporate the two-thirds ratio.

Selling on Installment. Instead of selling outright for cash, you also have the option of selling the property on installment and earning interest on a long-term sale. You could accept a reasonable down payment and finance the balance owing with a long-term mortgage loan for 30 years. Then, if you sold the property for $110,000 with a $10,000 down payment and financed the balance owing at 7 percent interest, you would earn $667 per month in principal and interest.

The installment sale, of course, is only feasible if you have surplus cash and don't need the proceeds from the sale of the property to reinvest in another property.

10

How to Profitably Manage Your Holdings

(Most of this chapter is taken from Chapter 10 of McLean, Buying and Managing Residential Real Estate, *2nd edition, published by McGraw-Hill in 2005.)*

In this chapter we will go into the issue of managing your tenants without the usual hassles many inexperienced landlords have to endure. Essentially, it's a guide to optimizing profits by using the proper techniques for screening tenants, hiring competent resident managers, collecting rents, overseeing maintenance and repairs, and setting up a necessary budget. By doing things efficiently, the right way, you learn how to avoid the usual nuisances—the ones uncaring and naive landlords face every day.

Being a successful landlord is no accident. It can be a wonderful learning experience as you reap all the rewards of operating a profitable moneymaking income property. On the other hand, poorly managed real estate can drain your resources and be a burdensome daily chore. It can turn a potentially great investment into an unwanted nightmare. However, when you hire the right people and do things the proper way, you not only make the most from your investment, but you will also be able to just about put all your realty holdings on automatic pilot and go away on a long vacation.

Making Your Rental Units Desirable

Far too many landlords are uncaring, miserly property managers who wrongly view their tenants as necessary evils. They look upon them not as valued customers, but instead as headaches who are always complaining and never seem to be satisfied. All of this presents a great opportunity for the smart investor who sees property management as a customer-service business and treats his or her tenants as valued customers. How can you make people want to be in your building? You do it in the following ways:

- Keep the property extraordinarily clean, inside and out. Tenants will pay more for an immaculately maintained building than they will for one that looks just so-so.
- Provide extra household features for tenants, instead of merely supplying them with living quarters. Invest your money in special features that can be readily seen, such as a center island in the kitchen, granite countertops, or top-of-the-line cabinets. In the bathroom, install a special lighted mirror for putting on makeup.
- Provide special customer service. For example, the resident manager or superintendent could perform a special service, such as receiving and mailing packages.
- Provide fast service for needed repairs. Hire a resident manager or an all-around maintenance worker who can do odd jobs so that someone with a pleasant customer-service attitude will be readily available most of the time.
- When you or your resident managers are truly orientated toward your customers, when you delight tenants with a pleasant and courteous attitude, and when you truly demonstrate a willingness to serve your customers' needs, you will gain a great advantage over the competition.

Managing Multiunit Buildings

Regardless of whether you own one rental home, a fourplex, or a large 20-unit apartment building, most of the guidelines presented in this chapter still apply. However, if you own more than one rental unit on a particular site—such as a duplex or a fourplex, instead of a single-family home—you need to have someone responsible for certain duties living on the premises. These duties include being responsible for showing vacancies, collecting rents, and generally overseeing the property.

In the 20-unit building, the responsible person is the resident manager the owner has delegated to assume certain responsibilities. But even with the smaller rental properties, the owner still needs to have someone on-site who is responsible for certain duties. This can include showing vacancies, maintaining the grounds, and opening a door for a locked-out tenant in the middle of the night. By delegating certain responsibilities to an on-site tenant, the owner alleviates many of the menial duties that can be a landlord's nuisance.

The responsible person is your liaison between you and the tenants. So, instead of having to drive to the property to show a vacant unit, you can have your manager do it. Or if a tenant has lost his or her key at two o'clock in the morning, the manager can let them in. Your manager can also be instructed on showing vacancies and having prospective tenants fill out the Application to Rent, which when completed can then be forwarded to you. (For sample forms, including the Application to Rent and Rental Agreement, see the Appendix.)

Choosing the Resident Manager

The ideal situation for resident manager is a husband and wife team. Typically, the wife will have the full-time responsibility, since it's more likely that she will be at home most of the time and not have a full-time job elsewhere. The husband will usually have a full-time job, but can still do some maintenance, such as mowing the lawn and function as a part-time maintenance and repair worker.

You should look for these characteristics in a resident manager:

- The ability to accept responsibility and adhere to the owner's guidelines.
- Has a spouse who has a full-time job, but at the same time is willing and able to be a part-time maintenance and repair worker on the property.

- Has a pleasant personality and is willing to give the tenants the ultimate in customer service.
- Willing to stay at home and assist in the overall operation of the property.

Duties of a Resident Manager

Above all, it's the manager's responsibility to adhere to the guidelines the owner of the property sets forth. Depending on the size of the property being managed, this can include rent collection, record keeping, showing vacancies, and maintaining the common grounds. When the resident manager or their spouse is capable of making repairs and taking care of the landscaping, you eliminate the need to hire a professional repair person or a lawn maintenance service.

It's very important that the resident manager agrees to stay at home and be on the job to show vacancies and keep order around the building. Someone active outside the home—a person with a full- or part-time job, or who has numerous social commitments—is not a good prospect. A parent who prefers to stay at home with children typically is better suited as an on-site manager.

What you pay a typical husband and wife management team depends on the size of the building being managed and the duties you assign them. Free rent on a two-bedroom apartment is common in a 20-unit apartment building. On a smaller building, such as a four- or six-unit building, a 25 percent reduction in rent would be common. Buildings larger than 20 units usually involve free rent plus a cash salary. For competitive salaries in your area, look in the classified section of the local newspaper under the column "Couples Wanted."

Supervising the Resident Manager

The duties of the resident manager must be fully explained at the outset of the owner-employee relationship. Be sure the manager knows exactly what is expected of him or her. Remember, the more responsibility you can delegate, the more time you'll have for other matters.

With small properties—less than four rental units—it's best to have the tenants mail the rental checks directly to the owner. With a four-unit rental or larger, however, the resident manager needs to handle rental income for the owner. Monthly reports (see the sample forms in the Appendix) submitted to the owner are necessary for efficient accounting and ready reference. These reports include a summary of rents (income) collected and bank deposits made (optional, depending on whether the manager or the owner makes the deposit).

Each entry on the summary of rents (income) collected should include the apartment number, rent-paid date and due date, amount paid, and type of income (such as rent, cleaning fee, key deposit, or security deposit). And whenever the manager receives tenant income, it should be recorded on a triplicate form of a rent receipt. One copy is kept on file by the manager, one copy is given to the owner, and the third copy is given to the tenant if he or she requests it.

Major expenditures, such as replacing carpet or a hot-water heater, should be handled only by the owner and billed directly to him or her. This will reduce the temptation for a manager to pad expense bills or receive kickbacks from salespeople. Often you can save on supplies when you buy them in volume, or have an established commercial account at major suppliers, such as Lowe's or Home Depot.

Once you have a qualified and responsible manager caring for your building, you'll find that an occasional monthly supervisory visit is all that you need to make. On such visits, you can make major decisions, such as whether to undertake expensive repairs like replacing the carpet in a unit. In addition, during these visits you can pick up the collected rent and any paperwork from the manager, and inspect the premises. Thus, the joys of being a landlord can be enriched by having a responsible manager, avoiding the headaches and hassles many amateur owners experience through slipshod management practices.

NOTEWORTHY
THE PERILS OF BEING AN ABSENTEE LANDLORD

One time when I was teaching a session of "Investing in Real Estate," I was discussing the pitfalls of being an absentee landlord and one of my students told the class the following story:

While I was in Hawaii for two years, I responsibly turned the management of my rental home over to a local realtor. After about four months the realtor called me in Hawaii and said the tenant had moved out. Meanwhile, I never received any rent for about six months. Then I phoned one of my neighbors who lived near the rental home and asked him to take a look at the property. He called me back the next day and said that the house was, in fact, occupied, and that the same people who had been my original tenants when I moved to Hawaii were still there. Obviously, the realtor thought I would never check up on the so-called vacancy, and he was keeping the monthly rent owed to me for himself.

This scenario is a common ruse crooked property managers use to cheat absentee landlords out of their hard-earned rental income. It's why you should always inspect your properties, in particular the vacant units, at least once every month.

What Goes with the Rental and What Doesn't?

Furnished vs. Unfurnished Units

Whether you supply the furniture in your rental units depends on who your intended tenants will be. If you intend to operate a boardinghouse and rent to college students, obviously it will be necessary to supply adequate furnishings. Or if you own small studio-type apartments that tend to attract transient clientele, then supplying furnishings would be advantageous. And, of course, you can then charge more in rent for the use of the furniture. If you do, however, it will be your responsibility to maintain and insure it from theft and fire damage.

The problem with furnished units is that they attract a transient clientele, which creates a lot of turnover. A rented home completely furnished is very easy to move away from. On the other hand, a home where the tenants supply all their own furnishings requires much more of an effort to move in and out. Invariably, once tenants take the time, effort, and expense to move all their belongings into a home, it's very likely they plan to stay a while.

Appliances

As a rule, I try not to get involved with supplying my tenants with mechanical appliances such as refrigerators, washers, and dryers. My reasoning: These items are usually expensive to purchase, and like all things mechanical, they will eventually break and need to be repaired or replaced. And unless you make special arrangements with your tenants, the cost to repair and maintain these appliances will come out of your pocket.

They do, however, make great amenities to feature in your rental units. So if you have the opportunity to purchase these appliances at bargain prices as part of the purchase price of the property you invest in, then by all means do so. But if you're going to furnish them in your rentals, you should give your tenants the responsibility for the repair and maintenance of the appliances, which you have to make clear to your tenants before they move in. That means spelling it out in the rental agreement.

Laundry Facilities

If you purchase a multiunit apartment building with nine or more rental units, you have to consider whether you should to supply a laundry facility with coin-operated washers and dryers, and whether you should purchase or lease the equipment. In smaller buildings—those with eight units or less—installing washers and dryers in a laundry room for tenant use would not be economically feasible because the usage would not pay for the cost of the utilities to run the machines.

Should you decide to purchase the coin-operated equipment, the machines would probably pay for themselves within two years. That's the good news. However, you have to maintain the equipment and be responsible for acts of vandalism and the unauthorized removal of coins from your machines.

On the other hand, you could lease your laundry equipment from a reputable rental company. The leasing company would be responsible for supplying and maintaining the equipment while at the same time collecting coins from the machines. Generally, when you lease laundry equipment, the leasing company retains 60 percent of the gross receipts and remits the remaining 40 percent to the owner. If you decide on leasing, be sure that a responsible person oversees the removal of coins from the rented equipment in order to help eliminate the temptation of skimming from the coin boxes.

Utilities and Trash Removal

Tenants who rent detached single-family residences or condominiums should be responsible for paying for utilities and trash removal. Also, most apartment buildings, especially those built more recently, have separate meters for gas and electricity consumption, and the respective companies bill the individual tenants. But the owner of the building is usually responsible for paying the water bill. When separate meters for each unit are not available for these utilities, the owner must add the cost to the rent. If this is the case, simply get an overall monthly estimate and divide it by the number of units in the complex.

Whenever you can, it's best to have your tenants on a separate electric meter and make it their responsibility to pay the bill. Otherwise, tenants tend to be more wasteful with their electric usage.

The removal of trash from multiunit buildings is best paid for by the owner, in order to maintain a cleaner common area around the building and avoid friction with the tenants as to whose responsibility it is.

Attracting Good Tenants and Avoiding Bad Ones

Having good tenants residing in your properties is the key to profitable and hassle-free property management. Good tenants always pay their rent on time, have clean living habits, respect for others, usually get along with their neighbors, and properly care for your property. But unfortunately, you also have to deal with the other kind—the bad tenants—and you have to learn how to screen them out and keep them from residing in your properties.

Generally speaking, bad tenants are usually associated with being irresponsible and having bad credit. In other words, they're not going to pay their bills, and it's very likely they won't care for your property either. So why bother with them? Bad tenants are a nightmare for landlords and their resident managers, and you don't need the headaches and extra aggravation that go along with having them occupying your property. Let the other, naive, landlords have all the headaches and horrors that go with nonpaying deadbeats who have no respect for someone else's property.

Bad tenants have the following habits:

- They're slow payers, or they simply don't like to pay their rent at all.
- They have little regard for anyone else's property and usually treat it with disdain and leave the landlord with the chore and expense of cleaning and repairing it. Usually their children are just like their parents, and they tend to be troublesome.
- They are noisy and always bothering the neighbors and the resident manager or landlord.

So you have to be wary of potentially bad tenants, people who have recently been evicted, owe money, and are desperately seeking and need an unsuspecting landlord who will allow them to occupy their property. If you want to avoid the hassles such bad tenants bring, it's your job to weed them out. If you're not careful and rent your available unit to an undesirable deadbeat, you will soon wish the unit was vacant! The surest way to financial suicide, or at least a horrendous nightmare, is to continually rent to flaky people who won't pay their rent. There are enough qualified prospects to fill your vacant units; all you have to do is advertise for them and properly qualify them.

How Do You Find Tenants?

Prequalification and Advertising

Finding tenants, which includes weeding out undesirable tenants before you make the mistake of renting to them, begins by "prequalifying" prospective tenants through your advertising.

For example, in the sample advertisement "3-bedroom, 2-bath apartment. $775/month. References required," the mention of "references" will help keep potentially bad tenants from calling you to inquire about the available unit. They usually won't call if they suspect that you're going to check their references, because, of course, the references will be bad! People with bad credit know who they are. And they know that most commercial landlords and savvy apartment owners do thorough credit checks. (You'll also do some further weeding out of your prospects later in this chapter in processing the Application to Rent.)

Advertising for Prospects

The best way to prospect for tenants is to post vacancy signs on the property and place classified advertising in your local newspaper. Vacancy signs must be precise and to the point, qualifying the prospective tenant to a certain degree. For example, your sign might say "Vacancy, 1-Bedroom, Kids OK," or "Vacancy, 2-Bedroom, Adults Only." Stating certain facts about the available unit eliminates a lot of unqualified prospects who are looking for something you don't have. Your vacancy signs also need to be bright (printed or painted in red or yellow) and legible, so they can easily be seen from a passing vehicle. Erect your vacancy signs on either side of your building, or post them on the lawn near the busiest street for maximum exposure.

Classified advertising should also be precise and qualifying in order to eliminate unnecessary calls from unqualified people. Good advertising copy achieves *attention, interest, desire,* and *action* (remember these as AIDA). To get attention, your headline should attract specific prospects. To stimulate interest, the headlines should be expanded to offer a benefit to the prospects that makes them read the rest of the advertisement. Arouse desire with good descriptive copy that makes the prospect want what you have to offer. Ask for the action by making it easy for the prospect to respond to your offer.

Here are some specific ideas for each objective:

- *Attention.* The purpose of the attention heading is to get the reader to distinguish your ad from the numerous other ads in the same column. Some examples are: "Newly Decorated," or "Large 3-Bedroom," or "Free Rent for one month." (This last type of ad could be used in a rental market already oversupplied with available units. Free rent would definitely get more attention than the other ads in the same column.)
- *Interest.* To develop interest, offer a benefit like "quiet country living" or "newly carpeted" or "great ocean view" to entice the reader to finish reading the rest of your advertisement.
- *Desire.* This will precisely describe what you have to offer. It's the body of the advertisement. Examples are: "2-Bedroom, Kids OK, $775" or "1-Bedroom, pet OK, Pool, $750."

- *Action.* The action getter can simply be a phone number that the prospect can call to get more information.

Classified advertising is printed under specific headings, so there's no need to duplicate information that's already available. In other words, you need not state that your apartment is unfurnished when your ad is running under the column "Unfurnished Apartments."

Begin your ad with the location, then the type of unit. For example, under a column heading of "Unfurnished Houses for Rent," you might say:

> *BILOXI, 2 miles N of I-10, quiet country living,*
> *Large 2br, 1ba on 3 acres, kids & pets OK.*
> *References required. $795. Call 555-1212.*

By beginning your ad with the location, you qualify prospects right from the start. People usually look for rentals based on areas they want to live in. Anyone looking for a quiet two-bedroom apartment out in the country will respond to this ad; anyone looking for a three-bedroom in a different area—like downtown—will look elsewhere.

After a full description, including any particular features, close the ad with the amount of rent you require and a phone number to call. Stating the amount of rent is important because it enables you, again, to qualify the prospect. If you're charging more rent than the prospect can afford to pay, he or she won't bother to call.

The following was a sample adve rtisement that proved very effective. It ran in the *Las Vegas Review Journal* under the section "Unfurnished Condominiums for Rent."

> *RENT WITH BUY OPTION ... Spring Mt. & Jones, 3-br, 2-ba,*
> *Neat & clean, beautifully landscaped & decorated, w/tennis*
> *cts, pool, Jacuzzi. References. $695. Call 555-1212.*

More Prequalifying: Answering the Ad Calls

In many situations the people calling on whatever it is you have for rent want to know the address so they can drive by and see it. But before you give them enough information to do that, you need to develop some rapport with them and do a little more prequalifying. You want to avoid showing it to people you might not want to rent to—such as those with bad credit or with too many pets.

Which brings us to an important issue: discrimination. Federal law prohibits you from explicitly excluding applicants because of their race, religion, sex, ethnicity, national origin, disability, or family status (households with children). But you should also note that federal civil rights law and nearly all state and local fair-housing ordinances exempt owner-occupied properties of one to four units. So, those exempt property owners may discriminate without legal penalty.

While you're on the phone with the prospect, find out as much as you can. Ask the following questions: Do they earn enough to afford your rental? How long have they lived in their present address? How long have they worked at their present job? How many people will occupy the property? Are there any pets? (If you plan to accept tenants with pets, you could require they pay a nonrefundable pet deposit. (More about deposits will be discussed later in this chapter.)

Creditworthiness and Conduct

Laws against stereotyping people because of their race, religion, or family status does not mean you're legally bound to accept tenants who do not meet your standards for creditworthiness and conduct. To the contrary, you have the legal right to refuse to rent to anyone—regardless of protected status—whose rental record, credit history, or income is below your standards. Unlike employers, who are often compelled to accept special hiring standards, landlords are not required to rent to everyone.

So begin by asking certain questions. For instance, someone calls on your ad for a two-bedroom, one-bath unit and says, "What's the address so we can come by and look at it?"

You reply with, "Yes, but first let me ask you a few questions: Tell me, how many people will occupy the property?"

The caller replies with, "Just my husband and five kids."

You think for a moment, Hmmm ... seven people in a small two-bedroom and only one bath, and then say, "Are there any pets?"

She says, "Just three dogs, but they're all well mannered and house-trained."

And you reply, "I'm sorry, but we don't allow pets."

In this scenario, you prequalified this prospect by asking certain pertinent questions. And by doing so, you saved a lot of time and effort by not showing the unit to someone to whom you have no intention of renting.

How to Maintain Harmony by Profiling Your Tenants

Single adults like to live with other singles. Folks with families usually prefer living in the same apartment building with other folks with kids, so their kids have someone to play with. And senior adults prefer to live with other senior citizens and in a place where they're not annoyed by barking dogs and children at play. With this concept in mind, set certain standards if you own a multiunit building, and don't try to mix the elderly with the young, or singles with families.

Showing and Renting Available Units

At this point your advertisement is running in the local paper, and vacancy signs are strategically located on the property. Now it's imperative that the vacant unit is ready to be shown, which means it should be neat and clean throughout. If, by chance, you're showing an occupied unit that the occupants will be moving out of shortly, inform them of your intentions. Request that they keep the unit tidy so you can show the unit to prospects.

Showing the Unit

While you're showing the unit, point out its features, such as storage, cabinets, view, and so on. Avoid bringing up anything you might consider negative, because what may be a negative aspect to some may not be to others. If they're interested in the unit, the prospects will usually begin by asking the following questions, which you should have the answers to:

- What is the square footage of the rental?
- What are the names of the schools in the district and where are they located?
- Where is the closest bus stop, grocery store, and so on?

Rental Applications

Once your prospects have seen the available unit and decided they want it, what's next? Start with the Application to Rent (see Appendix). Have them fill it out completely while you calculate how much money they are required to pay before moving in. This total amount should be the first and last months' rent, along with any required deposits and a cleaning fee. After they complete the application, be sure to get a minimum of a $100 deposit (the more the better). The deposit can be in the form of a check, cash, or money order. Find out when you can get the balance owing—first and last months' rent, security deposits, and fees—preferably as soon as you can and definitely prior to the move-in. Then check the application for any omissions; if there are none, notify your prospects that you will phone them about your decision once you've made some inquiries.

Qualifying the Prospects

From the information on the application, you now have to determine whether to accept your applicants as tenants. Again, you're essentially looking for tenants who will pay their rent on time, are clean living, will care for your property, and not be a nuisance. Keep in mind that you're about to enter into a long-term business relationship with these people, and you don't need the headaches associated with bad tenants. Once your prospects become tenants and gain possession of your property, if, for whatever reason, you want them removed, you must do it by due process of law, which is costly and time-consuming.

The best way to avoid this catastrophic situation is to do some investigating. Telephone a local credit agency and find out what it requires to do a credit check. If the prospects have no credit, then inquire into their rent-paying habits with their past two landlords. It's a good idea to check with the past two landlords anyway; that way you can inquire about their living habits. Incidentally, you can usually discover a lot about people's living habits by observing how they care for their vehicle. It's been my experience that people who take good care of their vehicle will, in most cases, take good care of the home they live in. Conversely, people who drive a dirty, ill-maintained car in almost every case will have dirty and messy homes and won't take good care of your property.

This observation also usually holds true for kids. If the children of the family are reasonably well dressed in clean clothes, it would be a good assumption on your part that the parents will also care for other things, such as your property. So, when prospective tenants arrive at your available unit, check out the condition of the car and the children, if any. Later, if you have any doubts about renting to them, let your observations assist in your decision.

Finally, the prospects have to be qualified on their capacity to pay the rent. Use similar guidelines to those lenders employ, including the same ratios for paying the rent. The monthly rent should not exceed 28 percent of the tenant's gross income. However, if they have no consumer debt (such as car loans or credit cards), then they can afford up to 33 percent of their gross monthly income.

Attract Tenants Through Their Pets

Keep in mind that you have to compete with other landlords, and many of them *do not* accept tenants with pets. A great marketing strategy to attract good-quality tenants is to be lenient in accepting pets. Perhaps, allow them one pet, and charge them accordingly. Typically, you can do several things to cover inclusion of a pet: One is to charge your tenants a nonrefundable deposit of between $200 and $400, and/or charge them substantially more rent for the addition of one pet. This means that you won't accept a menagerie of animals but will accept one animal as long as it is, say, less than 40 pounds.

Drafting the Best Rental Agreement

Although I have included a sample lease for your consideration and use (see the Appendix), you need to develop a practical lease that will serve your individual needs. In designing a lease to fit your particular purposes, try to keep your clauses, rules, and contingencies simple. Avoid the lengthy multipage fine-print leases written in lawyer jargon (legalese). Lawyers, of course, will argue that these lengthy leases cover every conceivable contingency no matter what happens. But these overburdened lists of authoritarian dos and don'ts tend to alienate and intimidate tenants, instead of portraying a cooperative business atmosphere.

When drafting your rental agreement, consider the following issues and clauses for possible inclusion.

Tenant Names and Signatures

All adult tenants and children who will occupy the premises should be named in the lease. Only the adults are required to sign the lease. As a rule, owners should not permit tenants to freely add more or substitute tenants for those moving out. Any new tenants must be fully approved by the owner.

Joint and Several Responsibility

If you rent a unit to more than one tenant, include a *joint and several responsibility clause*. This means married couples too, because divorces do occur. This clause makes every tenant signed on the lease both individually and jointly accountable for all rents owed and for tenant damages.

When this clause is omitted, individual cotenants can claim they're not responsible for the broken window, and they will say, "Collect from Frank, because he did it." Or they will say that they're only liable for their half of the rent. You'll find that in most cases, though, "Frank" has moved out of town. With a joint and several responsibility clause, you have the legal right to collect monies owed from the other tenants.

Guests

Protect yourself against unwanted guests who end up becoming unauthorized roommates (cotenants) by inserting a *guest clause* in the lease. This clause limits both the total number of people permitted to reside in the premises and the amount of time genuine guests can stay. Without this clause, you may show up at the property someday and wonder who these extra people are. (Calling them "guests" is a sneaky way of not listing roommates on the rental application.). When you ask who they are, you're told, "They're guests. Barbara is just down from Michigan for a couple of weeks." When you come back a month later, Barbara's three kids have also taken up residency.

Personal Property Description and Inventory

If you supply any personal property with the rental unit (stove, microwave oven, washer, dryer, refrigerator, blinds, or draperies), you need to inventory and describe each separate item as a lease addendum. If you can, keep a photograph and a record of the serial number for each item. Without this documentation, it's difficult to prove theft when a vacating tenant takes your new microwave and leaves a piece of junk in its place.

Discounts and Late Fees

To encourage early or on-time payment of rent, some landlords offer their tenants a discount of about $25 for prompt payment of rent prior to its due date. Other landlords discourage late payers by charging a late fee of 4 to 5 percent of the monthly rent amount when the rent is not paid within five days of its due date.

Your use of one of these strategies will let your tenants know that you intend to enforce your collection policies. Be firm in not allowing your tenants to take the discount or sidestep the late charge unless they pay the rent within the specified due dates. If a tenant is a chronic late payer, I try to arrange a new payment date that better matches his or her cash flow needs.

And this brings up another important issue: Never allow tenants to get behind more than five days in their rent without taking action. Initiate the eviction process as soon as local ordinances permit.

Bad-Check Fees

Also as part of your collection policy, you should never tolerate bad checks. If a tenant remits a bounced check, charge him or her a bad-check fee of $30. And from that point on you should no longer accept checks from the person—only cash (if you're doing the collecting) or money orders.

Tenant Improvements

You need to keep tenants from making unauthorized improvements on their own accord without your approval. Always include a clause in the lease that requires the tenants to obtain your permission *in writing* before they make any improvements. The purpose of this clause is to prevent tenants from diminishing the value of the property.

The clause is so important that you need to point it out to the tenants when they sign the lease, emphasizing that they must obtain your written permission before they alter the premises in any way. This includes such modifications to the leased property as paint, wallpaper, or any other type of redecoration.

Sublet and Assignment

When tenants are temporarily away from the premises, as they might be for an extended summer vacation, they may want to *sublet* the unit (rent to another party). Or when tenants permanently move away, they might be inclined to *assign* their lease to another party. To avoid this situation, which is tantamount to having unauthorized strangers you never qualified or approved occupying your property, make sure you include a no-right-to-sublet-or-assign clause in your lease.

Tenant Insurance

Since property owner's insurance only covers the structure of the premises, not the tenant's personal property within, it's a good idea to include a clause that requires the tenants to carry a renter's insurance policy for personal property.

Grounds Care

When you're the landlord of a rented detached single-family dwelling, it's likely you want the tenants to care for the grounds. To make sure they do that, it's important to precisely explain what this entails. To a tenant, "caring for the grounds" might mean simply mowing the lawn. To a caring landlord, it usually means keeping the lawn watered, along with caring for all the shrubs and flowers. If you want the tenants to properly care for your property, spell out the duties you expect them to perform.

Repairs

Part of the no-hassle management operations consists of avoiding some of the nuisances common to managing residential rentals. If you make the tenant responsible for the cost of repairs up to a certain limit, you will avoid many of the menial calls for certain minor repairs.

In the sample rental agreement shown in the Appendix, under line 19, "Tenant Maintenance," it says that "If a professional service call is required, the tenant shall pay the first fifty dollars ($50) of the total repair bill." Having this clause in your rental agreements will help make your tenants more responsible, because if they know they have to pay for repairs, they'll be more inclined not to recklessly break things. And it will help reduce troublesome phone calls to the landlord requesting repairs.

Landlord Access

Landlords need an access clause in the lease to enable them to conduct periodic inspections, make repairs, show the unit to prospective tenants, and, most important, to take care of emergencies (such as mending a broken water pipe or stopping an overflowing toilet). An access clause, however, should not give you unlimited freedom to access the premises any time you please. Tenants deserve a certain amount of privacy, and with this in mind, except for emergencies, landlords should always get the tenants' permission before accessing a rented unit.

Pets

Although the majority of households have a pet, many landlords refuse to accept pets of any kind. Because of this widespread restrictive policy, landlords who do accept pets have the opportunity to command higher rents and a nonrefundable pet fee. Typically you can charge $200 to $400 as a onetime fee for allowing one pet. If you do accept pets, be sure to include a pet-rules clause in your lease. Also, be careful in accepting tenants with more than one pet, and do not accept pets larger than 40 pounds.

Deposits and Fees

You have to consider security deposits for certain items of personal property the tenants use frequently that usually go with the property. These include such things as door keys and remote-control garage-door openers.

Also, you should charge your tenants certain fees to cover your costs for restoring their rental unit to good condition when they move out of it. Such fees might include a nonrefundable pet fee and/or an apartment cleaning fee to be paid in advance.

Regarding security deposits and fees, you need to address the following issues in your lease:

- The amounts and when they're due
- The conditions under which the tenants will forfeit all or part of the fees
- If and when the fees will be refunded

Not only do you need to spell out this information in your lease, you also need to go over each item with your tenants during the lease signing. Why? Because often tenants have the misconception that they can apply prepaid deposits to rent that they owe when they move out. To prevent such misunderstandings, it is helpful to explain these important money issues:

- *The amounts and when they are payable.* The more you can get in security deposits, the better. As a rule, try to base the amount on what it would cost to restore whatever it is you'll have to replace, plus something for your trouble. Regarding first and last months' rent, always get the full amount in advance prior to the tenants moving in. Never allow your tenants to pay the security deposit in monthly increments or permit postdated checks. Remember, you're not renting a flophouse run on charity; instead, you're looking for tenants who have the financial capacity and good rent-paying history to lease your desirable property.
- *Conditions of forfeiture.* It's important that your tenants know up front, before taking possession of the property, your forfeiture-of-deposit policy. Again, security deposits cover any damages to the property that the tenants have caused; it does not cover rent that may be due upon moving out. Furthermore, the tenants have to be made aware of the fact that if their liability for rent or actual damages exceeds the security deposit, they're responsible to pay the higher amount.
- *Final inspection.* The best time to do your final inspection is immediately after your tenants have vacated the premises. Do a walk-through inspection with your tenants present. Use the inventory-of-furnishings sheet you prepared when they first moved in to compare the condition of each item and every room. Take note of any damage, and estimate the cost.

- *Deposit refund.* Many penny-pinching landlords hold out for 30 or more days before returning a tenant's security deposit. Instead, as a courtesy to your customers, you should refund your tenant's deposits at the end of the final walk-through inspection. They will surely appreciate it, especially when they probably need it for expenses on the new residence.

The Move-In

Before your tenants are given the keys and take over residency of your rental unit, be sure that they've paid, in full, all monies owed you. If they paid by check, make sure the check has cleared before they move in. The total amount includes the first and last months' rent, cleaning fee, pet fee, and all security deposits. Be sure that the rental agreement is signed and that one copy is available for the tenants. Also make sure each adult tenant has one set of keys, plus written information on whom to call to have all utilities turned on, along with the name and number of the local cable television company. Finally, inform your tenants that you expect the rent to be paid on time and that there is a three-day grace period, after which a late fee will be charged.

Inventory of Furnishings

At the time of move-in, have the tenants go through the unit room by room with you. The tenants should fill out the inventory of furnishings form, make comments, and return the form to you. Also, they can note any damage to the ceiling, walls, or flooring. (See an example of an inventory-of-furnishings form in the Appendix.)

Rent Collection

Never allow your resident manager to accept cash for rent or deposits. Only in an emergency should you allow the manager to ever accept cash. However, your on-site managers can be allowed to accept checks or money orders. This helps eliminate the opportunity of theft or embezzlement of the owner's income receipts.

Checks should be acceptable from your tenants until you receive a bad check. From then on, you should accept only cash or money orders from that particular tenant. (The resident manager, though, can accept only money orders). On your monthly inspection visits to your property, you can either collect rent receipts from the resident manager or have him or her deposit the checks. To do this, order a rubber stamp that reads "For Deposit Only (to your account number)" from the printer, and then require the manager to stamp the back of each rent check. The resident manager can then deposit the checks in your bank account.

Occasionally, a tenant will request a receipt for the paid monthly rent. To be prepared for those instances, it's necessary to furnish the manager with a triplicate receipt pad. One copy of a rent receipt can then be available for the tenant, one for the manager, and one for the owner's records.

Reminders to Pay

Also, as part of your collection policy, you need to follow through with reminders to pay the rent if your tenants become delinquent. First, issue a three-day reminder when the rent is three days past its due date. When the rent is five days overdue, issue a more forceful five-day notice. (See examples of the three- and five-day reminders in the Appendix.)

Eviction Procedures (for Nonpayment of Rent)

Here's another good reason you need to be particular about who rents your property: Lawful actions to evict a deadbeat tenant will only bring a judgment for rent monies, court costs, and moving fees. Cases that go to court will undoubtedly require 30 days or more to remedy. The costs involved, plus additional loss of rent, can be very expensive to an owner when nonpaying tenants move into your property.

The following procedure is common in most states for the lawful eviction of a tenant for nonpayment of rent:

1. The tenant in default is served with a three-day notice to pay rent or quit the premises. To ensure proper legal procedure, the person serving the notice should be the marshal, not the owner or the resident manager.
2. An unlawful detainer is filed with the municipal court clerk, and a summons is issued.
3. The tenant is served with a summons and a complaint.

4. The tenant has the legal right to file against the complaint, pleading his or her case. In that event, a trial is held.
5. The default of tenant is taken and given to the owner.
6. The court issues the writ of possession.
7. The marshal receives the writ of possession.
8. The marshal evicts the tenant.

Budgeting

The successful operation of a rental building will ultimately depend on a carefully planned budget, which the building owner then sticks to without exception. Essentially, the budget is the financial planning for the upcoming years. Income and expenses are projected to provide an overall view of the building's financial well-being.

If you don't properly plan income and expenses, financial disaster is inevitable. Money must be allocated for certain replacement items over the years so they can be paid for when they need replacing. When owners fail to allocate funds to replace certain items, they defer maintenance. That, in turn, causes vacancies, which in turn causes loss of income and further deferred maintenance and eventual loss in value.

Good budgeting sets aside a proportionate allowance for the future replacement of certain expensive capital items, such as carpeting, roofs, elevators, pool equipment, air-conditioners, and furnishings. Thus, a contingency fund is set aside each month and held in reserve to replace these capital items when needed.

How much do you set aside each month? It depends on the amount of capital equipment you have. For example, carpeting usually has to be replaced, on average, about every seven years. New carpeting in today's market for a one-bedroom apartment costs about $700. Therefore, you budget $100 per year per apartment (about eight dollars per month), which is set aside in a contingency fund to replace carpeting. Likewise, a replacement reserve fund must be set up for other capital items as well. By preparing a budget, such as a reserve fund, you'll have money set aside when certain expensive things break down, instead of suddenly being faced with a large expenditure and not having adequate funds.

The best way to budget these items is to estimate total outlay for all future expenditures, maintaining the fund for each item in a savings account, to tap when the money is required. You determine, for instance, that the cost of a new roof is $2,400, and that it will last 20 years. Divide the total cost by the number of months, and the result is the amount that should be budgeted each month. So $2,400 divided by 240 months equals $10 per month allocated for a replacement reserve for roofing.

Expense items, such as property taxes and hazard insurance, also have to be budgeted if they're not part of your monthly impound account and paid by your lender. Both property taxes and insurance are projected at one-twelfth of the annual bill per month.

As a rule, 5 percent of gross collected rents is usually an adequate amount for all replacement reserves. However, this amount should be increased for additional capital equipment, such as a heated pool or spa.

Record Keeping

Proper record-keeping procedures are necessary so the information will be accessible when needed, especially when your accountant needs it, or if the IRS decides to make a surprise audit. Keeping records is simple when your investments are single-family homes. All you need is to keep all records and expense items inside an 8.5-by-11-inch manila envelope for each home. All income collected can be noted on the outside of the envelope, along with the addresses of note holders, balance owing on the notes, and initial cost of the property. At the end of each year you can start a new envelope for the upcoming year.

Multiunit buildings, such as apartment houses, require somewhat more elaborate record-keeping systems, with a separate set of records for each building. Make up file folders and label them "General Records," "Tenant Records," "Receipts and Expenses," and keep these files in a file cabinet. In the general records folder, retain such information as escrow papers, insurance policies, taxes, notes, and deeds. In the tenant record folder, maintain all rental applications, rental agreements, and any other data pertaining to your tenants. In the receipt folder, retain all paid receipts for all expenses related to the building and a copy of all rent receipts. Later you can arrange the expense items chronologically for tax purposes. At the end of the tax year, this envelope should be stored separately for at least five years, just in case you have to verify anything.

Tenant Records

For each tenant in an apartment building, set up a tenant record on a 5.5-by-8-inch file card, such as shown in Figure 10-1. Whenever a tenant makes a payment, record it on the tenant record file card.

Journals of Income, Expenses, and Depreciation

For each multiunit building, keep separate journals in which you post all relevant income and expense data monthly. These journals give you ready access to all current data relating to each property's monthly compilation of income and expenses. The journal of income in Figure 10-2, for example, takes into account all income collected for each unit in the building each month for the entire year. Figure 10-3 takes into account all the expenditures that have been made for the building. All the income and expense receipts you've been keeping in file folders are also posted in these journals each month. Anything you do not have receipts for can be recorded from your checking account record.

Once you've completed an entire page on the expense journal, as shown in Figure 10-3, total each column and bring the balance forward to the next sheet. Then start posting your subsequent later entries. After posting your last expenditure for the year, total the last sheet, and you'll have your year-end income and expense totals for each category of your building.

Be careful not to post on your expense record such capital items as carpeting or a new roof. These are depreciable items, not expenses, and are considered improvements to the property. (See Figure 10-4 for a sample depreciation record.)

Depreciation Records

Depreciable items are property or equipment that have an extended useful life and are considered to be improvements to the property. Some examples are carpeting, elevators, linoleum floors, roof replacements, and swimming

Figure 10-1 Tenant Record on File Card

Address _____ Key _____ Signature _____

Orig. Move-In Date _____

Lease Dated _____ Exp. _____

Tenant Tel. No. _____

Deposit

	Security Deposit	Cleaning Fee	Key Deposit #	Base Rent	Refrigerator	Furniture	Parking	Month to Month	Additional Occupancy	Other Fireplace & Dishwasher	Air-Conditioner	Utilities	Total Rent	Balance Due

Rent

Date Due	Date Paid	Receipt Number	Paid to Noon	Amount Paid										

BLDG. # _____ APT. _____ FL. PL. _____ CLR. _____ NAME _____ DATE DUE _____

Figure 10-2   Journal Income Record

Monthly Income Record   Page # _____

Address _____

Year _____

Unit	Jan.	Feb.	Mar.	Apr.	May	June	July	Aug.	Sept.	Oct.	Nov.	Dec.
1	400	400	400	400	400							
2	390	390	390	390	390							
3	425	425	425	425	425							
4	275	275	275	275	275							
5	415	415	415	415	415							
6	460	460	460	460	460							
7												
8												
Total	2,365	2,365	2,365	2,365	2,365							

Figure 10-3   Journal Expense Record

Expense and Payment Record

Address _____   Year # _____   Page # _____

Date	Paid to	Paid for	Total Paid	Mortgage Principal	Mortgage Interest	Tax	Ins.	Mgt.	Repairs and Maint.
1. 1/1	bank	1st mort	760.00	122.80	427.20	120.00	90.00		
2. 1/1	Smith	2nd	125.00	92.40	32.60				
3. 1/3	hdwr.	parts	9.60						
4. 1/7	water	water	56.71						
5. 1/8	muni ct	evict	21.00						
6. 2/1	bank	1st mort	760.00	124.06	425.94	120.00	90.00		
7.									

Figure 10-4   Depreciation Record

Location and description of capital improvement: 3750 Raymond, Los Angeles, CA: A 19-unit apartment building.

Date acquired:	January 1987
New or used:	Used
Cost or value:	$220,000
Land value:	$40,000
Salvage value:	0
Depreciable basis:	$180,000
Method of depreciation:	Straight line
Useful life:	27.5 years

Year	Prior Depreciation	Depreciation Balance	% of Year Held	Depreciation This Year
1987	0	$180,000	100%	$6,545
1988		173,455	100	6,545
1989		166,910	100	6,545

pools. Each of these items must be depreciated on a separate depreciation record form, as shown in Figure 10-4.

Annual Statement of Income

This statement brings together all relative income and expenses for the year and shows the net profit or loss of the subject property. Figure 10-5 provides an example. Notice how depreciation, not an out-of-pocket expense, is deducted last for tax. The bottom line is the net profit or loss shared with the IRS.

Chapter Lessons

Remember that the devil is in the details: Be as concerned about small details as about big ones. People will pay more to live in an immaculately maintained building than an average building. Make people want to be in

Figure 10-5   Annual Income Statement

Location: 3750 Raymond, Los Angeles, CA. Year: 1988
Annual income:

Rent	$28,471	
Laundry	629	
Total annual income		$29,100

Expenses:

Interest	$8,410	
Taxes	4,800	
Utilities	1,812	
Service, repairs	321	
Pest control	120	
Insurance	850	
Management	1,800	
Total expenses		18,113

Net income (before depreciation)	10,987
Less depreciation	−6,545
Net income for tax purposes	4,442

your building because of your eye for detail. You can impress existing and prospective tenants in the following ways:

- Make sure the premises, inside and out, are as clean as they can be at all times.
- Put money into items that offer services for the occupants. Rather than providing just a building, provide some customer services as well such as having the building superintendent available to receive packages delivered for the tenants.
- Provide tenants with a Jacuzzi tub, a steam unit in a stall shower, and a granite-looking countertop in the bathroom.

- Install special lighting in the bathroom for putting on makeup, great-looking cabinets and a center island in the kitchen, lots of storage space throughout the unit, and employ a well-thought-out design.
- Provide a resident manager or superintendent who is readily available and has a customer-service attitude.

The key to hassle-free property management is learning how to avoid many of the hassles that naive property owners have to deal with. Your objective is to rent *only* to qualified, responsible people who pay their bills on time and who know how to take care of your property. All you have to do is learn how to weed out the bad tenants and abide by some simple rules outlined in this book.

Investigate: Find out who your potential tenants are. Make them fill out a rental application, and call a past landlord or two. Also, get a thorough credit check on them. Check out the car they drove up in. If the inside is messy and uncared for, that's usually a telltale sign of how they will live in your rental property.

The Four "Nevers" of Successful Property Management

1. Never be an absentee landlord. Why? Because there are too many ways unscrupulous property managers can embezzle your hard-earned income when you cannot personally inspect your properties on a regular basis.
2. Never allow your resident manager to collect cash from tenants. You don't want to give anyone the opportunity to embezzle or steal your rent receipts.
3. Never accept tenants without thoroughly checking their credit history and getting references from their past landlords.
4. Never allow tenants to occupy the premises until they have paid all monies due in full.

11

How to Retire "On the House"

It has been said that a journey of a thousand miles must begin with a first step. With this in mind, your first step to becoming financially independent is the purchase of your first house. Beyond that, the amount of wealth you amass during your lifetime, though, depends on how much effort, time, and money you devote to the wealth-building process.

Consider several investment scenarios. In the first scenario, you buy just one house for $110,000 with a $10,000 down payment, along with a $100,000 mortgage loan for 30 years. Based on a very conservative annual rate of appreciation of 4 percent, look what happens to your small initial investment. After 30 years the mortgage loan is paid off and you own the home free and clear of any debt. So your small down payment of $10,000 had grown exponentially to a value of $300,140.

Yet 4 percent is a very conservative estimate of future appreciation in real estate, given that on average residential real estate over the past 30 years has appreciated at an annual rate of between 6 and 8 percent. Look what happens to the purchase of a similar house when more realistic rates of appreciation are factored in over 30 years. At 5 percent, you can expect a $10,000 down payment to increase to $491,350 in home equity. And at 6 percent, a similar down payment would grow to $589,350 in home equity.

In the other scenario, instead of just one house, you invest in three or four houses in the next 10 years, and at retirement your net worth could easily be in the range of $300,000 to $1 million or more. Presuming only modest increases in rents—at 4 percent annual appreciation, $1,000 rent today is equivalent to $2,000 in 18 years—the income from those rental houses could reach $10,000 per month. And that kind of income is generated from owning only three or four rental properties. Imagine how much income you could earn with even more rentals!

Use Built-Up Equity to Buy More Properties

After you've owned a house for several years, and with steady appreciation and pay-down of the mortgage loan, your initial small investment now has substantially grown into a sizable amount of equity. So what do you do with all this equity in your home?

You have several options. If all you have is one home, and you're living in a high-priced real estate market—such as the coastal areas of northern and southern California—you could downsize (trade down) and relocate to a more affordable part of the country. As an example, homeowners in the San Francisco area, where the average home is selling for $790,000, are selling their homes, taking their huge tax-free profits, and buying comparable homes for less than a third of the price in more affordable places like nearby Sacramento or Las Vegas, Nevada. They can live off the substantial price differential between the two homes, which is often in the neighborhood of $500,000.

You also have the option of arranging an installment sale on your home, instead of accepting all cash for it. This way you carry back a purchase-money mortgage and earn all that interest income over the next 30 years.

Still another alternative to tap the equity in your home is to refinance and pull out tax-free cash. You can use the proceeds to retire on, or do whatever you wish, including investing in rental property.

The Basics of "Retiring on the House"

Think of your first home as the foundation from which most of your future wealth will be derived. After it's purchased, you move in and begin making renovations to the house that eventually help to increase its value. Meanwhile, you continue saving to make another down payment on a second property. At some point in time you purchase a second property, move into it and rent out your original house. Now you have additional income coming in from the rental plus the benefit of appreciation and paying down the mortgage loans on two properties. After several years of appreciation and paying down the loans, you can refinance the loan on the first property, pull some of the cash out of the built-up equity, and invest the money in a third property.

Then, several years down the road, when you've accumulated substantial equity in the second and third properties you've invested in, do the same thing over again. You do it by renting out the house you're presently living in and moving into the property you just purchased. In this way you can utilize the benefits of owner-occupied financing (lower interest rates and smaller down payment requirements) discussed in Chapter 7.

Later on, when you've amassed more equity and paid down the loans, you can refinance one of your properties and use the proceeds to do the same procedure over again. When you properly utilize the success-proven guidelines outlined in this book, you could, realistically, retire comfortably on your income-producing realty holdings alone.

The Bright Future of Rental Housing

Predicting the long-term outlook for inflation or common stock prices is virtually impossible. But as long as America's population and economy continue to expand, which they're expected to do, there will always be great demand for rental housing. And don't forget about the finite supply of habitable land, which makes real estate more in demand because of its restricted supply. Real estate ownership will ultimately provide the most reliable and secure strategy to long-term wealth for the average person.

And there's more good news about the future of rental housing. You'll also enjoy the benefit of knowing your capital investment is safe in real estate. Even in the midst of a nationwide economic recession, property values endure and the landlord's rental income remains relatively stable. During these downturns of economic activity, the housing supply tightens as the number of home and apartment-building construction projects decline. Economic downturns—which are usually associated with high unemployment and tight credit markets—also have a propensity to draw more households toward renting and away from owning a home. And when the slumping economy finally reverses itself and the economy begins to grow and flourish, rising employment, more income, and general prosperity puts more pressure on an already tightened housing supply. The end result is higher rents and more appreciation in real estate values as more households, along with a growing population, strive to occupy a tight housing market.

A Lifetime of Rental Income

Many real estate owners who had the wisdom to hold on to their properties over the long haul are now, in the autumn of their life, able to live off their net rental income. Today's real estate investors have to be patient and realize that real estate is a much better long-term investment than a short-term one. That means that over a lifetime you'll make more money holding on to real estate than "flipping" it in a quick sale. That's because you benefit from the long-term effects of appreciation and mortgage pay-down. But when you sell a property soon after buying it, you not only have to find another investment to invest the proceeds in, but it's likely you'll have to pay taxes on the capital gain.

First-time investors who recently purchased rental property also have to be patient and realize that income property purchased today with a small down payment is unlikely to net an immediate positive cash flow. But as time passes, all the factors we discussed earlier that increase the demand for real estate go to work: The property steadily appreciates, and the rents are gradually raised year to year, which results in greater income and more equity gained in the property. So the lesson in a nutshell is: Buy all the real estate you can when you're young, then enjoy all the great tax-free income benefits when you're older.

To Sum Up ...

It's very important to choose fixed-rate long-term loans when it comes to financing real estate. Don't be enticed by the fancy introductory teaser rates primary lenders might tempt you with. When you get involved with adjustable-rate loans, eventually you'll be stuck with loan payments that will always be adjusted upward. The best choice for the long haul is always a traditional 30-year fixed rate loan.

When you're choosing types of real estate investments, avoid investing in unimproved land and attached dwellings, such as condominiums and cooperative apartments. Stay with detached single-family dwellings, which are in great supply and desired by most homeowners and tenants. And don't forget the key ingredients to making a superior realty investment, which we discussed in Chapter 5. If you follow them, you can rest assured that your real estate investments will reward you year after year.

Also, get to know the territory you intend to invest in. Learn about land values and the price per square foot that residential housing is selling for. This way you become very efficient and knowledgeable about values, which enables you to make concise and quick appraisals, which gives you the ability to know a good deal when you see one.

Finally, to optimize your profits and be a successful investor, you also have to abide by the following: Be very selective in both the property you buy and in choosing the tenants who will reside in your properties.

So get started now. By starting small; purchasing a home for yourself; always adding value with selective, appealing improvements; continually reinvesting that additional income into more rental property; and repeatedly adding value to your other properties—you can ultimately build a magnificent net worth to retire on!

Good luck with your real estate investing.

Sincerely,
A. J. McLean

Appendix
of Useful Forms

The forms in this section are for your use as you see fit, including duplicating of each page on any type of photocopying equipment.

Application to Rent

You can overcome many of the hassles frequently encountered by novice landlords by properly qualifying your prospective tenants. Conscientious people with good credit who will care for your property are a valuable asset. They're the good seeds in your garden of prosperity; you only need to weed out the so-called bad seeds to help ensure that your property management experience will be a fruitful one.

After your prospects have filled out the rental application (see Figure A-1), review it carefully, making sure that everything is legible and complete. Be certain the names are correct, because later on if Jim Jones skips the premises, he will be easier to trace with his complete name of James Anthony Jones. If more than one person will occupy the premises, get the names of all the adults, and make everyone responsible for rent payments.

Appendix of Useful Forms

Figure A-1 Application to Rent

Name of first applicant _____

Date of birth _____ Social security number_____

Present address _____

City _____ State _____ Zip _____

Home phone _____ Work phone _____

Unit to be occupied by _____ adults, _____ children, and _____ pets.

Diver's license/ID state _____ Driver's license/ID no. _____

Current landlord/mgr.'s name _____ Phone _____

Why are you leaving? _____

Previous address _____

City _____ State _____ Zip _____

First applicant's employer _____

Address _____ Gross monthly pay _____

Position _____ How long? _____

Credit references: Bank _____ Account no. _____ Type _____

Other active reference _____

In an emergency contact _____ Phone _____

City _____ State _____ Zip _____

Name of spouse/second applicant _____

Date of birth _____ Social security number_____

Present address _____

City _____ State _____ Zip _____

Home phone _____ Work phone _____

Driver's license/ID state _____ Driver's license no. _____

Current landlord/mgr's name _____ Phone _____

Why are you leaving? _____

Previous address _____

City _____ State _____ Zip _____

Second applicant's employer _____

Address _____ Gross monthly pay _____

Position _____ How long? _____

Credit references: Bank _____ Account no. _____ Type _____

Other active reference _____

In an emergency contact _____ Phone _____

City _____ State _____ Zip _____

List all major vehicles, including RVs, to be kept at the dwelling unit. Include make, model, year, and license plate number for each.

Vehicle no. 1 _____ License plate no. _____

Vehicle no. 2 _____ License plate no. _____

Vehicle no. 3 _____ License plate no. _____

I (we) declare that the above information is correct and that I (we) give my (our) permission for any reporting agency to release my (our) credit file to the undersigned landlord solely for the purposes of entering into a rental agreement. I (we) further authorize the landlord or his or her agent to verify the above information, including but not limited to contacting creditors, both listed herein or not, and present or former landlords.

First applicant _____ Date _____

Second applicant _____ Date _____

Be sure too that each adult includes his or her social security number. It is essential to conducting a thorough credit check.

Employment information is also very important. You definitely want to qualify the prospects on their ability to pay the rent. As a general rule of thumb, a range of 28 to 33 percent of gross monthly income can safely be paid in rent—28 percent if there are some other debt obligations, and 33 percent if there are not. If your prospects qualify based on their salary, then at a more appropriate time you should verify their employment. A simple phone call to the employer is sufficient.

Credit Check

Credit bureaus need a complete name, date of birth, present address, and a social security number to conduct a complete credit check on your applicants. You can also do some checking with the applicant's last landlord or second from last landlord by phoning him or her and inquiring about the applicant's conduct and rent-paying habits.

Multiple Tenants

You will have added protection by having each adult tenant sign all the documents of the rental agreement. This way the parties are jointly responsible, and if one of the lease signers skips out, it may still be possible and easier to locate one of the other tenants on the lease.

Inventory of Furnishings

An inventory of furnishings should accompany the rental agreement for each individual unit (see Figure A-2). Essentially, this form is used essentially to identify items supplied by the owner, such as the refrigerator, stove, washer, dryer, or couch, and to denote the present condition of each item. Later, if a lawsuit is necessary, the completed form can be used to support a claim of damage, excluding reasonable wear and tear, against the security deposit. Otherwise, the tenants may counter that the damage was there before they moved in, and except in cases of gross and negligent damage, such a defense is difficult to overcome without proper documentation.

Appendix of Useful Forms

At the time of move-in, have the tenants go through the unit room by room with you. Have them fill out the inventory, record any comments, and return the form to you. If the space provided for comments is too small, have your tenants make any additional comments on the reverse side of the form and note, "See reverse side."

Appendix of Useful Forms

Figure A-2   Inventory of Furnishings

Rental unit address _____

Tenant _____ Tenant _____

Date of inventory _____, 20_____.

Room	Item	Comments	Condition at move-out

Tenant agrees that the above information is an accurate inventory and description and assumes the responsibility for these items in the dwelling unit as of _____, 20 __.

Move-in   Move-out

_____ Date _____ _____ Date _____

_____ Date _____ _____ Date _____

Tenant Record on File Card

For multiunit buildings, keep tenant records on 5.5-by-8-inch cards. Each card is a ready reference of all monies paid by and due from the tenant, a description of the apartment type, including the floor plan (FL. PL), the color of carpet (CLR), plus other important tenant information (see Figure A-3).

Figure A-3   Tenant Record on File Card

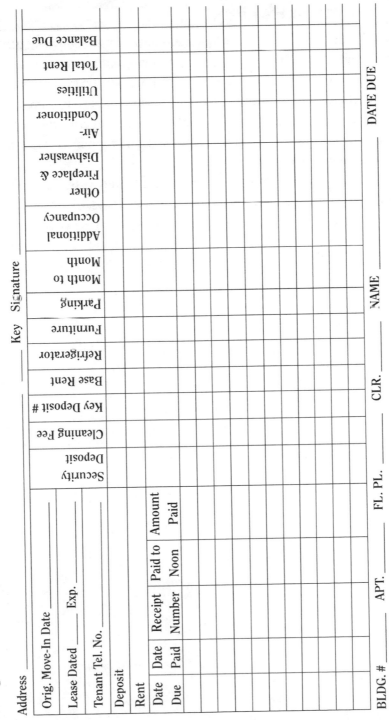

Reminders to Pay Rent

Efficient landlords should never tolerate their tenants being delinquent in paying their rent. You need to react predictably and immediately to non-payment of rent when it's due. Slow-paying tenants usually react to this predictability and make the rent a high priority on their list of payments. Normally there is a three-day grace period after the rent due date. If the rent is not received within three days of the due date, action has to be taken by the owner and/or manager.

Collection experts agree that a first notice should be sent within three days of the due date, and a second notice after five days. Use forms such as those in Figure A-4. If your slow-paying tenant has a history of continued delinquency, a Notice to Pay or Quit the Premises could be used in favor of the second notice. (For a sample of a pay-or-quit notice, see Figure A-5.)

Figure A-4   Reminders to Pay Rent

Three-Day Reminder to Pay Rent

To _____ Date _____

_____

Just a reminder that your rent was past due on _____.
According to the terms of your Rental Agreement, rent more than _____
days past due requires a late charge payment of $ _____.
We would appreciate your prompt payment.

Thank you,

_____
    Owner/manager

Figure A-4   *(Continued)*

Five-Day Reminder to Pay Rent

To _____ Date _____
    _____

Your rent is now past due as of _____. As of this date, the past due rent and late charges total $ _____.

You must settle this account, or our legal options will have to be considered. Therefore, please act to remedy this matter immediately.

Thank you,

_____
Owner/manager

Notice to Pay or Quit

The pay-or-quit notice, Figure A-5, gives the tenant three days from date of the notice to pay all monies in default or move out of the premises. This form is issued to the tenant only after you have attempted to procure the amount owed through other means, such as the three- and five-day reminders.

Note: Exercise caution in using a pay-or-quit notice because laws on this matter of eviction procedure vary throughout the country. This particular form may not conform to the laws in some states. If this is the case in your state, seek the appropriate form at a reputable legal stationery store or consult with an attorney who is familiar with the eviction procedure in your area.

Appendix of Useful Forms

Figure A-5 Notice to Pay Rent or Quit the Premises

To _____ Date _____

You are hereby notified that the rent for the period of _____, 20 ____, to _____, 20 _____, is now past due. As of this date, the total sum owing, including late charges, is $ _____. Unless the sum is received within three days of this dated notice, you will be required to vacate and surrender the premises.

   If it becomes necessary to proceed with legal action for the nonpayment of rent or to obtain possession of the premises, as per the terms of the Rental Agreement, you will be liable for recovery of our reasonable attorney's fees and expenses. You will also be liable for any additional rent for the time you are in possession of the premises.

_____
   Owner-manager

Rental Agreement

For your convenience, we have included a sample residential lease agreement in Figure A-6. You can modify this document for your needs, but note that both the tenant and owner or manager must initial any handwritten changes on the printed lease. Take special notice of the following three items that are an integral part of the rental agreement:

- *Term, Section 1.* In this section you need to specify whether the agreement is on a month-to-month or year-to-year basis. Be wary of committing to more than one year. If you do use a term of one year, specify graduated rent increases every 12 months, which can be tied to the rate of inflation, such as 1.5 times the CPI. This will protect you from losing money due to inflation.
- *Rent, Section 5.* Make sure the amount of rent is spelled out and that a late fee is specified, which is commonly 5 percent of the monthly rent.
- *Tenant maintenance, Section 19.* Under this heading note the clause "If a professional service call is required, the tenant shall pay the first $50 of the total repair bill." This is part of your hassle-free management program. By making the tenant partially responsible, he or she will be less likely to bother you or the resident manager with menial repairs and will be more conscientious about caring for the rental unit.
- *Pets, Section 3.* In this section of the agreement use the clause that's best suited for your particular unit and cross out the unused clauses you are not using. Then be sure both the owner and the tenant initial any changes to the lease at precisely where the change is made on the document.

Appendix of Useful Forms

Figure A-6 Residential Lease Agreement

This agreement made this date, _____, is between
_____, the "owner," and _____the
"tenant."

Description of leased property. Witnesseth, the owner, in consideration of the rents to be paid and the covenants and agreements to be performed by the tenant, does hereby lease unto the tenant the following described premises located thereon situated in the city of _____, county of _____, the state of _____, commonly known as _____
_____
_____.

1. *Term:* The term of this lease shall be _____months, beginning ___
   _____, 20____ and ending _____, 20_____.
   It is agreed that if the tenant is transferred or moved by an agency of the federal government or a branch of the military, this agreement becomes null and void and deposit money will be refunded after inspection of the unit.

2. *Security deposit.* The owner acknowledges receipt of $_____as security for the tenant's fulfillment of the conditions of this agreement. The owner shall return the security deposit to the tenant, without interest, within thirty (30) days after the tenant has vacated the premises. It is vacated if:
   a. The lease term has expired or the agreement has been terminated by both parties;
   b. All monies due the owner by the tenant have been paid; and
   c. The premises are not damaged and are left in their original condition, except for normal wear and tear.

   The tenant shall deliver possession of the premises in good order and repair to the owner, with all outstanding bills paid upon termination or expiration of this agreement. The security deposit may be applied by the owner to satisfy all or part of the tenant's obligations for the unit. Such an act shall not prevent the owner from claiming damages in excess of the deposit.

   The tenant may not apply the security deposit to any rent payment without the approval of the owner.

3. *Pets.* No animals, birds, or pets of any kind shall be permitted. (Or subsection optional a or b, in which case, the previous sentence needs to be crossed out.).
   a. One dog not to exceed 40 pounds is permitted, but the tenant must pay a nonrefundable pet fee deposit of $400.
   b. One cat not to exceed 15 pounds is permitted, but the tenant must pay a nonrefundable pet fee deposit of $400.

4. *Possession.* If there is a delay in delivery of possession by the owner, the rent shall be abated on a daily basis until possession is granted. If possession is not granted within two (2) days after the beginning of the initial term, then the tenant may void this agreement and receive a full refund of any deposit. The owner shall not be liable for damages for delay in possession.

Tenant's Renter's initials _____   Owner's initials_____

5. *Rent.* Rent is payable monthly in advance at a rate of $_____ per month during the term of this agreement, on the 1st day of each month, at such place that the owner may delegate.

6. *Late charge.* If rent is paid after the 5th day, a charge of $30 shall be added. After the 15th day, collection shall be turned over to the Justice Court and a $60 charge shall be added for court expenses. Any other court-related expenses shall be added.

7. *Returned-check charge.* If a returned check has to be collected, $30 shall be charged to the tenant for collection. If the check is not made good by the 15th day, it shall be turned over to the District Attorney's Office for collection and a $60 fee shall be added.

8. *Lease renewal.* Either party may terminate this agreement at the end of the initial term by giving the other party thirty (30) days' written notice prior to the end of the term. If no notice is given, this agreement shall be extended on a month to-month basis, with all terms remaining the same until terminated by either party upon thirty (30) days' written notice.

9. *Use.* The premises shall be used so as to comply with all state, county, and municipal laws and ordinances. The tenant shall not use the premises or permit it to be used for any disorderly or unlawful purpose or in any manner so as to interfere with the neighbors' quiet enjoyment of their homes.

The premises shall be used for residential purposes only and shall be occupied only by the following persons:

Name	Age	Social security number
Name	Age	Social security number
Name	Age	Social security number
Name	Age	Social security number

Tenant's initials _____   Owner's initials _____

10. *Sublet.* The tenant shall not sublet the premises or assign this lease without the written consent of the owner.

11. *Utilities.* The tenant shall pay for all charges for all water supplied to the premises and pay for all gas, heat, electricity, and other services supplied to the premises, except as herein provided: _____.

12. *Property loss.* The owner shall not be liable for damage to the tenant's property of any type for any reason whatsoever, except where such is due to negligence by the owner.

13. *Smoking.* Smoking shall not be allowed on the premises.

14. *Failure of the owner to act.* Failure of the owner to insist upon strict compliance with the terms of this agreement shall not constitute a waiver or any violation. Also, the waiver of one breach of any term, condition, covenant, obligation, or agreement of this lease shall not be considered to be a waiver of that or any other term, condition, covenant, obligation, or agreement or of any subsequent breach thereof.

15. *Fire.* If the premises are made uninhabitable by fire not the fault of the tenant, this agreement shall be terminated.

16. *Indemnification.* The tenant agrees to indemnify and release the owner from and against all loss, damage, or liability incurred as a result of:
    a. The tenant's failure to fulfill the conditions of this agreement;
    b. Any damage or injury happening in or about the premises to the tenant's family, friends, relatives, visitors, invitees, or such person's property unless caused by the negligence of the owner.
    c. The tenant's failure to comply with any requirements imposed by any governmental authority; and
    d. Any judgment, lien, or other encumbrance filed against the premises as a result of the tenant's action.

Tenant's initials _____   Owner's initials _____

17. *Cumulative remedies.* All remedies under this agreement, or by law or equity, shall be cumulative. If a suit for any breach of this agreement established a breach by the tenant, the tenant shall pay to the owner all expenses incurred in connection herewith.

18. *Notices.* Any notice required by this agreement shall be in writing and shall be deemed to be given if delivered personally or mailed by registered or certified mail.

19. *Tenant maintenance.* The tenant agrees to maintain the premises in good repair and to cause no damage to, or allow anyone else to cause any damage to, the premises. If a professional service call is required, the tenant shall pay the first fifty dollars ($50) of the total repair bill. The owner shall enter the premises each month to replace the central air-conditioning unit filter.

20. *Alterations and additions.* The tenant shall not make any alterations, additions, or improvements to said premises without the owner's written consent. All alterations, additions, or improvements made by either of the parties hereto upon the premises, except movable furniture, shall be the property of the owner and shall remain upon and be surrendered with the premises at the termination of this lease.

21. *Entry.* The owner or his or her representatives shall have the right to enter the premises at all reasonable times to inspect, make repairs to or alterations to, or show the premises to prospective purchasers, tenants, or lenders. The tenant shall not be entitled to abatement of the rent by reason thereof.

22. *Insurance.* The tenant understands and agrees that it shall be the tenant's own obligation to insure his or her personal property.

23. *Abandonment.* If the tenant removes or attempts to remove property from the premises, other than through the usual course of continuing occupancy, without having first paid the owner all monies due, the premises may be considered abandoned and the owner shall have the right, without notice, to store or dispose of any property left on the premises by the tenant. The owner shall also have the right to store or dispose of any of the tenant's property remaining in the premises after the termination of this agreement. Any such property shall be considered the owner's property and title thereto shall vest in the owner.

24. *Mortgagee's rights.* The tenant's rights under this lease shall at all times be automatically junior and subject to any mortgage debt that is now or shall hereafter be placed on the premises. If requested, the tenant shall promptly execute any certificate that the owner may request to specifically implement the subordination of this paragraph.

Tenant's initials _____   Owner's initials_____

25. *Sale of property.* All parties understand that if the owner agrees to sell the property during the term of the lease, the lease and future rents shall transfer to the new owner.
26. *Entire agreement.* This agreement and attached addendums constitute the entire agreement between the parties, and no oral statements shall be binding.

The undersigned tenant(s) hereby acknowledge receipt of a copy of this lease.

_____Tenant(s)/date

_____Tenant(s)/date

_____

Tenant's phone   Social security number

_____

Tenant's phone   Social security number

_____Owner /date

Owner's phone _____

Mail rent to:

_____

_____

_____

Index

Index

Index

Index

Index

Index

About the Author

With more than 35 years experience, Andrew James McLean has served as a real estate developer, appraiser, licensed realtor, and has managed millions of dollars in foreclosure property for a major savings and loan association. McLean is also a graduate of Michigan State University, and the published author of 17 nonfiction books.

Other books by the author include *Buying and Managing Residential Real Estate*, 2nd edition, and *Investing in Real Estate*, 5th edition. He is also the coauthor with George H. Ross of *Trump Strategies for Real Estate*.